Microsoft©

Windows® 7

Introductory

Gary B. Shelly

Steven M. Freund

Raymond E. Enger

Microsoft®

Windows® 7

Introductory

Gary B. Shelly
Steven M. Freund
Raymond E. Enger

COURSE TECHNOLOGY
CENGAGE Learning™

Australia • Brazil • Japan • Korea • Mexico • Singapore • Spain • United Kingdom • United States

COURSE TECHNOLOGY
CENGAGE Learning™

Microsoft© Windows® 7
Introductory
Gary B. Shelly
Steven M. Freund
Raymond E. Enger

Executive Editor: Kathleen McMahon

Product Manager: Klenda Martinez

Associate Product Manager: Jon Farnham

Editorial Assistant: Lauren Brody

Print Buyer: Julio Esperas

Director of Production: Patty Stephen

Content Project Manager: Matthew Hutchinson

Developmental Editor: Karen Stevens

Director of Marketing: Cheryl Costantini

Marketing Manager: Tristen Kendall

Marketing Coordinator: Stacey Leasca

QA Manuscript Reviewers: John Freitas,
   Danielle Shaw

Art Director: Marissa Falco

Cover Designer: Lisa Kuhn, Curio Press, LLC

Cover Photo: Tom Kates Photography

Compositor: Pre-Press PMG

Copyeditor: Karen Annett

Proofreader: Kathy Orrino

Indexer: Alexandra Nickerson

For product information and technology assistance, contact us at
Cengage Learning Customer & Sales Support, 1-800-354-9706

For permission to use material from this text or product, submit all requests online at **cengage.com/permissions**
Further permissions questions can be emailed to
permissionrequest@cengage.com

Library of Congress Control Number: 2009942962

ISBN-13: 978-1-4390-8103-7

ISBN-10: 1-4390-8105-0

Course Technology
20 Channel Center Street
Boston, MA 02210
USA

Cengage Learning is a leading provider of customized learning solutions with office locations around the globe, including Singapore, the United Kingdom, Australia, Mexico, Brazil, and Japan. Locate your local office at:
international.cengage.com/region

Cengage Learning products are represented in Canada by Nelson Education, Ltd.

Visit our website **www.cengage.com/ct/shellycashman** to share and gain ideas on our textbooks!

To learn more about Course Technology, visit **www.cengage.com/coursetechnology**

Purchase any of our products at your local college store or at our preferred online store **www.CengageBrain.com**

Printed in the United States of America
2 3 4 5 6 16 15 14 13 12 11

Microsoft®
Windows® 7
Introductory

Contents

Appendices

Preface

The Shelly Cashman Series® offers the finest textbooks in computer education. We are proud of the fact that our Microsoft Windows 3.1, Microsoft Windows 95, Microsoft Windows 98, Microsoft Windows 2000, Microsoft Windows XP, and Microsoft Windows Vista books have been so well received by students and instructors. With each new edition of our Windows books, we have made significant improvements based on the software and comments made by instructors and students.

Microsoft Windows contains many changes in the user interface and feature set. Recognizing that the new features and functionality of Microsoft Windows 7 would impact the way that students are taught skills, the Shelly Cashman Series development team carefully reviewed our pedagogy and analyzed its effectiveness in teaching today's student. An extensive customer survey produced results confirming what the series is best known for: its step-by-step, screen-by-screen instructions, its project-oriented approach, and the quality of its content.

We learned, though, that students entering computer courses today are different than students taking these classes just a few years ago. Students today read less, but need to retain more. They need not only to be able to perform skills, but to retain those skills and know how to apply them to different settings. Today's students need to be continually engaged and challenged to retain what they're learning.

As a result, we've renewed our commitment to focusing on the user and how they learn best. This commitment is reflected in every change we've made to our Windows 7 books.

Objectives of This Textbook

Microsoft© Windows® 7: Introductory is intended for a course that includes an introduction to Windows 7. No experience with a computer is assumed, and no mathematics beyond the high school freshman level is required. The objectives of this book are:

- To teach the fundamentals of Microsoft Windows 7
- To expose students to practical examples of the computer as a useful tool
- To acquaint students with the proper procedures to manage and organize document storage options for coursework, professional purposes, and personal use
- To help students discover the underlying functionality of Windows 7 so they can become more productive
- To develop an exercise-oriented approach that allows learning by doing

Distinguishing Features

A Proven Pedagogy with an Emphasis on Project Planning Each chapter presents a practical problem to be solved, within a project planning framework. The project orientation is strengthened by the use of Plan Ahead boxes, that encourage critical thinking about how to proceed at various points in the project. Step-by-step instructions with supporting screens guide students through the steps. Instructional steps are supported by the Q&A, Experiment Step, and BTW features.

A Visually Engaging Book that Maintains Student Interest The step-by-step tasks, with supporting figures, provide a rich visual experience for the student. Call-outs on the screens that present both explanatory and navigational information provide students with information they need when they need to know it.

Supporting Reference Materials (Appendices) The appendices provide additional information about Windows 7, such as the security features and distinguishing between editions.

Integration of the World Wide Web The World Wide Web is integrated into the Windows 7 learning experience through step-by-step instruction on Internet Explorer, as well as the Learn It Online section for each chapter.

End-of-Chapter Student Activities Extensive end of chapter activities provide a variety of reinforcement opportunities for students where they can apply and expand their skills through individual and group work.

Instructor Resources CD-ROM

The Instructor Resources include both teaching and testing aids.

INSTRUCTOR'S MANUAL Includes lecture notes summarizing the chapter sections, figures and boxed elements found in every chapter, teacher tips, classroom activities, lab activities, and quick quizzes in Microsoft Word files.

SYLLABUS Easily customizable sample syllabi that cover policies, assignments, exams, and other course information.

FIGURE FILES Illustrations for every figure in the textbook in electronic form.

POWERPOINT PRESENTATIONS A multimedia lecture presentation system that provides slides for each chapter. Presentations are based on chapter objectives.

SOLUTIONS TO EXERCISES Includes solutions for all end-of-chapter and chapter reinforcement exercises.

TEST BANK & TEST ENGINE Test Banks include 112 questions for every chapter, featuring objective-based and critical thinking question types, and including page number references and figure references, when appropriate. Also included is the test engine, ExamView, the ultimate tool for your objective-based testing needs.

DATA FILES FOR STUDENTS Includes all the files that are required by students to complete the exercises.

ADDITIONAL ACTIVITIES FOR STUDENTS Consists of Chapter Reinforcement Exercises, which are true/false, multiple-choice, and short answer questions that help students gain confidence in the material learned.

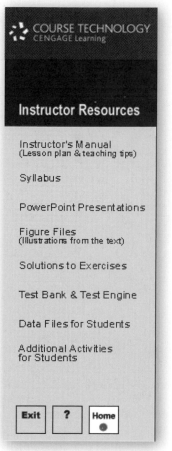

Blackboard

course|notes™
quick reference guide

Content for Online Learning

Course Technology has partnered with Blackboard, the leading distance learning solution provider and class-management platform today. The resources available for download with this title are the test banks in Blackboard- and WebCT-compatible formats. To access this material, simply visit our password-protected instructor resources available at www.cengage.com/coursetechnology. For additional information or for an instructor username and password, please contact your sales representative.

Guided Tours

Add excitement and interactivity to your classroom with "*A Guided Tour*" product line. Play one of the brief mini-movies to spice up your lecture and spark classroom discussion. Or, assign a movie for homework and ask students to complete the correlated assignment that accompanies each topic. "*A Guided Tour*" product line takes the prep-work out of providing your students with information on new technologies and software applications and helps keep students engaged with content relevant to their lives, all in under an hour!

CourseNotes

Course Technology's CourseNotes are six-panel quick reference cards that reinforce the most important concepts and features of a software application in a visual and user-friendly format. CourseNotes serve as a great reference tool during and after the student completes the course. CourseNotes are available for software applications, such as Microsoft Office 2007, Word 2007, PowerPoint 2007, Excel 2007, Access 2007, and Windows 7. There are also topic-based CourseNotes available for Best Practices in Social Networking, Hot Topics in Technology, and Web 2.0. Visit www.cengage.com/ct/coursenotes to learn more!

SAM: Skills Assessment Manager

SAM is designed to help bring students from the classroom to the real world. It allows students to train and test on important computer skills in an active, hands-on environment.

SAM's easy-to-use system includes powerful interactive exams, training and projects on the most commonly used Microsoft® Office applications. SAM simulates the Office 2010 application environment, allowing students to demonstrate their knowledge and think through the skills by performing real-world tasks such as bolding word text or setting up slide transitions. Add in live-in-the-application projects and students are on their way to truly learning and applying skills to business-centric document.

Designed to be used with the Shelly Cashman Series, SAM includes handy page references, so students can print helpful study guides that match the Shelly Cashman Series textbooks used in class. For instructors, SAM also includes robust scheduling and reporting features.

Textbook Walk-Through

The Shelly Cashman Series Pedagogy:
Project-based — Step-by-Step — Variety of Assessments

Plan Ahead boxes prepare students to create successful projects by encouraging them to think strategically about what they are trying to accomplish before they begin working.

Step-by-step instructions now provide a context beyond the point-and-click. Each step provides information on why students are performing each task, or what will occur as a result.

Microsoft **Windows 7**

3 | File and Folder Management

Introduction

In Chapter 2, you used Windows 7 to create documents on the desktop and work with documents and folders in the Documents library. Windows 7 also allows you to examine the files and folders on the computer in a variety of other ways, enabling you to choose the easiest and most accessible manner when working with the computer. The Computer folder window and the Documents library provide two ways for you to work with files and folders. In addition, the Pictures library allows you to organize and share picture files, and the Music library allows you to organize and share your music files. This chapter illustrates how to work with files in the Computer folder, as well as the Documents, Pictures, and Music libraries.

Overview

As you read this chapter, you will learn how to work with the Computer folder window, as well as the Pictures and Music libraries, by performing these general tasks:

- Opening and using the Computer folder window
- Searching for files and folders
- Managing open windows
- Opening and using the Pictures library
- Using Windows Photo Viewer
- Opening and using the Music library
- Playing a music file in Windows Media Player
- Backing up and restoring a folder

Plan Ahead

> **Working with Files and Folders**
> Working with files and folders requires a basic knowledge of how to use the Windows 7 desktop.
>
> 1. **Be aware that there might be different levels of access on the computer you will be using.** A user account can be restricted to a certain level of access to the computer. Depending on the level of access that has been set for your account, you might or might not be able to perform certain operations.
>
> 2. **Identify how to connect a USB flash drive to your computer.** Depending upon the setup of your computer, there might be several ways to connect a USB flash drive to your computer. You should know which USB ports you can use to connect a USB flash drive to your computer.
>
> 3. **Determine if your computer has speakers.** Some computer labs do not provide speakers. If you are going to be using a computer in a lab, you need to know if the computer has speakers or if you will need to bring earbuds.
>
> *(continued)*

To Open the Getting Started Window

If you are new to using Windows 7, you can open the Getting Star~~ted~~ allows you to complete a set of tasks to optimize the computer. The task~~s~~ transferring files and settings from another computer, and backing up yo~~ur~~ Started window to perform these tasks, but it can assist you with configu~~ring~~ open the Getting Started window. If the Getting Started window alread~~y~~ without performing them.

①
- Click the Start button on the taskbar to display the Start menu (Figure 1–13).

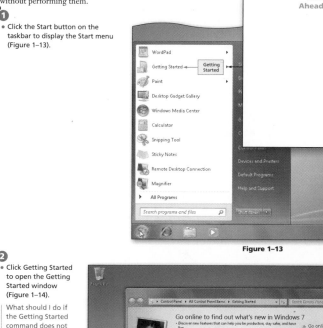

Figure 1–13

②
- Click Getting Started to open the Getting Started window (Figure 1–14).

Q&A What should I do if the Getting Started command does not display on the Start menu?

Depending upon how your computer is configured, you might find the Getting Started command in the Accessories list instead.

Other Ways
1. Display Start menu, click All Programs, click Accessories, click Getting Started

Figure 1–14

BTW
Screen Shots
Callouts in screenshots give students information they need, when they need to know it. The Series has always used plenty of callouts to ensure that students don't get lost. Now, color is used to distinguish the content in the callouts to make them more meaningful.

Navigational callouts in red show students where to click.

Explanatory callouts summarize what is happening on screen.

Textbook Walk-Through

Q&A boxes offer questions students may have when working through the steps and provide additional information about what they are doing right where they need it.

Experiment Steps within our step-by-step instructions, encourage students to explore, experiment, and take advantage of the features of Windows 7. These steps are not necessary to complete the projects, but are designed to increase the confidence with the software and build problem-solving skills.

To Collapse the Local Disk (C:) List

The following step collapses the Local Disk (C:) list.

1
- Click the arrow next to Local Disk (C:) to collapse the Local Disk (C:) list (Figure 1–30).

Q&A
Should I keep the list expanded or collapsed?

If you need to use the contents in the list, it is handy to keep the list expanded. You can collapse the list when the information is not needed.

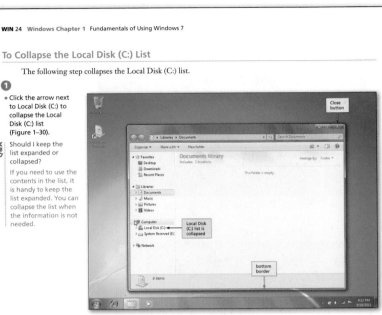

Figure 1–30

The Windows 7 Desktop **WIN** 25

w to its original size. To return the ibrary, complete the following steps.

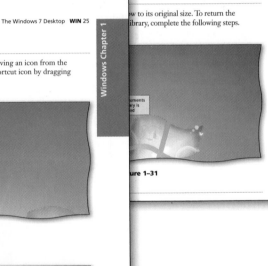

ure 1–31

To Delete a Desktop Icon by Dragging it to the Recycle Bin

Although Windows 7 has many ways to delete desktop icons, one method of removing an icon from the desktop is to drag it to the Recycle Bin. The following steps delete the Documents - Shortcut icon by dragging the icon to the Recycle Bin.

1
- Point to the Documents - Shortcut icon on the desktop and press the left mouse button to select the icon (Figure 1–32). Do not release the left mouse button.

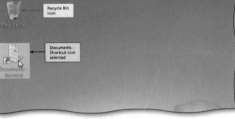

Figure 1–32

2
- Drag the Documents - Shortcut icon over the Recycle Bin icon on the desktop, and then release the left mouse button to place the shortcut in the Recycle Bin (Figure 1–33).

Experiment
- Double-click the Recycle Bin icon on the desktop to open a window containing the contents of the Recycle Bin. The Documents - Shortcut icon you have just deleted will display in this window. Close the Recycle Bin window.

Q&A
Why did the Documents - Shortcut icon disappear?

Releasing the left mouse button moved the icon from the desktop to the Recycle Bin.

Figure 1–33

Other Ways
1. Right-click icon, click Delete, click Yes button
2. Right-click icon and hold, drag to Recycle Bin, release right mouse button, click Move Here

Textbook Walk-Through

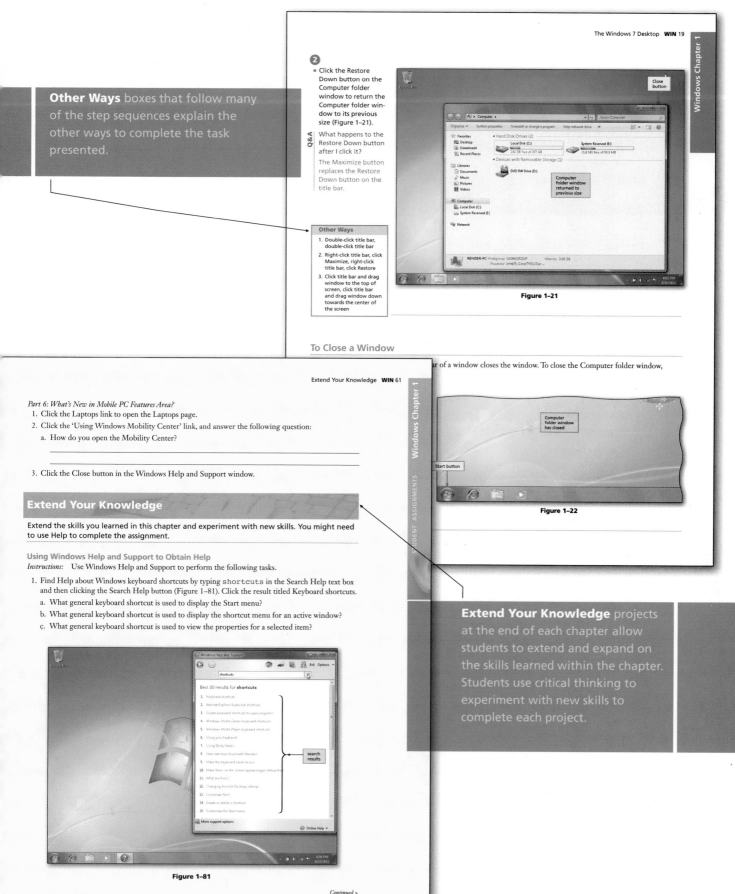

Other Ways boxes that follow many of the step sequences explain the other ways to complete the task presented.

2
- Click the Restore Down button on the Computer folder window to return the Computer folder window to its previous size (Figure 1–21).

Q&A What happens to the Restore Down button after I click it?

The Maximize button replaces the Restore Down button on the title bar.

Other Ways
1. Double-click title bar, double-click title bar
2. Right-click title bar, click Maximize, right-click title bar, click Restore
3. Click title bar and drag window to the top of screen, click title bar and drag window down towards the center of the screen

Figure 1–21

To Close a Window

...ar of a window closes the window. To close the Computer folder window,

Figure 1–22

Part 6: What's New in Mobile PC Features Area?
1. Click the Laptops link to open the Laptops page.
2. Click the 'Using Windows Mobility Center' link, and answer the following question:
   a. How do you open the Mobility Center?

   _____

3. Click the Close button in the Windows Help and Support window.

Extend Your Knowledge

Extend the skills you learned in this chapter and experiment with new skills. You might need to use Help to complete the assignment.

Using Windows Help and Support to Obtain Help
Instructions: Use Windows Help and Support to perform the following tasks.

1. Find Help about Windows keyboard shortcuts by typing shortcuts in the Search Help text box and then clicking the Search Help button (Figure 1–81). Click the result titled Keyboard shortcuts.
   a. What general keyboard shortcut is used to display the Start menu?
   b. What general keyboard shortcut is used to display the shortcut menu for an active window?
   c. What general keyboard shortcut is used to view the properties for a selected item?

Figure 1–81

Extend Your Knowledge projects at the end of each chapter allow students to extend and expand on the skills learned within the chapter. Students use critical thinking to experiment with new skills to complete each project.

Continued >

Textbook Walk-Through

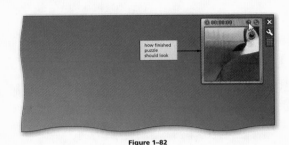

Figure 1–82

The in-depth **In the Lab** assignments require students to utilize the chapter concepts and techniques to solve problems.

3. Play the Picture Puzzle game, by moving the puzzle tiles around by clicking on them when they are near the empty slot. Continue to rearrange the tiles until you have completed the picture (you can show the picture at any time to determine if you are close to the solution). Record your time here:

4. Click the Close button on the gadget to remove the gadget from the desktop.

In the Lab

Lab 2: Switching through Open Windows

Instructions: Perform the following steps to launch multiple programs using the Start menu and then use different methods to switch through the open windows (Figure 1–83 on the next page).

Part 1: Launching the Getting Started Window, WordPad, and Internet Explorer
1. Click the Start button, click the All Programs command, and then click the Internet Explorer command to launch Internet Explorer.
 ll Programs command, click the Accessories folder, and then click isplay the Getting Started window.
 ll Programs command, click the Accessories folder, and then click

 xt open window.
 press the TAB key two times to switch to the next open window.
 open programs. Press TAB. Click the WordPad window to switch

 w the open programs. Press TAB. Click the Internet Explorer lorer.

 ssing ALT+TAB and pressing WINDOWS+TAB? _____

 ssing ALT+TAB and CTRL+ALT+TAB? _____

Continued >

Cases and Places

Apply your creative thinking and problem-solving skills to design and implement a solution.

• **EASIER**   •• **MORE DIFFICULT**

• 1 Finding Programs
You are interested in identifying which programs are installed on your computer. To find all the programs, you decide to search the Program Files folder on your computer. Using techniques you learned in this chapter, open the Program Files folder on the C drive. Search for *.exe files. Summarize your findings in a brief report. Be sure to indicate the number of programs you found.

• 2 Filter Searching
Your employer suspects that someone has used your computer during off-hours for non–company business. She has asked you to search your computer for files that have been created or modified during the last week. Search for files in the Windows 7 libraries using the Date modified filter. When you find the files, determine if any are WordPad files or Paint files that you did not create or modify. Summarize the number and date they were created or modified in a brief report.

•• 3 Researching Backups
Backing up files is an important way to protect data and ensure that it is not lost or destroyed accidentally. You can use a variety of devices and techniques to back up files from a personal computer. Using Windows Help and Support, research the Backup and Restore. Determine what backup tools Windows 7 provides. Write a brief report of your findings.

•• 4 Researching Photo Printing Sites
Make It Personal
Now that you know how to work with the Pictures library, you want to find Web sites where you can upload and print your photos. Using the Internet, search for three photo printing Web sites. Find the prices per 4 x 6 photo, which file formats are required, and explore any other photo products that you would be interested in purchasing. Write a brief report that compares the three Web sites and indicate which one you would use.

•• 5 Researching Data Security
Working Together
Data stored on disk is one of a company's most valuable assets. If that data were to be stolen, lost, or compromised so that it could not be accessed, the company could go out of business. Therefore, companies go to great lengths to protect their data. Working with classmates, research how the companies where you each work handle their backups. Find out how each one protects its data against viruses, unauthorized access, and even against natural disasters such as fire and floods. Prepare a brief report that describes the companies' procedures. In your report, point out any areas where you find a company has not protected its data adequately.

Found within the Cases & Places exercises, the **Make It Personal** exercise calls on students to create an open-ended project that relates to their personal lives.

Microsoft®

Windows® 7

Introductory

1 | Fundamentals of Using Windows 7

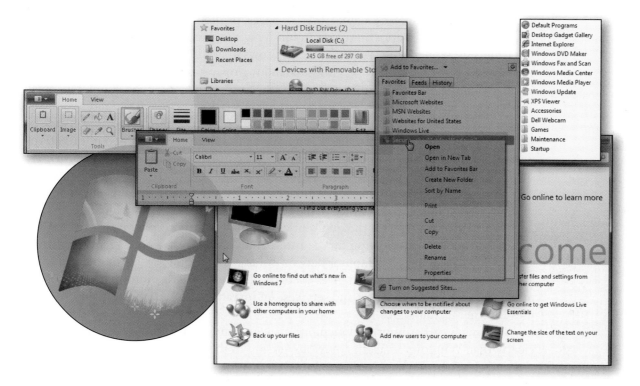

Objectives

You will have mastered the material in this chapter when you can:

- Describe Windows 7
- Explain the following terms: operating system, server, workstation, and user interface
- Log on the computer
- Identify the objects on the Windows 7 desktop
- Display the Start menu
- Add gadgets to the desktop
- Identify the Computer folder window and the Documents library

- Add and remove a desktop icon
- Open, minimize, maximize, restore, and close a window
- Move and size a window on the Windows 7 desktop
- Scroll a window
- Launch a program
- Switch between running programs
- Use Windows 7 Help and Support
- Log off the computer and turn off the computer

1 | Fundamentals of Using Windows 7

What is Windows 7?

An **operating system** is the set of computer instructions that controls the allocation of computer hardware such as memory, disk devices, printers, and optical disc drives, and provides the capability for you to communicate with the computer. The most popular and widely used operating system is the Windows operating system from Microsoft. **Windows 7** is the newest version of the Windows operating system.

Windows 7 is commonly used on desktop computers, notebook computers, including netbooks and Tablet PCs, and workstations. A **workstation** is a computer connected to a server. A **server** is a computer that controls access to the hardware and software on a network and provides a centralized storage area for programs, data, and information. Figure 1–1 illustrates a simple computer network consisting of a server, three workstations, and a printer connected to the server.

Windows 7 is easy to use and can be customized to fit individual needs. The operating system simplifies working with documents and programs, transferring data between documents, interacting with the different components of the computer, and using the computer to access information on the Internet or an intranet. The **Internet** is a worldwide group of connected computer networks that allows public access to information about thousands of subjects and gives users the ability to use this information, send messages, and obtain products and services. An **intranet** is an internal network that uses Internet technologies.

Windows 7 has improved memory management so that it runs faster and more efficiently than Windows Vista, the previous version of the Windows operating system. The user interface also has been enhanced to create a more friendly and customizable experience. Several other improvements over previous versions of Windows make Windows 7 a suitable choice for all users.

This book demonstrates how to use Windows 7 to control the computer and communicate with other computers both on a network and the Internet. In Chapter 1, you will learn about Windows 7 and how to use the Windows 7 user interface.

Overview

As you read this chapter, you will learn how to use the Windows 7 user interface by performing these general tasks:

- Start Windows 7 and log on
- Display the Start menu and expand and close a list
- Work with Windows gadgets
- Launch and switch between programs
- Open, minimize, restore, move, size, scroll, and close a window
- Use the Help system to answer questions
- Log off and turn off the computer

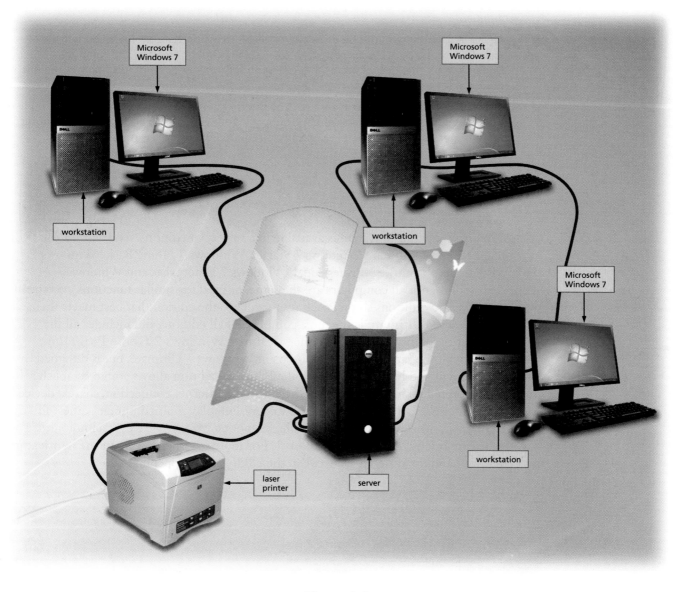

Figure 1–1

Working with Windows 7

Plan
Ahead

Working with an operating system requires a basic knowledge of how to start the operating system, log on and off the computer, and identify the objects on the Windows 7 desktop.

1. **Determine how you will be logging on to computer.** Depending on the setup of the computer you are using, you might need a user account, consisting of a user name and password. If it is a computer provided in a work or education setting, you might be assigned an account.

2. **Establish which edition of Windows 7 is installed.** There are six different editions of Windows 7, each containing different features. You should know which edition is installed on the computer you will be using.

(continued)

(continued)

3. **Be aware that there might be different levels of access on the computer you will be using.** A user account can be restricted to a certain level of access to the computer. Depending on the level of access that has been set for your account, you might or might not be able to perform certain operations.

4. **Determine if you have Internet access.** The Internet contains useful material for Windows 7, such as Windows Help and Support. You will want to know if your computer has Internet access and whether anything is required of you to use it.

Multiple Editions of Windows 7

The Windows 7 operating system is available in a variety of editions. The editions that you most likely will encounter are Windows 7 Starter, Windows 7 Home Basic, Windows 7 Home Premium, Windows 7 Professional, Windows 7 Enterprise, and Windows 7 Ultimate. Because not all computers are the same, or used for similar functions, Microsoft offers these various editions so that each user can have the edition that best meets their needs. **Windows 7 Ultimate** is the most complete of all editions and includes all the power, security, mobility, and entertainment features. **Windows 7 Home Premium** contains many of the same features as Microsoft Windows 7 Ultimate, but is designed for entertainment and home use. The Home Premium edition allows you to establish a network of computers in the home that share a single Internet connection, share a device such as a printer or scanner, share files and folders, and play multicomputer games. You can create a home network using Ethernet cable, telephone wire, or wireless technologies. The six editions are briefly described in Table 1–1. For more information about the new features of Windows 7 and the differences between the editions, see Appendix A.

Table 1–1 Windows 7 Editions	
Edition	**Description**
Windows 7 Starter	This edition contains the least number of features and mostly is used for computers with limited capabilities. Windows 7 Starter typically is installed by computer manufacturers and is generally not available in retail outlets.
Windows 7 Home Basic	This edition is designed for use in emerging markets only and lacks several new features. Similar to the Starter edition, Windows 7 Home Basic is installed by computer manufacturers and generally is not available in retail outlets.
Windows 7 Home Premium	This edition is designed for home users and includes features such as Windows Media Center, Windows Aero, and touch screen controls. This edition is available in retail outlets and is installed on new computers.
Windows 7 Professional	This edition is designed for small business users. It includes network and productivity features, backup and restore capabilities, and the ability to join domains. This edition is available in retail outlets and on new computers.
Windows 7 Enterprise	This edition is designed for enterprise customers who plan to install Windows 7 enterprise-wide. This edition includes additional features such as support for Multilingual User Interface packages and BitLocker Drive Encryption.
Windows 7 Ultimate	This edition contains all Windows 7 features and is designed for home and small business users who want all the features Windows 7 offers. This edition is the most expensive of the six Windows 7 editions.

Windows 7

Windows 7 is an operating system that performs the functions necessary for you to communicate with and use the computer. Windows 7 is available in 32-bit and 64-bit versions for all editions except Windows 7 Starter Edition.

Windows 7 is used to run **programs**, which are a set of computer instructions that carries out a task on the computer. **Application software** consists of programs designed to make users more productive and assist them with personal tasks, such as word processing. Windows 7 includes several programs, including Windows Internet Explorer and Windows Media Player. **Windows Internet Explorer**, also known as Internet Explorer, is a Web browser that integrates the Windows 7 desktop and the Internet. Internet Explorer allows you to work with programs and files in a similar fashion, regardless of whether they are located on the computer, a local network, or the Internet. **Windows Media Player** lets you create and play CDs, watch DVDs, listen to radio stations originating from all over the world, and search for and organize digital media files.

Some features of Windows that previously were available within the operating system are now only available online by downloading Windows Live Essentials. **Windows Live Essentials** is a suite of free downloadable programs, including Windows Live Movie Maker and Windows Live Mail. **Windows Live Movie Maker** can transfer recorded audio and video from analog camcorders or digital video cameras, also called DV cameras, to the computer, import existing audio and video files, and distribute finished movies, either in an e-mail message or by posting the movies on the World Wide Web. **Windows Live Mail** is an e-mail program that lets you exchange e-mail messages with friends and colleagues, manage your calendar and contacts, and view RSS feeds.

Windows 7 offers a variety of features that you can customize. Depending upon your personal preferences, you can change the appearance of various components such as the desktop, the taskbar, and the Start menu. As you proceed through this book, you will learn many ways to customize your experience. To use programs with Windows 7, you first should understand the Windows 7 user interface.

User Interface

A **user interface** is the combination of software and input devices that you use to communicate with and control the computer. Through the user interface, you are able to make selections on the computer, request information from the computer, and respond to messages displayed by the computer. Thus, a user interface provides the means for dialogue between you and the computer.

The computer software determines the messages you receive, the means of your response, and the actions that occur based on your responses. The goal of an effective user interface is to be **user-friendly**, which means that the software is easy to use by people with limited training.

A **graphical user interface**, or **GUI** (pronounced gooey), is a user interface that relies on graphics in addition to text to communicate with the user. Windows 7 has two user interfaces: Windows 7 Basic and Windows 7 Aero. The Basic interface appears in all editions of Windows 7. If your hardware configuration supports it, the Aero interface appears in all editions, except for the Starter or Home Basic editions.

BTW

Determining Edition Support
Before you upgrade an existing Windows operating system to Windows 7, you should determine which edition your computer will support by installing and running the Windows 7 Upgrade Advisor. To access the Windows 7 Upgrade Advisor, visit http://www .microsoft.com/windows/ windows-7/get/ upgrade-advisor.aspx.

BTW

Aero Enhancements
The Windows 7 Aero experience has been improved from the Windows Vista version. It now is designed to be easier to customize and is considered faster and more efficient than before. For example, Aero now allows live preview to display a window preview at full-screen size, along with a thumbnail size.

Windows Aero

The **Aero** interface, also known as the Aero experience, features translucent colors along with various animations. To use Aero, your computer must have a compatible video card and an edition of Windows 7 installed that supports Aero. The first thing you will notice about Aero is **Aero Glass**, which is a translucent glass effect around the borders of the windows that allows you to partially see the items behind the windows. **Aero Flip 3D**, another component of the Aero experience, makes switching between your programs as visual and tactile as flipping through papers on your desk.

Aero provides a simple and entertaining interface for interacting with Windows 7. Figure 1–2 shows examples of the Basic experience and the Aero experience. The figures in this book were created using the Aero interface in Windows 7 Ultimate.

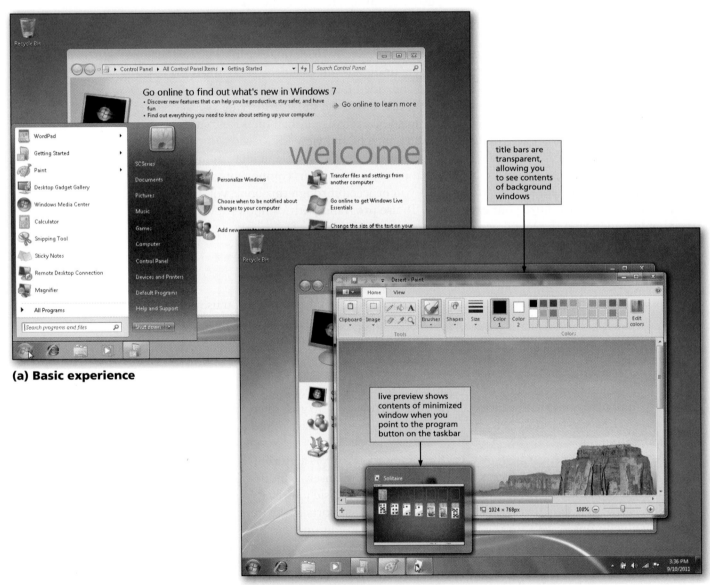

(a) Basic experience

(b) Aero experience

Figure 1–2

Launching Windows 7

When you turn on the computer, an introductory screen consisting of the Windows logo and copyright messages is displayed. The Windows logo is animated and glows as the Windows 7 operating system loads. After the Windows logo appears, if your computer is configured to start with **automatic logon**, your desktop will display on the screen without first asking you to type a user name or password. If your computer is not configured for automatic logon, the Welcome screen displays (Figure 1–3).

The Welcome screen shows the user icons and names of every user on the computer. The Ease of Access button, in the lower-left corner of the Welcome screen, allows you to change accessibility options as long as you have permission to change them. In the lower-right corner of the Welcome screen is the Shut down button. The Shut down command shuts down Windows 7 and turns off the computer.

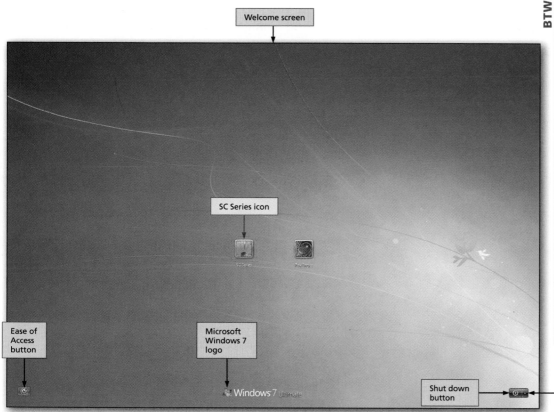

Figure 1–3

At the bottom-center of the Welcome screen is the Windows logo and the name of your Windows 7 edition, for example, Windows 7 Ultimate. In the middle of the Welcome screen is a list of the user icons and user names for all authorized computer users. The list of user icons and user names on the Welcome screen on your computer might be different. Clicking the user icon or user name begins the process of logging on the computer. If the user account you clicked does not require a password, you will be taken to your desktop; otherwise, you will be prompted to enter your password to log on.

If, after logging on the computer, you leave the computer unattended for a predetermined period of time, the computer might go to sleep automatically. In **sleep mode**, your work is saved and the computer is placed in power saving mode. When you start using your computer again, the Welcome screen will display and you will have to log on the computer again to access your account.

To Log On the Computer

After starting Windows 7 and before working, you must log on the computer. For this section, it is assumed that automatic logon is turned off and that you have to type in a password. Logging on the computer opens your user account and makes the computer available for use. In the following steps, the SC Series icon and the Next button are used to log on the computer and enter a password. When you perform these steps, you will want to log on the computer by clicking *your user icon* on the Welcome screen and typing *your password* in the text box instead of the password shown in the steps.

1

- Click the SC Series icon (or the icon representing your user account) on the Welcome screen to display the password text box.

- Type your password in the password text box (Figure 1–4).

Q&A Why do I not see an SC Series icon?

The SC Series icon is not present as the SC Series account is not a user account on your computer.

Q&A Where is my password text box?

You will not see a password text box if your account does not require a password. You only have to select your user icon to log on.

Q&A Why do I have an icon and a password text box?

If there only is one user account, the password text box automatically displays, as there are no other accounts to select.

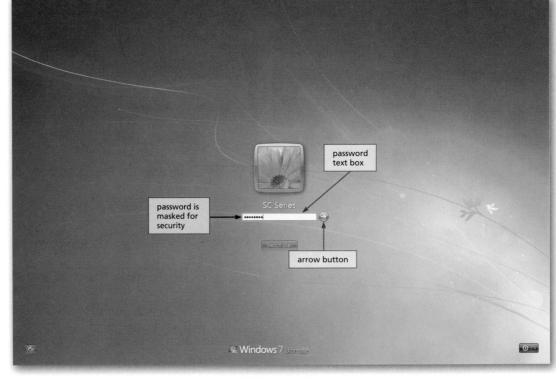

Figure 1–4

2

- Click the arrow button to log on the computer and display the Windows 7 desktop (Figure 1–5).

Q&A

Why does my desktop look different from the one in Figure 1–5?

The Windows 7 desktop is customizable and your school or company might have modified the desktop to meet their needs. For example, some schools customize their computer desktops with a picture of the school and/or the school name.

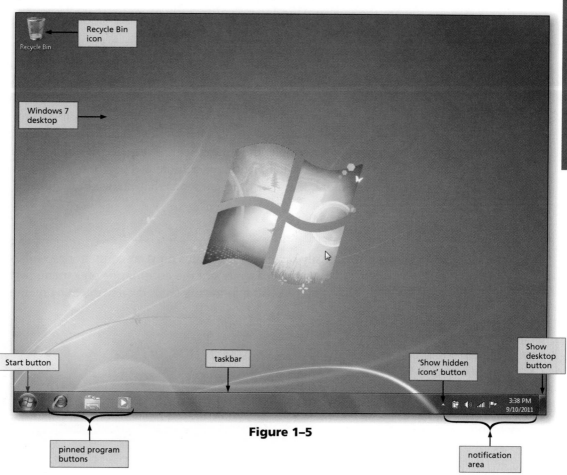

Figure 1–5

The Windows 7 Desktop

The Windows 7 desktop, and the objects on the desktop, emulate a work area in an office. You can think of the desktop as an electronic version of the top of your desk. You can perform actions such as placing objects on the desktop, moving the objects around the desktop, and looking at objects and then putting them aside.

Although the Windows 7 desktop can be arranged to meet your needs, it does contain some standard elements. The items on the desktop in Figure 1–5 include the Recycle Bin icon and name in the upper-left corner of the desktop and the taskbar at the bottom. The **Recycle Bin** allows you to discard unneeded objects. Your computer's desktop might contain more, fewer, or different icons, depending on how the desktop was modified.

The taskbar shown at the bottom of the screen in Figure 1–5 contains the Start button, taskbar button area, and notification area. The Start button, which displays the Start menu, allows you to perform many tasks such as launching a program, finding or opening a document, changing the computer's settings, obtaining help, and shutting down the computer. The taskbar button area contains buttons to indicate which windows are open on the desktop. When a program has been **pinned** to the taskbar, a button with the program icon appears, regardless of whether the program is open or closed. You can access the program quickly by clicking the pinned program button. Pinned programs usually are the programs that you use most frequently and appear first in the taskbar button area.

BTW

The Notification Area
The 'Show hidden icons' button displays on the left edge of the notification area if one or more inactive icons are hidden from view in the notification area. Clicking the 'Show hidden icons' button displays all of the inactive icons in a pop-up window. Moving the mouse pointer away from the notification area, or clicking the 'Show hidden icons' button again, hides the inactive icons.

By default, Internet Explorer, Windows Explorer, and Windows Media Player are pinned to the taskbar. **Windows Explorer** is a program that allows you to browse the files and folders on your computer.

The notification area contains the 'Show hidden icons' button, notification icons, and the current time and date. The 'Show hidden icons' button indicates that one or more inactive icons are hidden from view in the notification area. The notification icons provide quick access to programs that are currently running in the background on your computer. A program running in the background does not show up on the taskbar, but is still working. Icons may display temporarily in the notification area when providing status updates. For example, the printer icon is displayed when a document is sent to the printer and is removed when printing is complete. The notification area on your desktop might contain more, fewer, or different icons than shown in Figure 1–5.

To Display the Start Menu

The Start menu allows you to easily access the programs on your computer as well as other frequently used features and files. A **menu** is a list of related commands and the **commands** on a menu perform a specific action, such as launching a program or obtaining help. The following steps display the Start menu.

1

- Click the Start button on the Windows 7 taskbar to display the Start menu (Figure 1–6).

Q&A

Why does my Start menu look different?

Depending upon your computer's configuration, the Start menu can look different. In a work or school environment, it might be customized for any number of reasons, such as usage requirements or security policies.

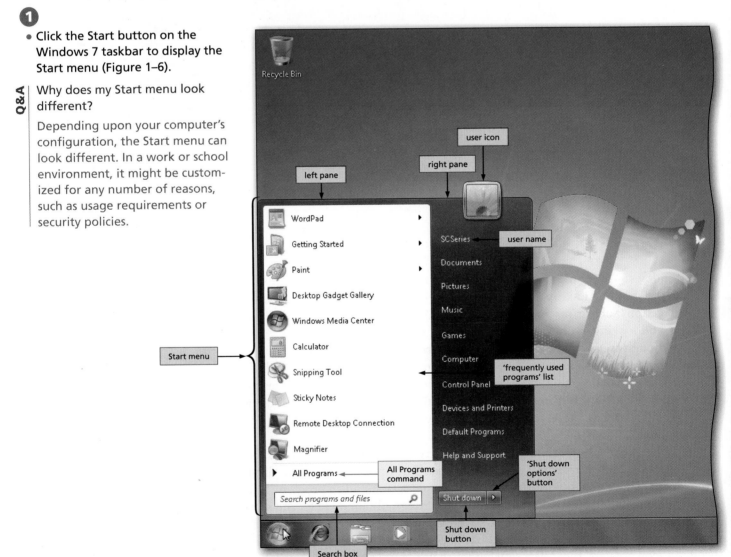

Figure 1–6

2

• Click the All Programs command on the Start menu to display the All Programs list (Figure 1–7).

Q&A Why does my All Programs list look different than the All Programs list in Figure 1–7?

The programs installed on your computer might differ. Your All Programs list will show the programs that are installed on your computer.

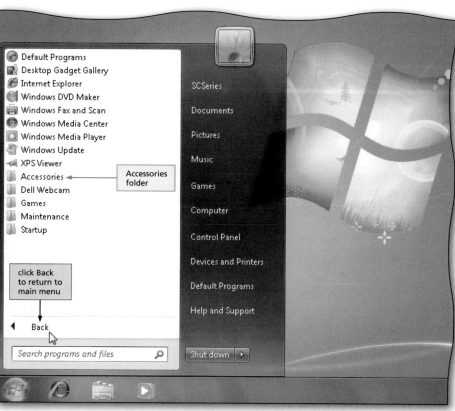

Figure 1–7

3

• Click the Accessories folder to display the Accessories list (Figure 1–8).

Q&A What can I expect to find in the Accessories list?

The Accessories list contains programs that accomplish a variety of tasks commonly required on a computer. Most of these programs are installed with the Windows 7 operating system, such as Calculator, Snipping Tool, Windows Mobility Center (if you have a portable computer), and WordPad. Your Accessories list might contain additional or fewer programs.

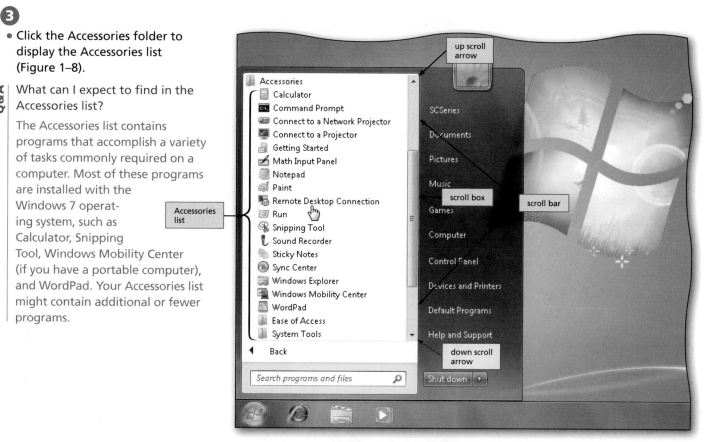

Figure 1–8

To Scroll Using Scroll Arrows, the Scroll Bar, and the Scroll Box

A **scroll bar** is displayed when the contents of an area are not completely visible. A vertical scroll bar contains an up scroll arrow, a down scroll arrow, and a scroll box that enables you to view areas that currently are not visible. In Figure 1–8, a vertical scroll bar displays along the right side of the All Programs list. Scrolling can be accomplished in three ways: (1) Click a scroll arrow, (2) click the scroll bar, or (3) drag the scroll box. You **drag** an object by pointing to it, holding down the left mouse button, moving the object to the desired location, and then releasing the left mouse button. The following steps scroll the items in the All Programs list.

❶

- Click the down scroll arrow on the scroll bar to display additional folders at the bottom of the All Programs list (Figure 1–9). You might need to click more than once to reach the bottom of the All Programs list.

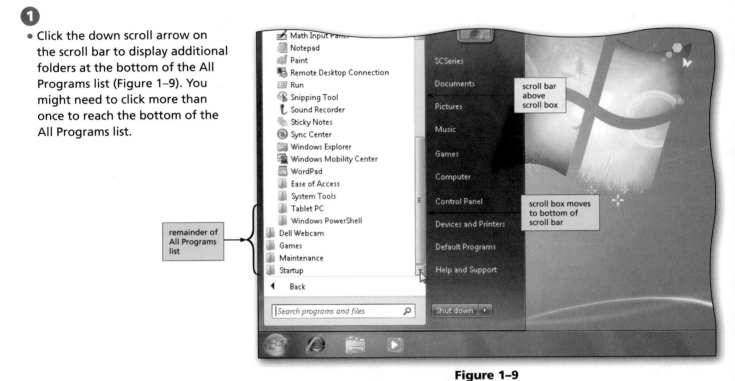

Figure 1–9

❷

- Click the scroll bar above the scroll box to move the scroll box to the top of the All Programs list (Figure 1–10). You might need to click more than once to reach the top of the All Programs list.

Q&A

Why does it take more than one click on the scroll bar to move the scroll box to the top of the scroll bar?

There might be more programs installed on your computer than on the one in the figure. As the number of programs on your computer increases, you might need to click the scroll box multiple times to reach the top of the list.

Figure 1–10

- Click the scroll box and drag down to the bottom of the scroll bar to display the bottom of the All Programs list (Figure 1–11).

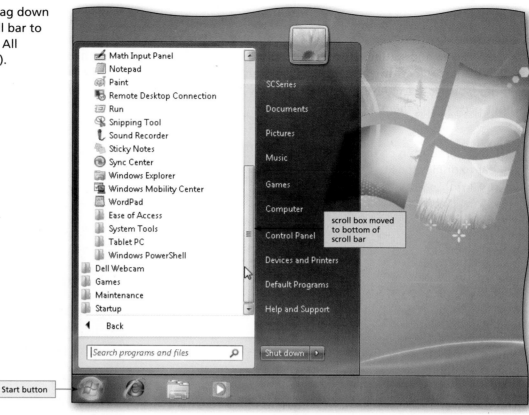

Figure 1–11

- Click the Start button to close the Start menu (Figure 1–12).

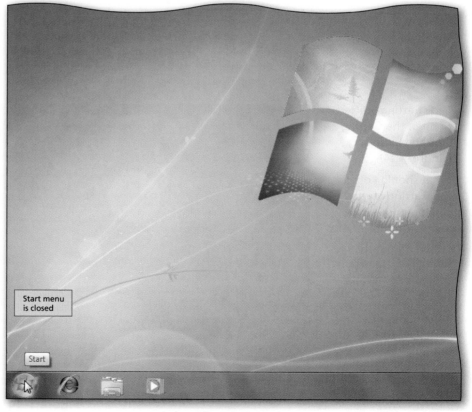

Figure 1–12

To Open the Getting Started Window

If you are new to using Windows 7, you can open the Getting Started window. The **Getting Started window** allows you to complete a set of tasks to optimize the computer. The tasks might include adding user accounts, transferring files and settings from another computer, and backing up your files. You do not have to use the Getting Started window to perform these tasks, but it can assist you with configuring your computer. The following steps open the Getting Started window. If the Getting Started window already is visible on your desktop, read these steps without performing them.

1

● Click the Start button on the taskbar to display the Start menu (Figure 1–13).

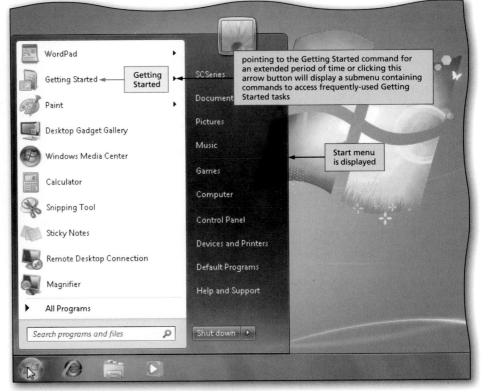

pointing to the Getting Started command for an extended period of time or clicking this arrow button will display a submenu containing commands to access frequently-used Getting Started tasks

Getting Started

Start menu is displayed

WordPad

Getting Started

Paint

Desktop Gadget Gallery

Windows Media Center

Calculator

Snipping Tool

Sticky Notes

Remote Desktop Connection

Magnifier

All Programs

Search programs and files

SCSeries

Documents

Pictures

Music

Games

Computer

Control Panel

Devices and Printers

Default Programs

Help and Support

Shut down

Figure 1–13

2

● Click Getting Started to open the Getting Started window (Figure 1–14).

Q&A

What should I do if the Getting Started command does not display on the Start menu?

Depending upon how your computer is configured, you might find the Getting Started command in the Accessories list instead.

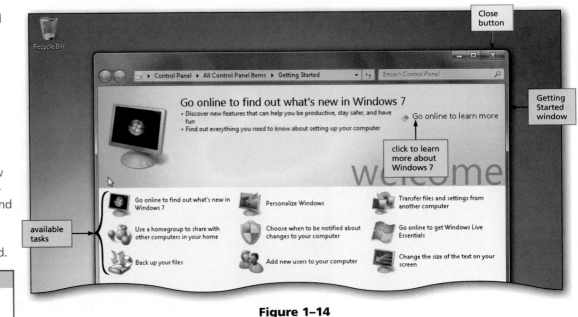

Recycle Bin

Close button

Control Panel ▶ All Control Panel Items ▶ Getting Started

Search Control Panel

Getting Started window

Go online to find out what's new in Windows 7

• Discover new features that can help you be productive, stay safer, and have fun
• Find out everything you need to know about setting up your computer

Go online to learn more

click to learn more about Windows 7

welcome

available tasks

Go online to find out what's new in Windows 7

Use a homegroup to share with other computers in your home

Back up your files

Personalize Windows

Choose when to be notified about changes to your computer

Add new users to your computer

Transfer files and settings from another computer

Go online to get Windows Live Essentials

Change the size of the text on your screen

Figure 1–14

Other Ways

1. Display Start menu, click All Programs, click Accessories, click Getting Started

To Close the Getting Started Window

After reviewing the options available in the Getting Started window, you can close it. The following step closes the Getting Started window.

1

• Click the Close button on the Getting Started window to close the Getting Started window (Figure 1–15).

Getting Started window is closed

Start button

Figure 1–15

To Open the Computer Folder Window

The Computer folder is accessible via the Start menu. When opened, the Computer folder opens in a folder window. The Computer folder is the place you can go to access hard disks, optical disc drives, removable media, and network locations that are connected to your computer. You also can access other devices such as external hard disks or digital cameras that might be connected to your computer. The following steps open the Computer folder window.

1

• Click the Start button on the Windows 7 taskbar to display the Start menu (Figure 1–16).

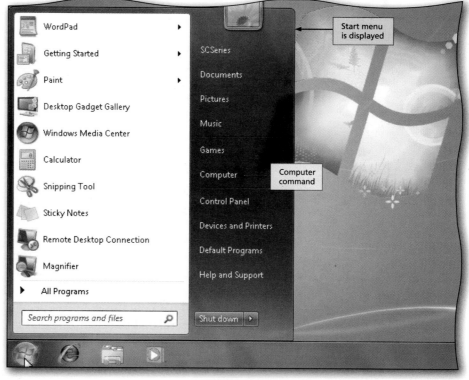

WordPad

Getting Started

Paint

Desktop Gadget Gallery

Windows Media Center

Calculator

Snipping Tool

Sticky Notes

Remote Desktop Connection

Magnifier

▶ All Programs

Search programs and files

SCSeries

Documents

Pictures

Music

Games

Computer

Control Panel

Devices and Printers

Default Programs

Help and Support

Shut down ▶

Start menu is displayed

Computer command

Figure 1–16

2

- Click the Computer command on the right pane of the Start menu to open the Computer folder window (Figure 1–17).

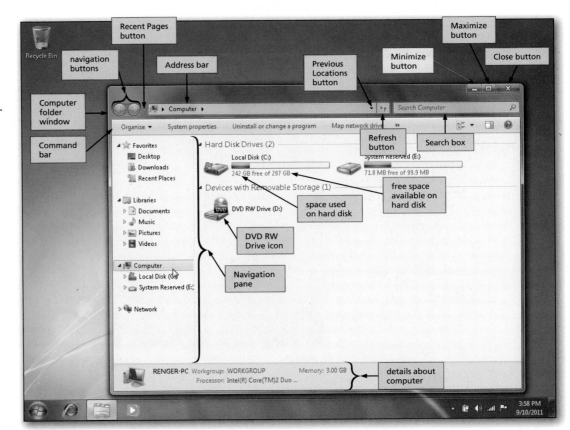

Figure 1–17

Other Ways

1. Click Start button, right-click Computer, click Open
2. Press WINDOWS+E

Folder Windows

Folder windows are the key tools for finding, viewing, and managing information on the computer. Folder windows have common design elements, as shown in Figure 1–17. The three buttons to the left of the Address bar allow you to navigate the contents of the right pane and view recent pages. The Recent Pages button saves the locations you have visited and displays the locations in a list. On the right of the title bar are the Minimize button, the Maximize button, and the Close button, which can be used to reduce the window to the taskbar, increase the window to the full screen, or close the window.

The Previous Locations button and the Refresh button are on the right side of the Address bar. The Previous Locations button displays a list of recently visited file locations. The Refresh button refreshes the contents of the window. The Search box to the right of the Address bar contains the dimmed word, Search, followed by the location you currently are viewing. For example, in Figure 1–17, the Search box displays Search Computer because the Computer folder window is open. You can type a term into the Search box to search for files, folders, shortcuts, and programs containing that term within the specified location.

The Command bar contains context-specific buttons used to accomplish various tasks on the computer related to organizing and managing the contents of the open window. Depending upon the selections you make in the Computer folder window, the Command bar buttons will change to reflect the selections. If you navigate to an optical disc drive, the Command bar would display the appropriate buttons for an optical disc drive. For example, you might see a Burn button for burning an optical disc. The area below the Command bar is separated into two panes; the left pane contains the Navigation pane and the right pane displays the contents of the location you currently are viewing.

The Navigation pane on the left contains the Favorites section, Libraries section, Computer folder section, Network folder section, and if your computer is connected to a network, the Homegroup section. The Favorites section contains links to your favorite locations. By default, this list contains only links to your desktop, downloads, and recent places. The Libraries section shows links to files and folders that have been included in a library.

A **library** is designed to help you manage multiple folders and files stored in various locations on your computer. It does not store the files and folders, but rather displays links to them so that you can access them quickly. For example, you can save pictures from your digital camera in any folder in any storage location on your computer. Normally, this would make management of the different folders difficult; however, if you add the folders to the Pictures library, you can access all your pictures no matter where they are stored.

Expanding the Computer folder section displays all your folders in the classic folder list, or folder tree, that you might be familiar with from previous versions of Windows. Finally, the Network folder section allows you to browse network locations.

To Minimize and Redisplay a Window

Two buttons on the title bar of a window, the Minimize button and the Maximize button, allow you to control the way a window displays or does not display on the desktop. The following steps minimize and restore the Computer folder window.

1

- Click the Minimize button on the title bar of the Computer folder window to minimize the Computer folder window (Figure 1–18).

Q&A What happens to the Computer folder window when I click the Minimize button?

The Computer folder window remains available, but no longer is an active window. It collapses down to a button on the taskbar.

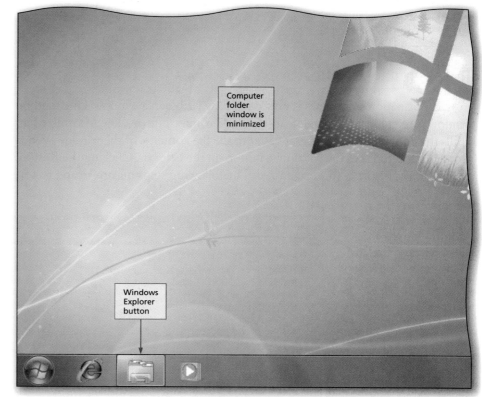

Computer folder window is minimized

Windows Explorer button

Figure 1–18

2

- Click the Windows Explorer button on the taskbar to display the Computer folder window (Figure 1–19).

Q&A Why does the Windows Explorer button on the taskbar change?

The button changes to reflect the status of the Computer folder window. A highlighted button indicates that the Computer folder window is active on the screen. An unhighlighted button indicates that the Computer folder window is open but not active.

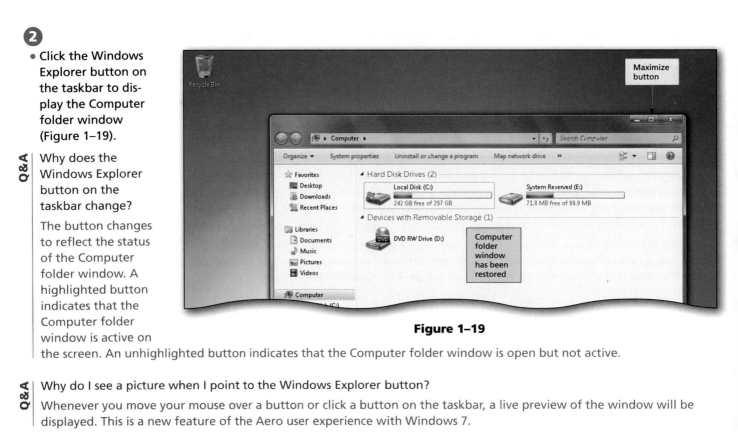

Figure 1–19

Q&A Why do I see a picture when I point to the Windows Explorer button?

Whenever you move your mouse over a button or click a button on the taskbar, a live preview of the window will be displayed. This is a new feature of the Aero user experience with Windows 7.

Other Ways

1. Right-click title bar, click Minimize; in taskbar button area, click taskbar button
2. Press WINDOWS+M, press WINDOWS+SHIFT+M

To Maximize and Restore a Window

Information sometimes is not completely visible in a window. One method of displaying the entire contents of a window is to enlarge the window using the Maximize button. The Maximize button increases the size of a window so that it fills the entire screen, making it easier to see the contents of the window. When a window is maximized, the Restore Down button replaces the Maximize button on the title bar. Clicking the Restore Down button will return the window to the size it was before it was maximized. The following steps maximize and restore the Computer folder window.

1

- Click the Maximize button on the title bar to maximize the Computer folder window (Figure 1–20).

Q&A When a window is maximized, can you also minimize it?

Yes. Click the Minimize button to minimize the window to the taskbar. Clicking the button on the taskbar will return the window to its maximized size.

Figure 1–20

• Click the Restore Down button on the Computer folder window to return the Computer folder window to its previous size (Figure 1–21).

Q&A

What happens to the Restore Down button after I click it?

The Maximize button replaces the Restore Down button on the title bar.

Other Ways

1. Double-click title bar, double-click title bar

2. Right-click title bar, click Maximize, right-click title bar, click Restore

3. Click title bar and drag window to the top of screen, click title bar and drag window down towards the center of the screen

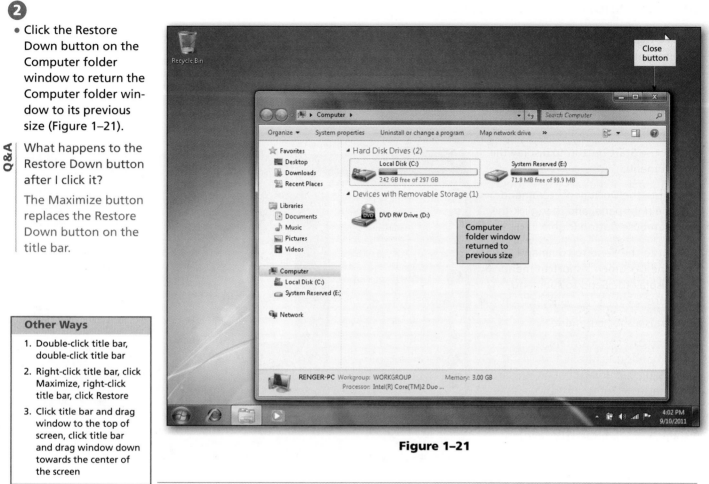

Figure 1–21

To Close a Window

The Close button on the title bar of a window closes the window. To close the Computer folder window, complete the following step.

• Click the Close button on the title bar of the Computer folder window to close the Computer folder window (Figure 1–22).

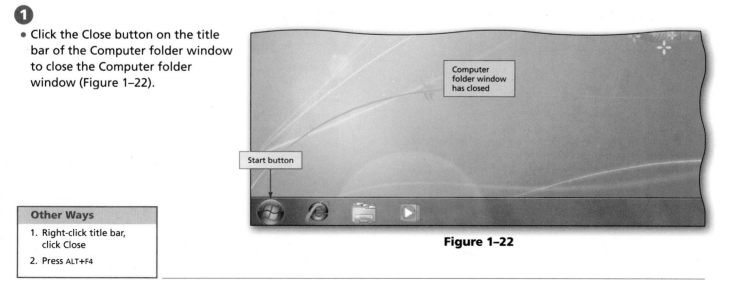

Figure 1–22

Other Ways

1. Right-click title bar, click Close

2. Press ALT+F4

To Add a Shortcut to the Desktop

Once you start doing more work on your computer, you might want to add shortcuts to the desktop. For example, you might want to add the Documents library shortcut to the desktop so that you can access the Documents library quickly. The **Documents library** is a central location for the storage and management of documents. This library is optimized for faster searching and organizing. The following steps add a shortcut to the Documents library to your desktop.

1

- Click the Start button to display the Start menu.

- Point to the Documents command in the right pane, and then click the right mouse button (right-click).

- Point to the Send to command on the Documents shortcut menu to display the Send to submenu (Figure 1–23).

Q&A What is a shortcut menu?

A shortcut menu contains commands specifically for use with that object. Shortcut menus often appear when you right-click an object. Using shortcut menus can speed up your work and add flexibility to your interaction with the computer by making often-used items easily accessible.

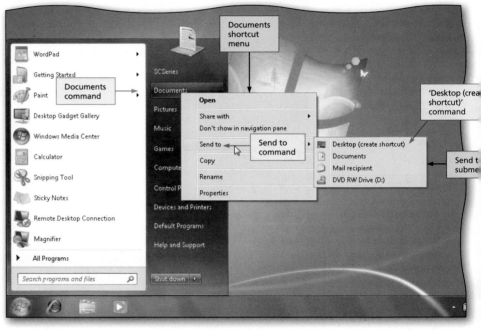

Figure 1–23

2

- Click the 'Desktop (create shortcut)' command on the Send to submenu to place a shortcut to the Documents library on the desktop (Figure 1–24).

Q&A Why am I unable to add an item to my desktop?

On some work or school computers, users are not allowed to add items to the desktop.

Q&A How many icons should I have on my desktop?

Icons can be added to your desktop by programs or by users; however, it is considered a best practice to keep your desktop as clutter free as possible. If you are not using an icon on the desktop, consider removing it from the desktop.

3

- Click the Start button to close the Start menu.

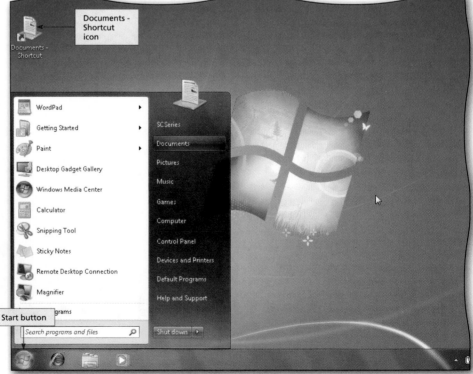

Figure 1–24

To Open a Window Using a Desktop Shortcut

The following step opens the Documents library using the shortcut you have just created on the desktop.

1

- Double-click (click the left mouse button twice, in rapid succession) the Documents - Shortcut icon on the desktop to open the Documents library (Figure 1–25).

Why are the contents of my Documents library different from Figure 1–25?

The Documents library in the figure is empty because there are no files or folders added. Because you might have different documents and folders on your computer, the contents of your Documents library might be different from the one in Figure 1–25.

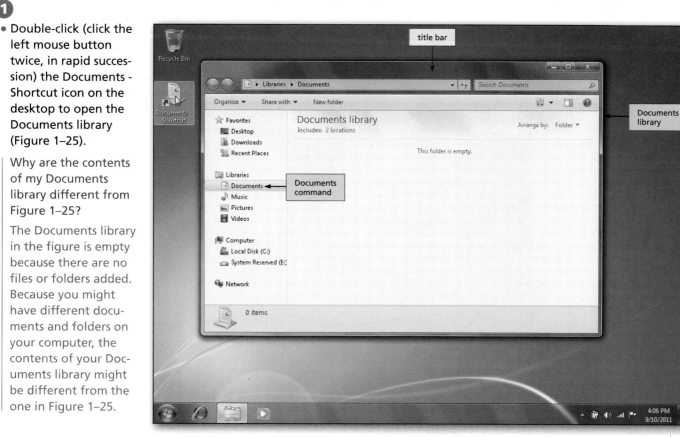

Figure 1–25

Other Ways

1. Right-click desktop icon, click Open on shortcut menu

Double-Clicking Errors

When double-clicking an object, it is easy to click once instead of twice. When you click an object such as the Documents - Shortcut icon once, the icon becomes active and highlighted. To open the Documents library after clicking the Documents - Shortcut icon once, double-click the icon as if you had not clicked it at all.

Another possible error occurs when the mouse moves after you click the first time and before you click the second time. In most cases when this occurs, the icon will appear highlighted as if you had clicked it just one time.

A third possible error is moving the mouse while you are pressing the mouse button. In this case, the icon might have moved on the screen because you inadvertently dragged it. To open the Documents library after dragging it accidentally, double-click the icon as if you had not clicked it at all.

To Move a Window by Dragging

You can move any open window to another location on the desktop by dragging the title bar of the window. The following step drags the Documents library to the center of the desktop.

1

- Drag the title bar of the Documents library so that the window appears at the center of the screen, as shown in Figure 1–26.

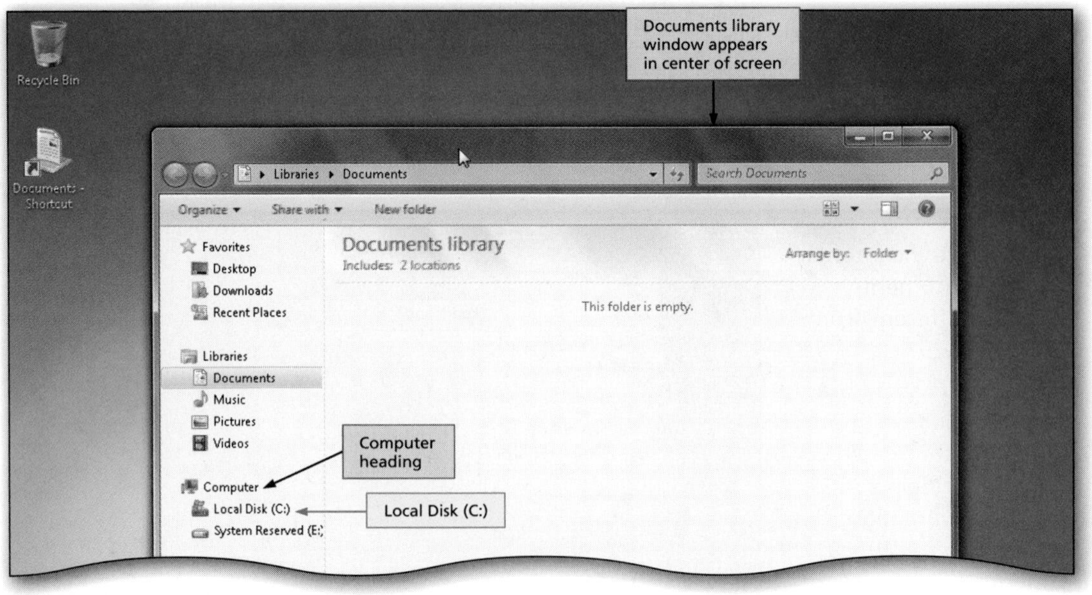

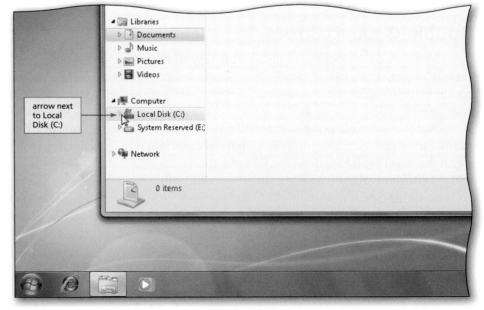

Documents library window appears in center of screen

Computer heading

Local Disk (C:)

Figure 1–26

Other Ways

1. Right-click title bar, click Move, drag window

To Expand the Contents of Local Disk (C:)

In Figure 1–26, the Local Disk (C:) list in the Documents library is collapsed. The Navigation pane displays arrows that can be used to expand and collapse the different sections in the Navigation pane. Clicking the arrow that appears next to Local Disk (C:) expands and reveals the contents of Local Disk (C:). The following steps expand the Local Disk (C:) list.

1

- Point the mouse to the arrow next to Local Disk (C:) below the Computer heading in the Navigation pane (Figure 1–27).

arrow next to Local Disk (C:)

Figure 1–27

2

- Click the arrow to expand the contents of Local Disk (C:) in the Navigation pane of the Documents library (Figure 1–28).

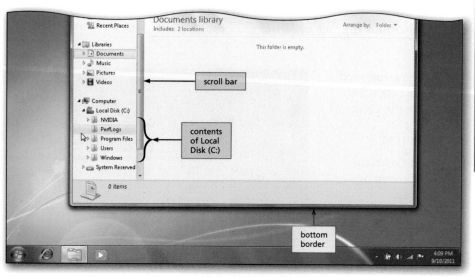

Figure 1–28

To Size a Window by Dragging

Sometimes information is not completely visible in a window. You have learned how to use the Maximize button to increase the size of a window. Another method to change the size of the window is to drag the window borders. The following step changes the size of the Documents library.

1

- Point to the bottom border of the Documents library until the mouse pointer changes to a two-headed arrow.

- If necessary, drag the bottom border downward to display more of the Navigation pane so that your screen looks similar to Figure 1–29.

Q&A Can I drag other borders besides the bottom border to enlarge or shrink the window?

Yes, you can drag the left, right, and top borders and any window corner to resize the window.

Q&A Will Windows 7 remember the new size of the window after I close it?

Yes. Windows 7 remembers the size of the window when you close the window. When you reopen the window, the window will display at the same size as when you closed it.

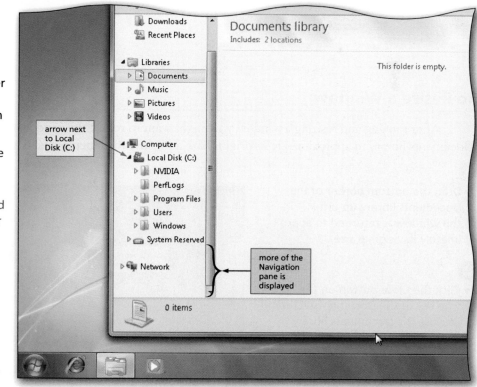

Figure 1–29

To Collapse the Local Disk (C:) List

The following step collapses the Local Disk (C:) list.

1

- Click the arrow next to Local Disk (C:) to collapse the Local Disk (C:) list (Figure 1–30).

Q&A

Should I keep the list expanded or collapsed?

If you need to use the contents in the list, it is handy to keep the list expanded. You can collapse the list when the information is not needed.

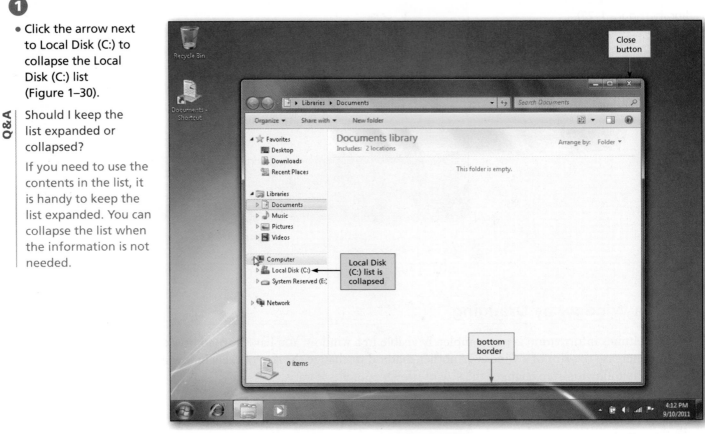

Figure 1–30

To Resize a Window

After moving and resizing a window, you might want to return the window to its original size. To return the Documents library to approximately its original size and close the Documents library, complete the following steps.

1

- Drag the bottom border of the Documents library up until the window is returned to approximately its original size.

2

- Click the Close button on the title bar of the Documents library to close the Documents library (Figure 1–31).

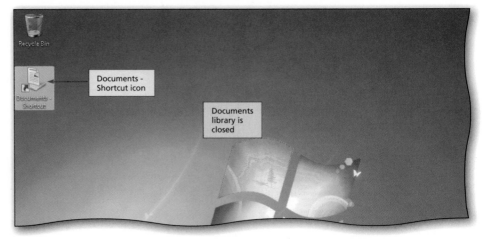

Figure 1–31

To Delete a Desktop Icon by Dragging it to the Recycle Bin

Although Windows 7 has many ways to delete desktop icons, one method of removing an icon from the desktop is to drag it to the Recycle Bin. The following steps delete the Documents - Shortcut icon by dragging the icon to the Recycle Bin.

1

- Point to the Documents - Shortcut icon on the desktop and press the left mouse button to select the icon (Figure 1–32). Do not release the left mouse button.

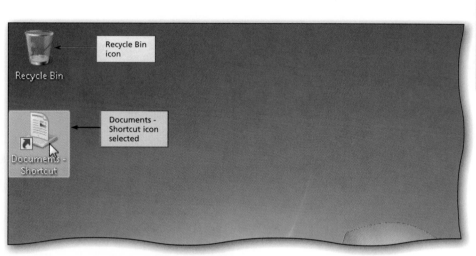

Recycle Bin icon

Documents - Shortcut icon selected

Figure 1–32

2

- Drag the Documents - Shortcut icon over the Recycle Bin icon on the desktop, and then release the left mouse button to place the shortcut in the Recycle Bin (Figure 1–33).

Experiment

- Double-click the Recycle Bin icon on the desktop to open a window containing the contents of the Recycle Bin. The Documents - Shortcut icon you have just deleted will display in this window. Close the Recycle Bin window.

Q&A

Why did the Documents - Shortcut icon disappear?

Releasing the left mouse button moved the icon from the desktop to the Recycle Bin.

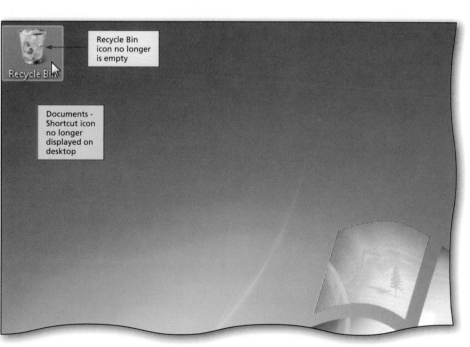

Recycle Bin icon no longer is empty

Documents - Shortcut icon no longer displayed on desktop

Figure 1–33

Other Ways
1. Right-click icon, click Delete, click Yes button
2. Right-click icon and hold, drag to Recycle Bin, release right mouse button, click Move Here

To Empty the Recycle Bin

The Recycle Bin prevents you from deleting files you actually might need. Until you empty the Recycle Bin, you can recover deleted items from it. The following steps empty the Recycle Bin. If you are not sure that you want to permanently delete all the files in the Recycle Bin, read these steps without performing them.

1

- Right-click the Recycle Bin to display the shortcut menu (Figure 1–34).

2

- Click the Empty Recycle Bin command to permanently delete the contents of the Recycle Bin.

- Click the Yes button to confirm the operation.

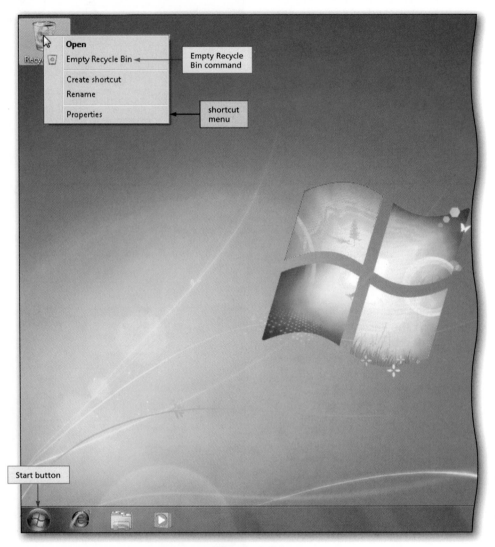

Figure 1–34

Other Ways

1. Right-click Recycle Bin icon, click Open, click Empty the Recycle Bin, click Yes button, click Close button

2. Double-click Recycle Bin icon, click Empty the Recycle Bin, click Yes button, click Close button

To Add a Gadget to the Desktop

Gadgets are miniprograms that display information and provide access to various useful tools. Gadgets can be found in the Gadget Gallery or you can download gadgets from the Internet. Gadgets can include games, viewers for RSS feeds, and even online auction updates. The first step when using a gadget is to add the gadget to the desktop. One way to add a gadget to the desktop is to double-click the gadget in the Gadget Gallery. The following steps open the Gadget Gallery and add a gadget to the desktop.

1

- Click the Start button to display the Start menu.

- Click All Programs to display the All Programs list (Figure 1–35).

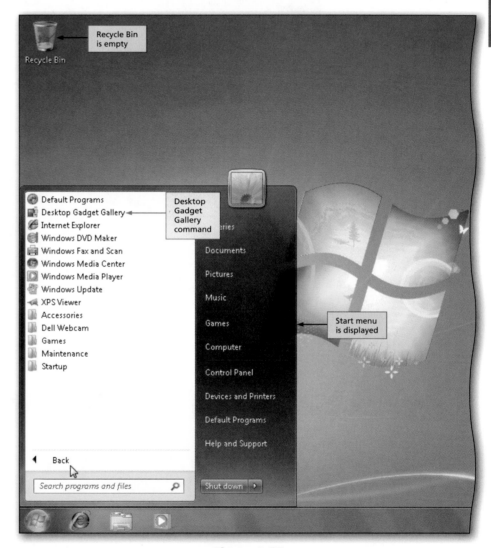

Figure 1–35

②

- Click the Desktop Gadget Gallery command to open the Gadget Gallery (Figure 1–36).

Q&A

Where can I find more gadgets?

You can download additional gadgets by clicking the Get more gadgets online link, by downloading gadgets from http://gallery.live.com, or by searching online to locate other gadget collections.

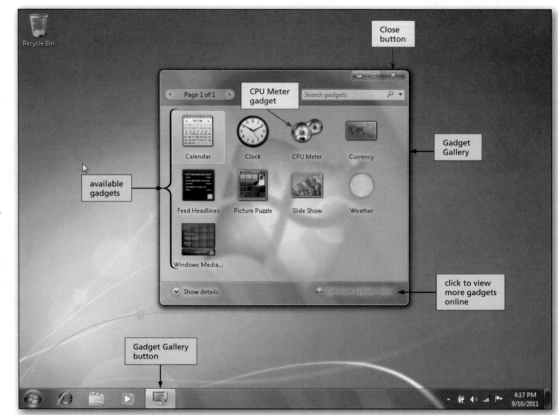

Figure 1–36

③

- Double-click the CPU Meter gadget in the Gadget Gallery to add the gadget to the desktop and display the performance measurements for your CPU (Figure 1–37).

- Click the Close button to close the Gadget Gallery.

Q&A

Can I change the position of gadgets on the desktop?

Yes, you can move them to any location you desire on the desktop by clicking and dragging them to your preferred location.

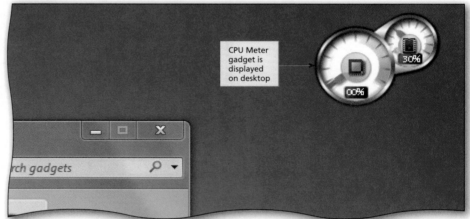

Figure 1–37

To Remove a Gadget from the Desktop

In addition to adding gadgets to the desktop, you can remove gadgets. The following steps remove the gadget from the desktop.

- Point to the CPU Meter gadget to make the Close button visible (Figure 1–38).

- Click the Close button to remove the CPU Meter gadget from the desktop.

Figure 1–38

Launching a Program

One of the basic tasks you can perform using Windows 7 is to launch a program. Recall that a program is designed to perform a specific user-oriented task. For example, a **word-processing program** allows you to create written documents; a **presentation program** allows you to create graphical presentations for display on a computer; and a **Web browser** allows you to explore the Internet and display Web pages.

Internet Explorer, the default Web browser in Windows 7, appears as a pinned program on the taskbar. Because you can change which Web browser is the default, the Web browser on your computer might be different. For example, you could install another frequently used Web browser such as **Mozilla Firefox** and set it as the default Web browser.

BTW

Programs
Many programs (for example, Internet Explorer, WordPad, Paint) are installed with Windows 7. Most programs, however, such as Microsoft Office or Adobe® Photoshop®, must be purchased separately. Other programs, such as Mozilla Firefox or OpenOffice, are available to download for free.

To Start a Program Using the Start Menu

The most common activity performed on a computer is using a program to accomplish tasks. You can start a program by using the Start menu. **Paint** is a popular program available with Windows 7 that allows you to create and edit simple graphics. The following steps start Paint using the Start menu.

1

- To display the Start menu, click the Start button.

- Display the All Programs list.

- Display the Accessories list (Figure 1–39).

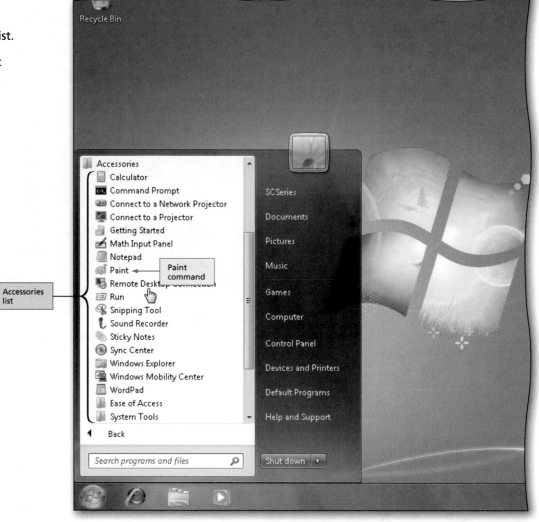

Figure 1–39

2

- Click the Paint command to start Paint and display the Untitled - Paint window (Figure 1–40).

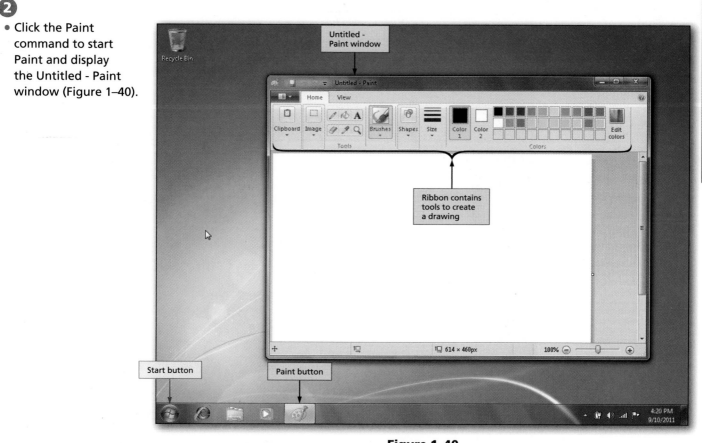

Figure 1–40

To Start a Program Using the Search Box

If you are unsure of where to find the program you want to open in the Start menu, you can use the Start menu Search box to search for the program. The following steps search for the WordPad program using the Search box.

1

- Display the Start menu.

- Type wordpad in the Search box to have Windows 7 look for WordPad (Figure 1–41).

Q&A

Why did different items display as I typed in the Search box?

As you type in the Search box, Windows 7 automatically tries to find items matching the text you type.

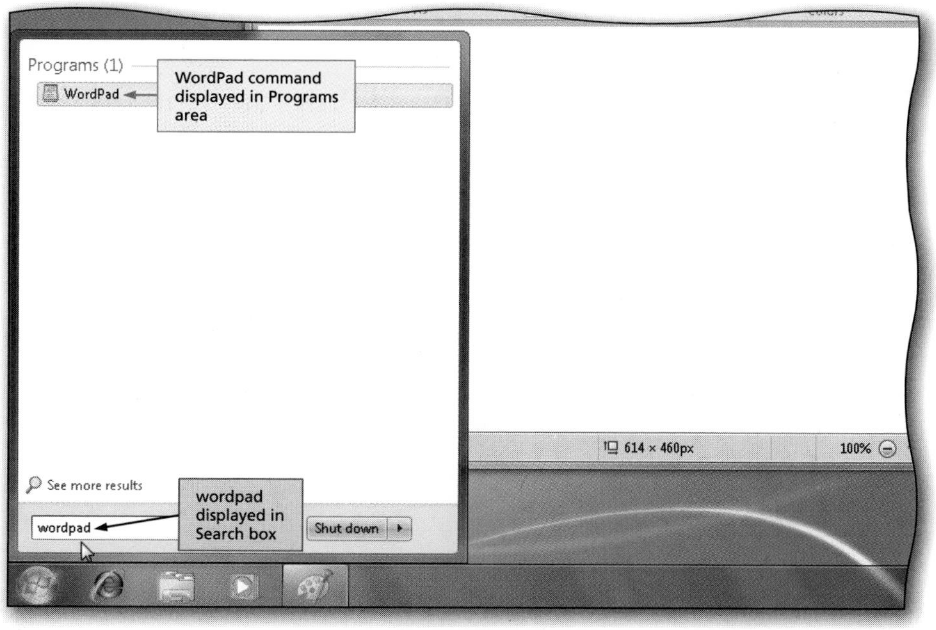

Figure 1–41

2

- Click the WordPad command in the Programs area to start WordPad and display the Document - WordPad window (Figure 1–42).

Do I have to type the entire word before clicking the result?

No. As soon as you see the result you are looking for in the Programs area above the Search box, you can click it.

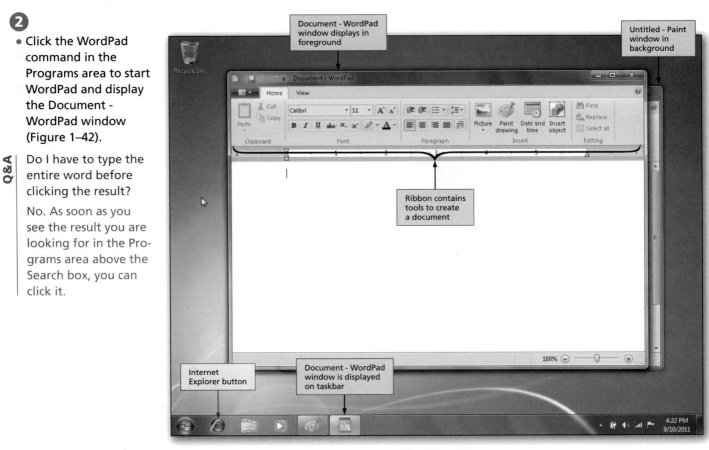

Figure 1–42

Other Ways

1. Open Start menu, type `wordpad` in Search box, press ENTER
2. Open Start menu, click All Programs, open Accessories list, click WordPad

To Start a Program Using a Pinned Program Icon on the Taskbar

Windows 7 allows users to access selected programs with one click of the mouse button when the program icon is pinned to the taskbar. The following step launches the Internet Explorer program using the pinned program icon on the taskbar.

- Click the Internet Explorer button on the taskbar to start Internet Explorer (Figure 1–43).

Q&A What if the Internet Explorer icon does not appear on my taskbar?

The pinned items on the taskbar are customizable, and yours might differ. Use one of the previous methods to open Internet Explorer instead.

Figure 1–43

Other Ways

1. Display Start menu, click All Programs, click Internet Explorer

To Switch Programs Using Aero Flip 3D

When you have multiple programs open simultaneously, invariably you will need to switch between them. Aero Flip 3D provides an easy and visual way to switch between the open programs on your computer. The following steps switch from Internet Explorer to WordPad using Aero Flip 3D.

- Press CTRL+ WINDOWS+TAB to start Aero Flip 3D (Figure 1–44).

Q&A Why does this effect not appear three-dimensional on my computer?

Your computer is set up to use the Basic experience, so you are seeing the basic program switching method, which is not three-dimensional. Aero Flip 3D is part of the Aero experience.

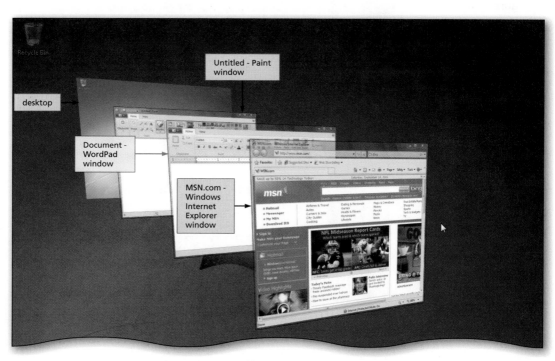

Figure 1–44

2

● Press the TAB key
repeatedly until the
Document - WordPad
window appears at
the front of the pro-
grams displayed in
Aero Flip 3D
(Figure 1–45).

Q&A

Do I have to use the
TAB key?

You also can scroll the
mouse wheel, if your
mouse has one, until
the WordPad window
is at the front.

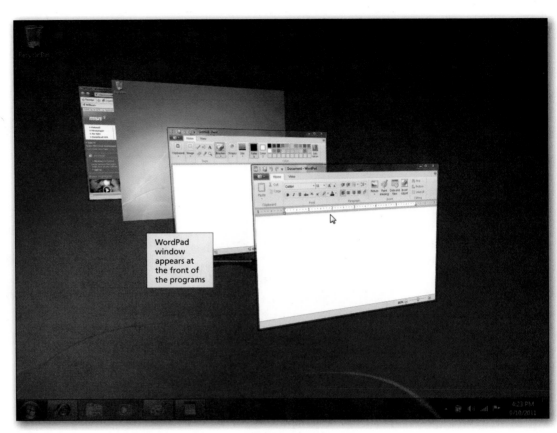

Figure 1–45

3

● Click the WordPad
window to exit Aero
Flip 3D and make
the WordPad window
the active window
(Figure 1–46).

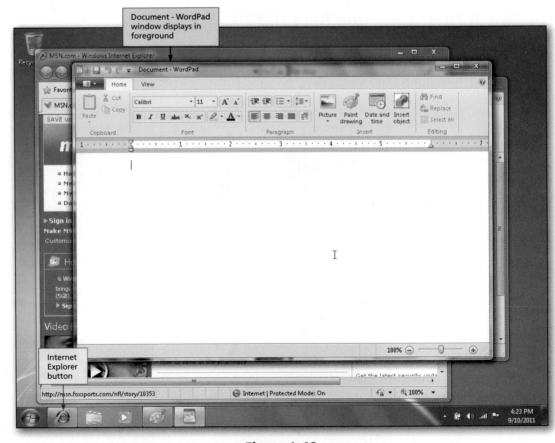

Figure 1–46

To Switch Between Programs Using the Taskbar

You also can switch between programs using the taskbar. By clicking the button for the program, you make that program active by bringing the window to the front. If the button represents multiple windows or there are multiple files open in a program, you will need to click the button for the program and then the particular file or window you want to make active. The following steps switch between programs using the taskbar.

1

• Click the Windows Internet Explorer button on the taskbar to make the MSN.com - Windows Internet Explorer window the active window (Figure 1–47).

Figure 1–47

2

• Click the Untitled - Paint button on the taskbar to make the Paint window the active window (Figure 1–48).

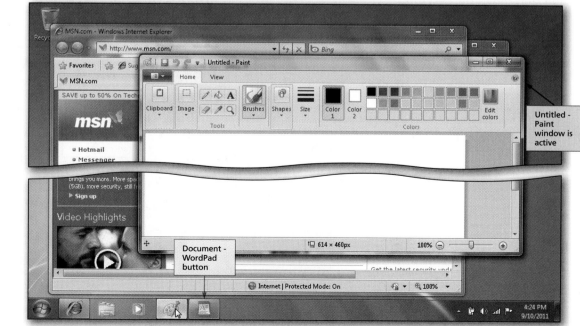

Figure 1–48

3

- Click the Document - WordPad button on the taskbar to make WordPad the active window (Figure 1–49).

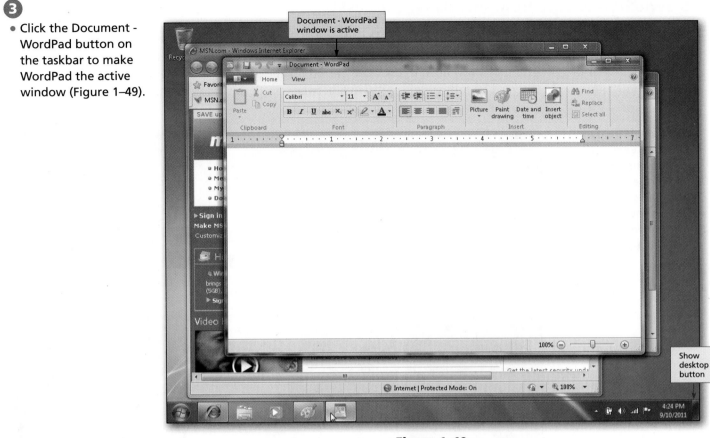

Figure 1–49

To Show the Desktop Using the Show Desktop Button

When you have several windows open at the same time and need to reveal the desktop without closing all of the open windows, you can use the Show desktop button on the taskbar to quickly display the desktop. The following step shows the desktop.

1

- Click the Show desktop button on the taskbar to show the desktop (Figure 1–50).

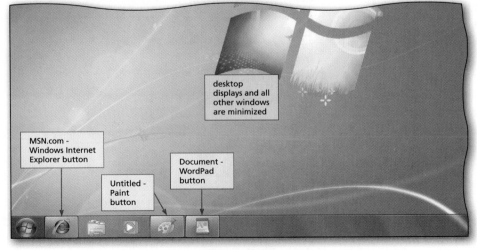

Figure 1–50

To Close Open Windows

After you are done viewing windows or using programs in Windows 7, you should close them. The following steps close the open programs.

1 Click the Document - WordPad button on the taskbar to display the WordPad window. Click the Close button on the title bar of the WordPad window to close WordPad.

2 Click the Internet Explorer button on the taskbar to display the MSN.com - Windows Internet Explorer window. Click the Close button on the title bar to close Internet Explorer.

3 Display the Untitled - Paint window and click the Close button to close Paint.

Other Ways

1. Right-click taskbar button of the program you want to close, click Close window

Using Windows Help and Support

One of the more powerful Windows 7 features is Windows Help and Support. **Windows Help and Support** is available when using Windows 7 or when using any Microsoft program running under Windows 7. This feature is designed to assist you in using Windows 7 or the various other programs. Table 1–2 describes what can be found in Windows Help and Support.

Table 1–2 Windows Help and Support Content Areas	
Area	**Function**
Find an answer quickly	This area contains instructions about how to perform a quick search using the Search Help box.
Not sure where to start?	This area displays three links to topics to help guide users: How to get started with your computer, Learn about Windows Basics, and Browse Help topics. Clicking one of the options takes you to corresponding Help and Support pages.
More on the Windows website	This area contains links to online content from the Windows Web site. Clicking one of the links takes you to the corresponding Web pages on the Web site.

To Start Windows Help and Support

Before you can access the Windows Help and Support services, you must start Windows Help and Support. One method of launching Windows Help and Support uses the Start menu. The following steps start Windows Help and Support.

1

- Display the Start menu (Figure 1–51).

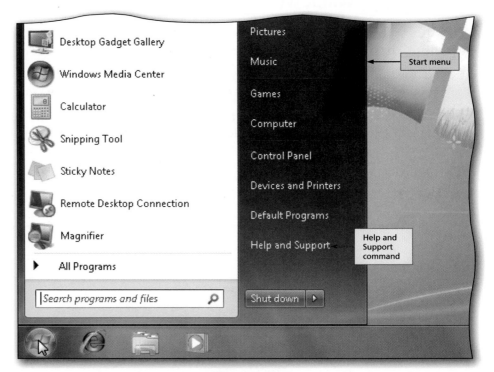

Figure 1–51

2

- Click the Help and Support command to display the Windows Help and Support window (Figure 1–52).

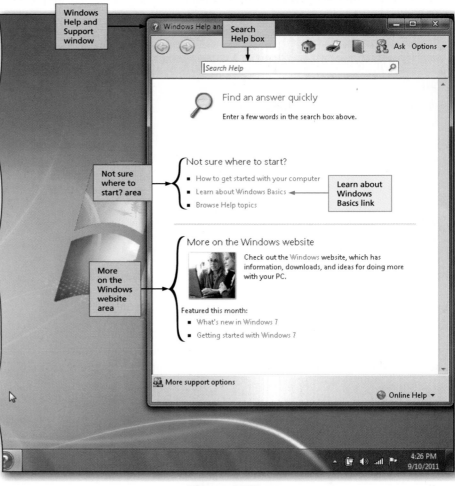

Other Ways

1. Press CTRL+ESC, press RIGHT ARROW, press UP ARROW, press ENTER
2. Press WINDOWS+F1

Figure 1–52

To Browse for Help Topics in Windows Basics

After launching Windows Help and Support, your next step is to find Help topics that relate to your questions. The following steps use the Not sure where to start? area in the Windows Help and Support to locate a Help topic that describes how to use the Windows Help and Support.

1

- Click the Learn about Windows Basics link in the Not sure where to start? area to display the Windows Basics: all topics page (Figure 1–53).

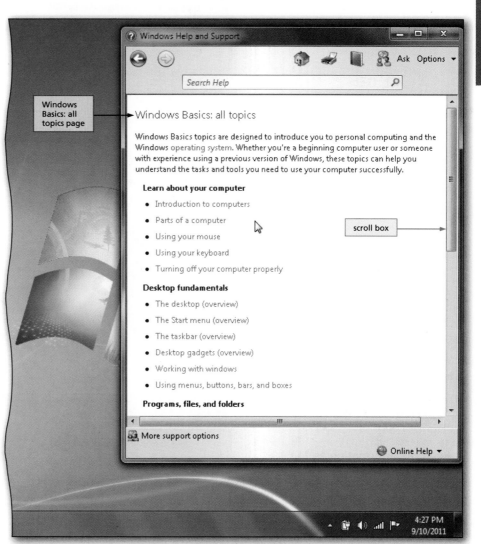

Figure 1–53

2

- Scroll down until you can see the Getting help link under the 'Help and support' heading (Figure 1–54).

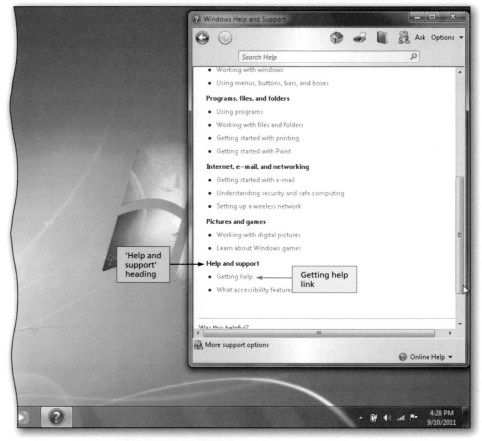

Figure 1–54

3

- Click the Getting help link to display the Getting help page (Figure 1–55).

- Read the information on the Getting help page.

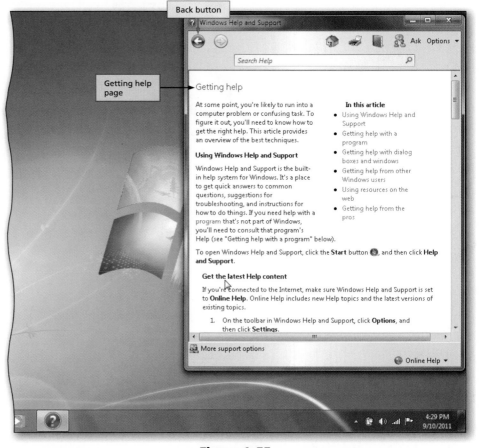

Figure 1–55

4

- Click the Back button on the Navigation toolbar two times to return to the Help and Support home (Figure 1–56).

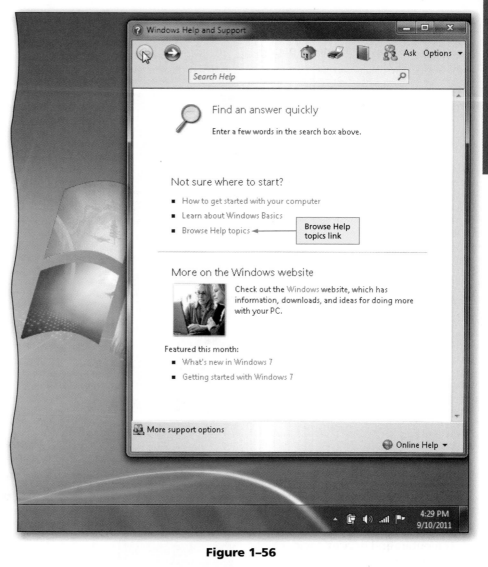

Figure 1–56

To Search for Help Topics Using the Table of Contents

A second method for finding answers to your questions about Windows 7 is to use the Browse Help topics link. Browse Help topics contains a list of categories, organized like a table of contents. Each category contains links to help pages and subtopics, which allow you to refine your search until you find the material that answers your question. The steps on the following pages locate help and information about what you need to set up a home network.

1

- Click the Browse Help topics link in the 'Not sure where to start?' area to display the Contents page (Figure 1–57).

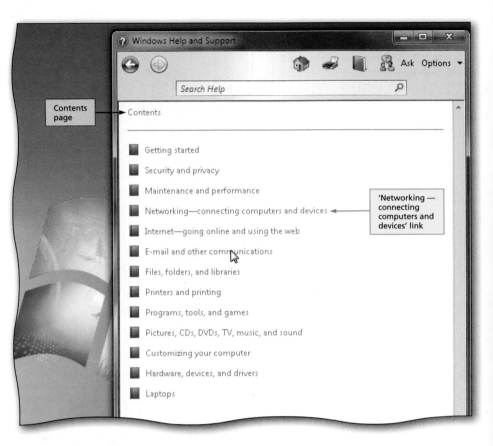

Figure 1–57

2

- Click the 'Networking—connecting computers and devices' link on the Contents page to display the links in the 'Networking—connecting computers and devices' topic (Figure 1–58).

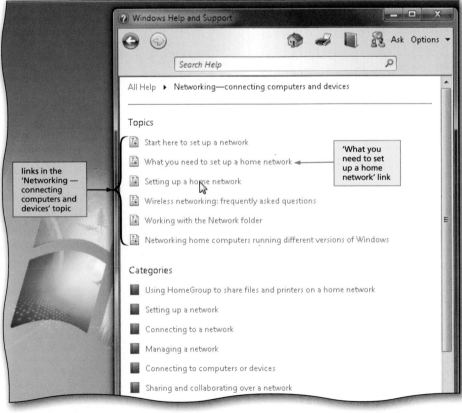

Figure 1–58

3

- Click the 'What you need to set up a home network' link to display the 'What you need to set up a home network' help page (Figure 1–59).

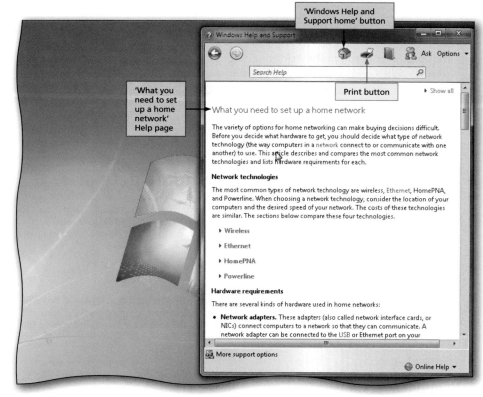

Figure 1–59

Other Ways

1. Press TAB until category or topic is highlighted, press ENTER, repeat for each category or topic

To Print a Help Topic

There are times when you might want to print a help topic so that you can have a printout for reference. The following steps show you how to print a Help topic. If you do not have access to a printer, read the following steps without performing them.

1

- Click the Print button on the Help toolbar to display the Print dialog box (Figure 1–60).

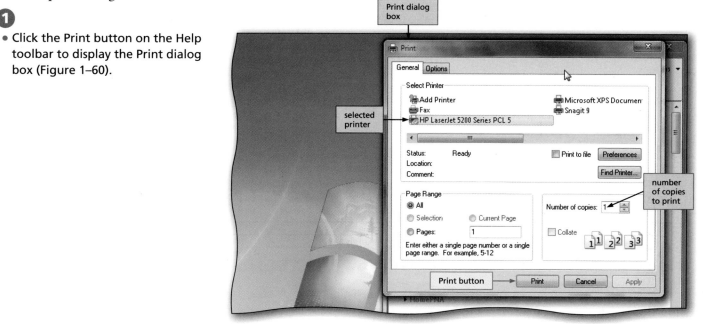

Figure 1–60

2

- Verify that the correct printer is selected, and ready the printer according to the printer instructions.

- Click the Print button in the Print dialog box to print the Help topic (Figure 1–61).

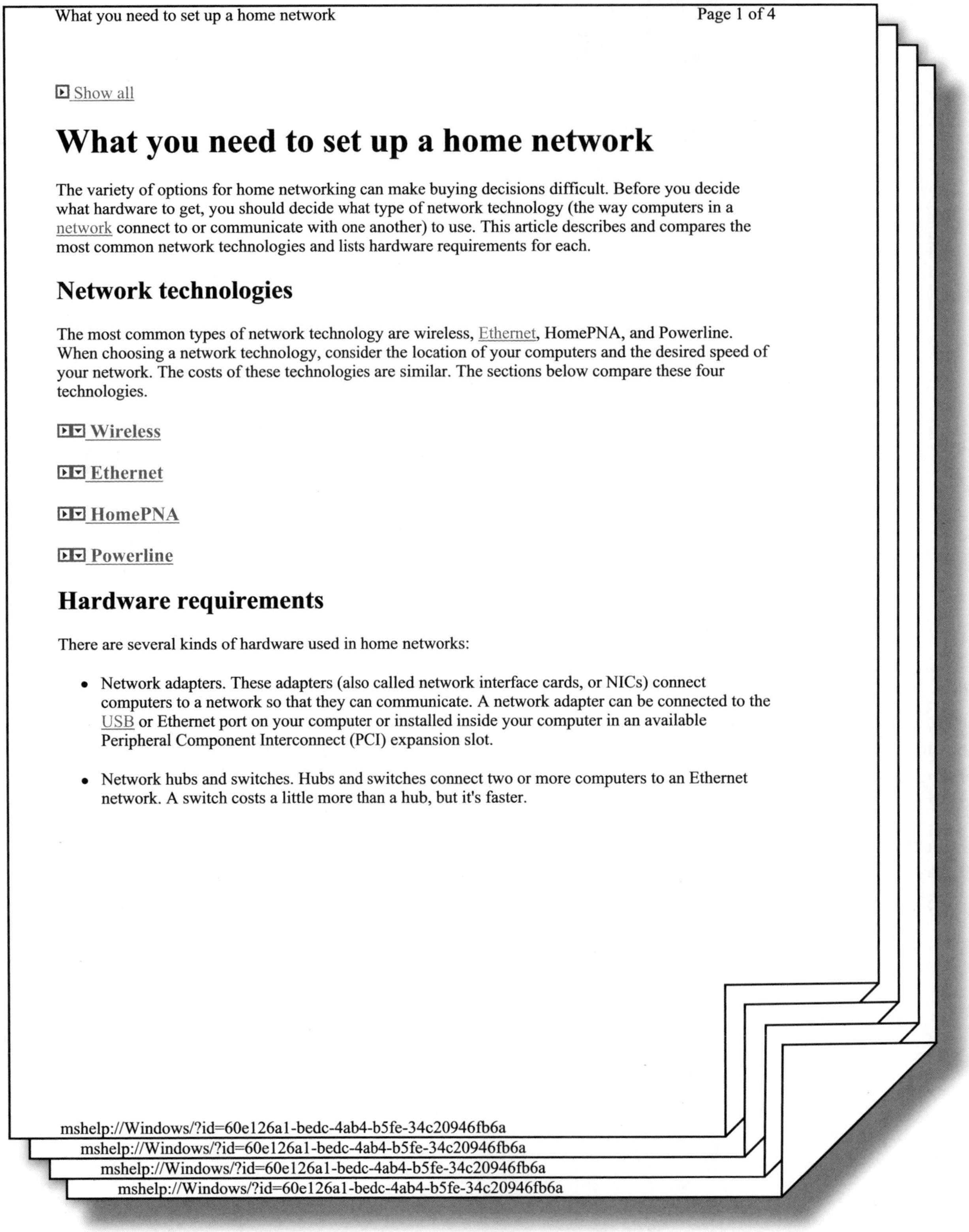

What you need to set up a home network   Page 1 of 4

▶ Show all

What you need to set up a home network

The variety of options for home networking can make buying decisions difficult. Before you decide what hardware to get, you should decide what type of network technology (the way computers in a network connect to or communicate with one another) to use. This article describes and compares the most common network technologies and lists hardware requirements for each.

Network technologies

The most common types of network technology are wireless, Ethernet, HomePNA, and Powerline. When choosing a network technology, consider the location of your computers and the desired speed of your network. The costs of these technologies are similar. The sections below compare these four technologies.

▶▾ **Wireless**

▶▾ **Ethernet**

▶▾ **HomePNA**

▶▾ **Powerline**

Hardware requirements

There are several kinds of hardware used in home networks:

- Network adapters. These adapters (also called network interface cards, or NICs) connect computers to a network so that they can communicate. A network adapter can be connected to the USB or Ethernet port on your computer or installed inside your computer in an available Peripheral Component Interconnect (PCI) expansion slot.

- Network hubs and switches. Hubs and switches connect two or more computers to an Ethernet network. A switch costs a little more than a hub, but it's faster.

mshelp://Windows/?id=60e126a1-bedc-4ab4-b5fe-34c20946fb6a
mshelp://Windows/?id=60e126a1-bedc-4ab4-b5fe-34c20946fb6a
mshelp://Windows/?id=60e126a1-bedc-4ab4-b5fe-34c20946fb6a
mshelp://Windows/?id=60e126a1-bedc-4ab4-b5fe-34c20946fb6a

Figure 1–61

To Return to Windows Help and Support Home

The following step returns to Windows Help and Support home.

1

- Click the 'Help and Support home' button on the Navigation toolbar to return to Windows Help and Support home (Figure 1–62).

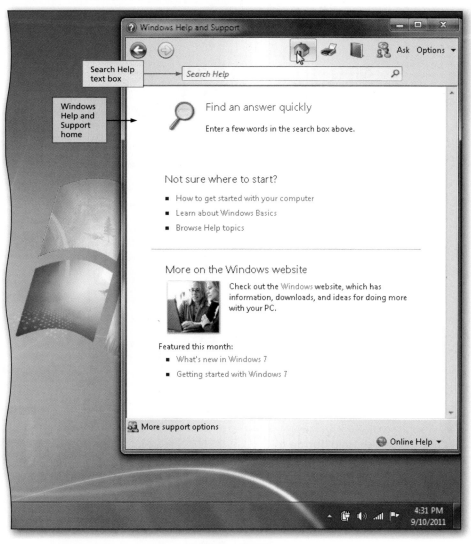

Figure 1–62

To Search Windows Help and Support

A third method for obtaining help about Windows 7 is to use the Search Help text box in the Windows Help and Support window. The Search Help text box allows you to enter a keyword and search for all Help topics containing the keyword.

When you search Help, the results of the search are sorted to produce the best matches for your keyword. When the computer is connected to the Internet, Windows Help and Support also searches the Microsoft Knowledge Base Web site for topics or articles that are relevant to the keyword you enter. If there are 30 results or less, all results are displayed. If there are more than 30 results for your keyword, a link to view more results will appear at the end of the Best 30 results list. The total number of results will depend upon the search keywords. The following steps use the Search Help text box to locate information about computer viruses.

1

- Click the Search Help text box and type `virus` in the Search Help text box to provide a keyword for searching (Figure 1–63).

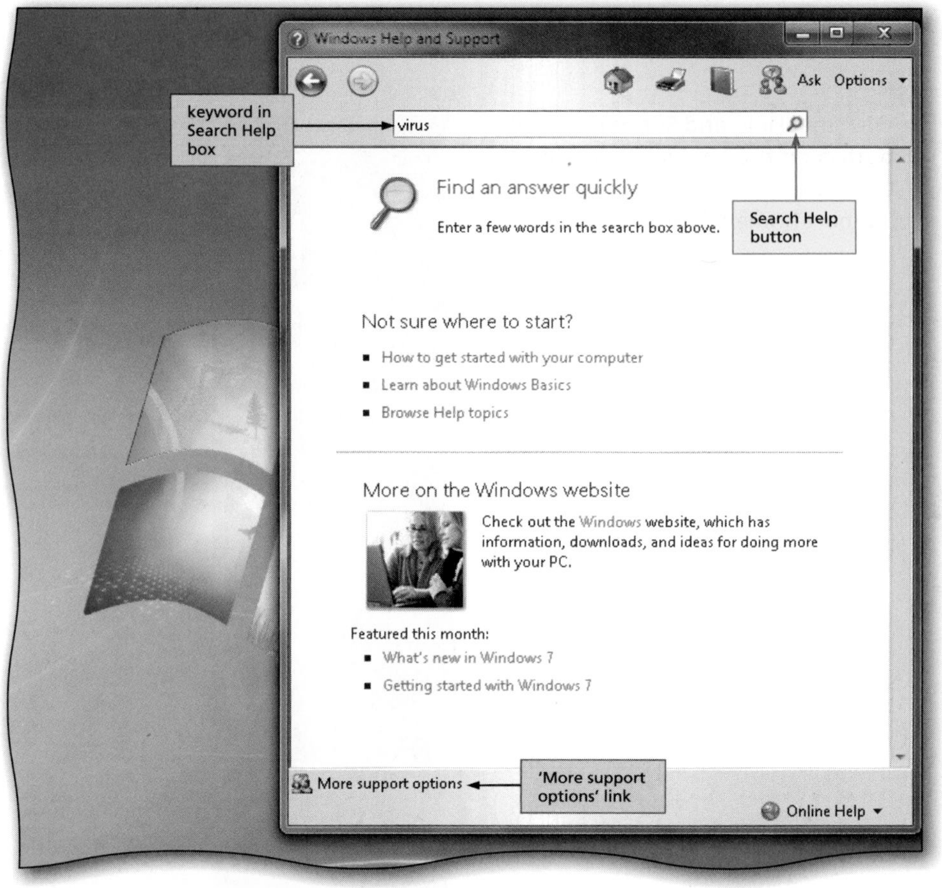

keyword in Search Help box

virus

Find an answer quickly

Enter a few words in the search box above.

Search Help button

Not sure where to start?

- How to get started with your computer
- Learn about Windows Basics
- Browse Help topics

More on the Windows website

Check out the Windows website, which has information, downloads, and ideas for doing more with your PC.

Featured this month:

- What's new in Windows 7
- Getting started with Windows 7

More support options

'More support options' link

Online Help ▼

Figure 1–63

2

- Click the Search Help button to search for items matching your keyword (Figure 1–64).

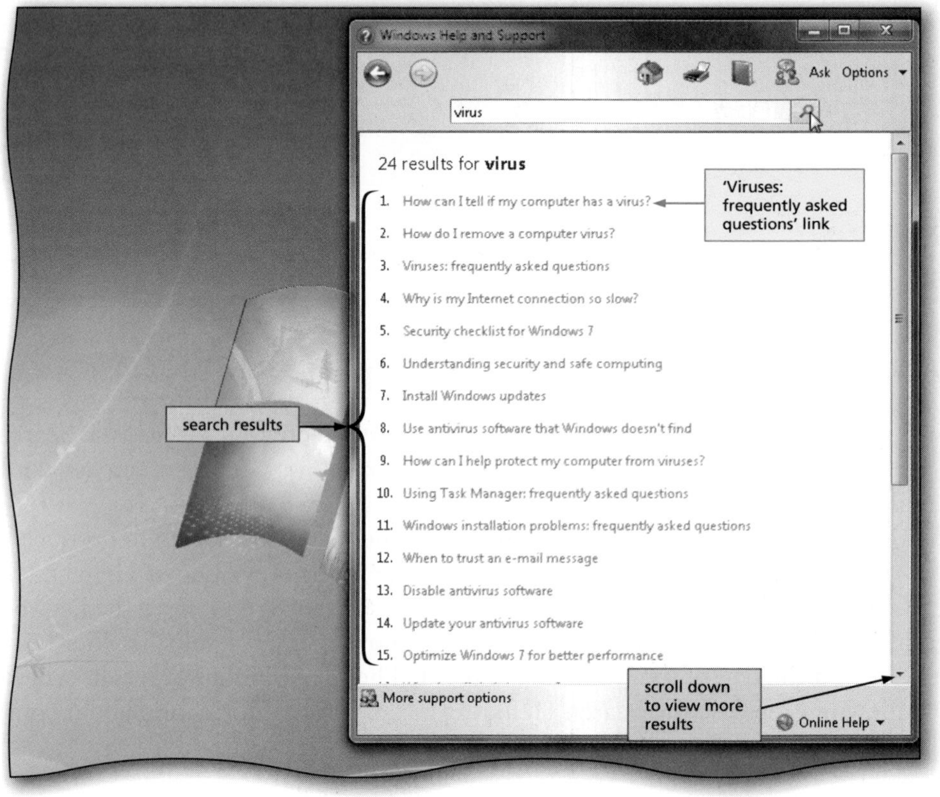

Windows Help and Support

Ask Options ▼

virus

24 results for **virus**

1. How can I tell if my computer has a virus?
2. How do I remove a computer virus?
3. Viruses: frequently asked questions
4. Why is my Internet connection so slow?
5. Security checklist for Windows 7
6. Understanding security and safe computing
7. Install Windows updates
8. Use antivirus software that Windows doesn't find
9. How can I help protect my computer from viruses?
10. Using Task Manager: frequently asked questions
11. Windows installation problems: frequently asked questions
12. When to trust an e-mail message
13. Disable antivirus software
14. Update your antivirus software
15. Optimize Windows 7 for better performance

'Viruses: frequently asked questions' link

search results

More support options

scroll down to view more results

Online Help ▼

Figure 1–64

❸
- Click the 'Viruses: frequently asked questions link' to display the 'Viruses: frequently asked questions' help page (Figure 1–65).

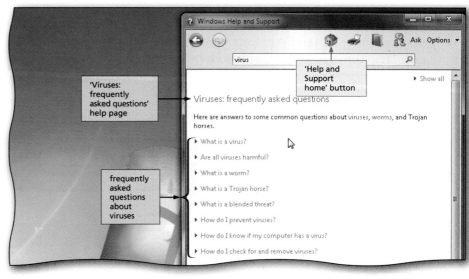

Figure 1–65

Other Ways

1. Press ALT+S, type keyword, press ENTER

To Get More Help

If you do not find the answers you are seeking, the 'More support options' link offers additional methods for asking for and receiving help. The following step opens the 'More support options' area.

❶
- Click the Help and Support home button to return to the Windows Help and Support home page.

- Click the 'More support options' link at the bottom of the Windows Help and Support window to open the 'More support options' page (Figure 1–66).

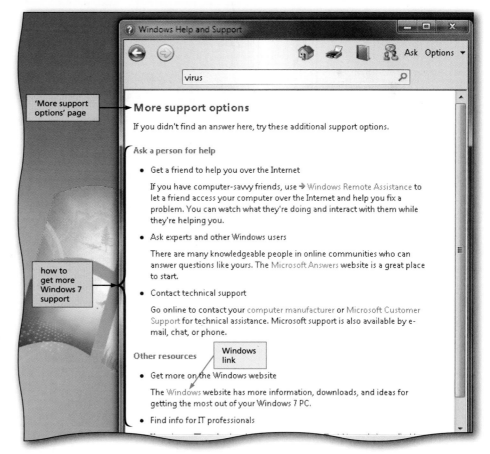

Figure 1–66

To Search Windows 7 Help & How-to Online

The Windows link on the 'More support options' page launches your Web browser and opens the Microsoft Windows Web site. From the Windows Web site, you can search a broader range of content, get help from others, share a Help topic, or save a link to a Help topic for future reference by adding it to your Favorites in Internet Explorer. The following steps open Internet Explorer to access the Windows Web site.

1

- Click the Windows link to open Internet Explorer.

- Point to the Help & How-to link and then click Windows 7 to display the Windows 7 Help & How-to Web page (Figure 1–67).

- If necessary, click the Maximize button on the Internet Explorer title bar to maximize the Internet Explorer window.

Q&A

Why am I unable to access Windows Help online?

You must have an active Internet connection to use Windows Help online.

Figure 1–67

2

• Click the Security checklist link on the Windows 7 Help & How-to Web page to display the Security checklist for Windows 7 Web page (Figure 1–68).

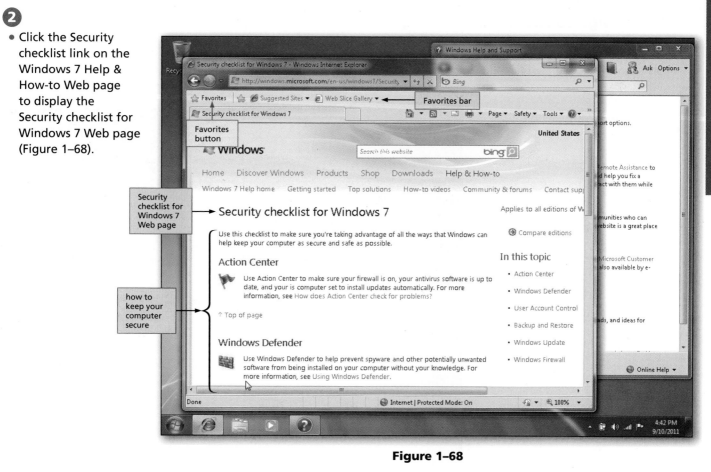

Figure 1–68

To Add a Page to Favorites

When you know you will want to return to a Windows Help Web page in the future, you can add it to your Favorites Center in Internet Explorer. The following steps add the Security checklist for Windows 7 page to your favorites.

1

• Click the Favorites button to display the Favorites Center (Figure 1–69).

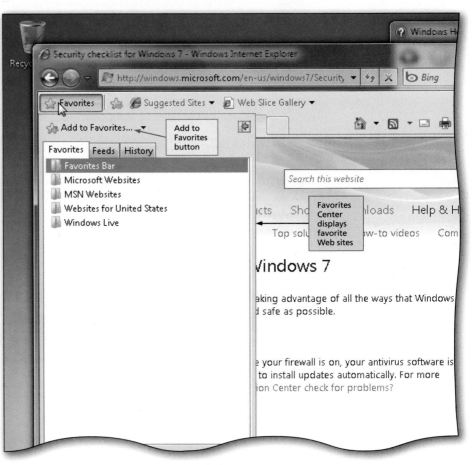

Figure 1–69

2

• Click the Add to Favorites button in the Favorites Center to display the Add a Favorite dialog box (Figure 1–70).

Figure 1–70

- Click the Add button to add the Security checklist for Windows 7 page to your Favorites Center (Figure 1–71).

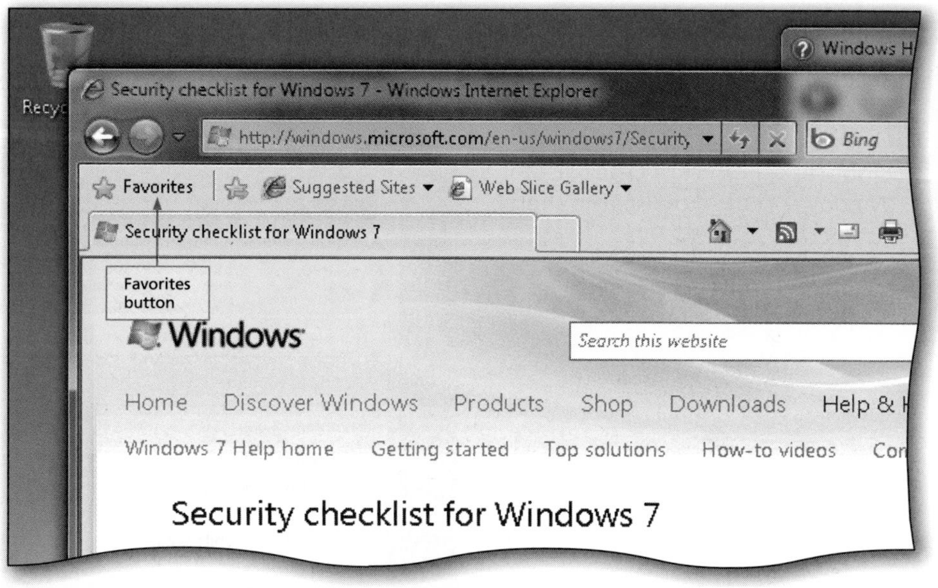

Figure 1–71

❹

- Click the Favorites button on the Favorites bar to display the Favorites Center and view the Security checklist for Windows 7 link (Figure 1–72).

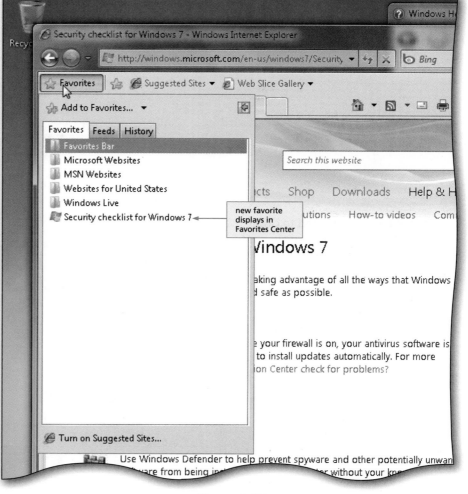

Figure 1–72

To Delete a Link from Favorites

When you are through referring to a Help topic stored in your Favorites Center, you might want to delete the link. The following steps delete the Security checklist for Windows 7 Web page from your Favorites Center.

1

- Right-click the Security checklist for Windows 7 entry to display a shortcut menu (Figure 1–73).

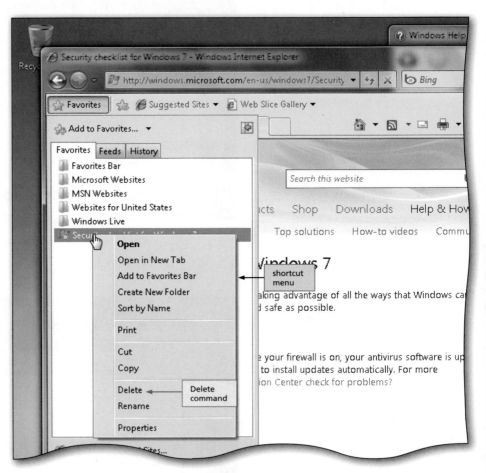

Figure 1–73

2

- Click the Delete command to close the shortcut menu and display the Delete Shortcut dialog box (Figure 1–74).

- Click the Yes button in the Delete Shortcut dialog box to delete the Security checklist for Windows 7 Favorite from the Favorites Center.

Q&A Why does the dialog box ask me if I want to delete a shortcut?

Internet Explorer and Windows 7 store your favorites as small text files in a special folder on your computer. When you add a favorite, you are creating a shortcut. When you delete a favorite, you are deleting a shortcut.

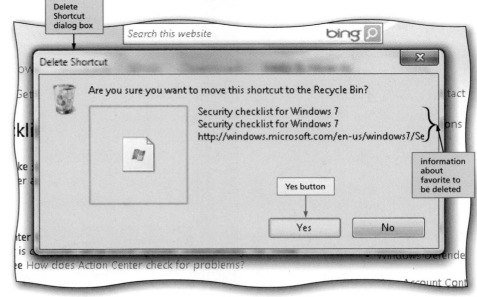

Figure 1–74

To Close Windows Internet Explorer and Windows Help and Support

When you have finished using a program, you should close it. The following steps close Windows Internet Explorer and Windows Help and Support.

1 Click the Close button on the title bar of the Windows Internet Explorer window.

2 Click the Close button on the title bar of the Windows Help and Support window.

To Empty the Recycle Bin

When you decide that you no longer need files located in the Recycle Bin, you can empty the Recycle Bin. The following steps empty the Recycle Bin and permanently delete the files it contains.

1 Right-click the Recycle Bin to display the shortcut menu.

2 Click the Empty Recycle Bin command to permanently delete the contents of the Recycle Bin.

3 Click the Yes button to confirm the operation.

Logging Off and Turning Off the Computer

After completing your work with Windows 7, you should close your user account by logging off the computer. In addition to logging off, there are several options available for ending your Windows 7 session. Table 1–3 describes the various options for ending your Windows 7 session.

BTW

Sleep Command
When a computer has been put to sleep using the Sleep command, you can bring it out of the sleep state in a variety of ways. Depending on the computer, you might press the power button, press a key on the keyboard, click the mouse, or open the lid, if it is a notebook computer.

Table 1–3 Options for Ending a Windows 7 Session

Option	Description
Switch user	Click the Start button, point to the arrow next to the Shut down button, and then click the Switch user command to keep your programs running in the background (but inaccessible until you log on again), and allow another user to log on.
Log off	Click the Start button, point to the arrow next to the Shut down button, and then click the Log off command to close all your programs and close your user account. This method leaves the computer running so that another user can log on.
Lock	Click the Start button, point to the arrow next to the Shut down button, and then click the Lock command to deny anyone except those who have authorized access to log on the computer.
Restart	Click the Start button, point to the arrow next to the Shut down button, and then click the Restart command to close all open programs, log off, and restart the computer.
Sleep	Click the Start button, point to the arrow next to the Shut down button, click the Sleep command, wait for Windows to save your work to memory and then power down your computer to a low-power state. This is useful if you are expecting to return to your computer in a short amount of time.
Hibernate	Click the Start button, point to the arrow next to the Shut down button, and then click the Hibernate command. Windows will save your session to the hard disk and turn off your computer. When you turn the computer on again, Windows restores your session. This is useful if you are expecting to not use your computer for at least several hours.
Shut down	Click the Start button and then click the Shut down button to close all your programs and turn off the computer.

To Log Off the Computer

Logging off the computer closes any open programs, giving you the opportunity to save any unsaved documents, and then makes the computer available for other users. A logging off message displays briefly as Windows 7 logs you off. When the process is finished, the Welcome screen appears. At this point, another user can log on the computer. The following steps log off the computer. If you do not want to end your session on the computer, read the following steps but do not perform them.

- Display the Start menu (Figure 1–75).

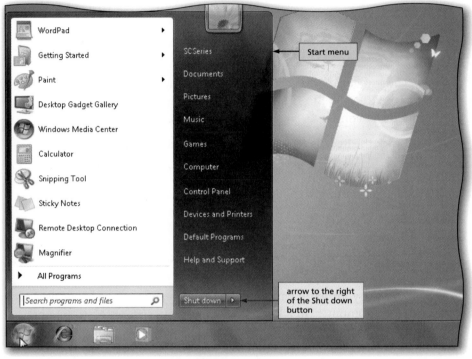

Figure 1–75

- Point to the arrow to the right of the Shut down button to display the 'Shut down options' menu (Figure 1–76).

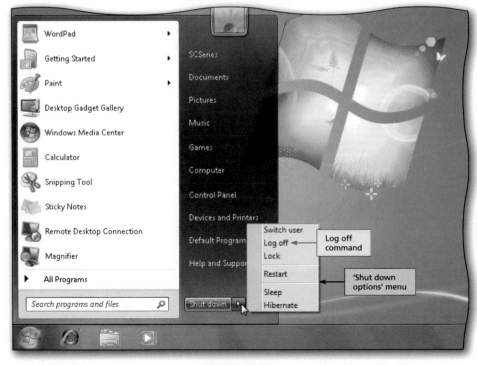

Figure 1–76

3

- Click the Log off command, and then wait for Windows 7 to prompt you to save any unsaved data, if any, and log off (Figure 1–77).

Q&A

Why should I log off the computer?

Some Windows 7 users have turned off their computers without following the log off procedure only to find data they thought they had stored on disk was lost. Because of the way Windows 7 writes data on the hard disk, it is important you log off the computer so that you do not lose your work. Logging off a computer is also a common security practice to prevent unauthorized users from tampering with the computer or your user account.

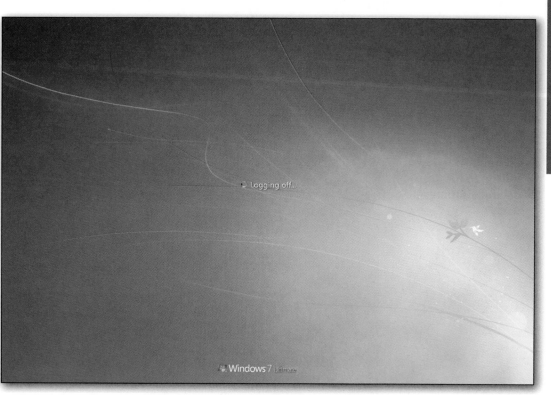

Figure 1–77

Other Ways

1. Press CTRL+ESC, press RIGHT ARROW, press RIGHT ARROW, press L

To Turn Off the Computer

After logging off, you also might want to turn off the computer. Using the Shut down button on the Welcome screen to turn off the computer shuts down Windows 7 so that you can turn off the power to the computer. Many computers turn the power off automatically as part of shutting down. While Windows 7 is shutting down, a message shows stating "Shutting down" along with an animated progress circle. When Windows 7 is done, the computer will shut off. You should not turn off your computer during this process, as you could lose data. The following step turns off the computer. However, if you do not want to turn off the computer, read the step without performing it.

1
- Click the Shut down button to turn off the computer (Figure 1–78).

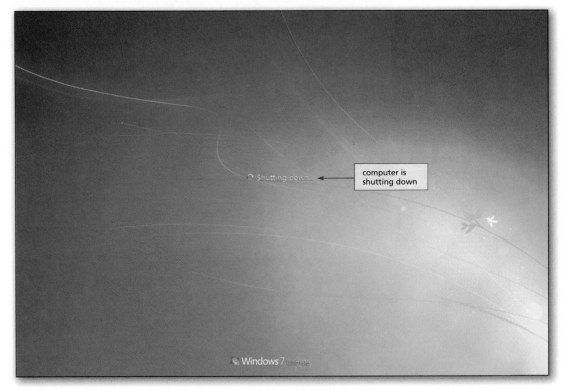

Figure 1–78

Other Ways
1. Press ALT+F4, select Shut down, click OK

Chapter Summary

In this chapter, you have learned how to work with the Microsoft Windows 7 user interface. You launched Windows 7, logged on the computer, learned about the parts of the desktop, and added and removed a gadget from the desktop. You opened, minimized, maximized, restored, and closed Windows 7 windows. You launched programs and used Aero Flip 3D to switch between them. Using Windows Help and Support, you located Help topics to learn more about Microsoft Windows 7. You printed a Help topic and learned how to find Help topics online. You logged off the computer using the Log off command and then shut down Windows 7 using the Shut down button on the Welcome screen. The items listed below include all of the new Windows 7 skills you have learned in this chapter.

1. Log On the Computer (WIN 8)
2. Display the Start Menu (WIN 10)
3. Scroll Using Scroll Arrows, the Scroll Bar, and the Scroll Box (WIN 12)
4. Open the Getting Started Window (WIN 14)
5. Close the Getting Started Window (WIN 15)
6. Open the Computer Folder Window (WIN 15)
7. Minimize and Redisplay a Window (WIN 17)
8. Maximize and Restore a Window (WIN 18)
9. Close a Window (WIN 19)
10. Add a Shortcut to the Desktop (WIN 20)
11. Open a Window Using a Desktop Shortcut (WIN 21)
12. Move a Window by Dragging (WIN 22)
13. Expand the Contents of Local Disk (C:) (WIN 22)
14. Size a Window by Dragging (WIN 23)
15. Collapse the Local Disk (C:) List (WIN 24)
16. Resize a Window (WIN 24)
17. Delete a Desktop Icon by Dragging it to the Recycle Bin (WIN 25)
18. Empty the Recycle Bin (WIN 26)
19. Add a Gadget to the Desktop (WIN 27)
20. Remove a Gadget from the Desktop (WIN 29)
21. Start a Program Using the Start Menu (WIN 30)
22. Start a Program Using the Search Box (WIN 31)
23. Start a Program Using a Pinned Program Icon on the Taskbar (WIN 32)
24. Switch Between Programs Using Aero Flip 3D (WIN 33)
25. Switch Between Programs Using the Taskbar (WIN 35)
26. Show the Desktop Using the Show Desktop Button (WIN 36)
27. Start Windows Help and Support (WIN 37)
28. Browse for Help Topics in Windows Basics (WIN 39)
29. Search for Help Topics Using the Table of Contents (WIN 41)
30. Print a Help Topic (WIN 43)
31. Return to Windows Help and Support Home (WIN 45)
32. Search Windows Help and Support (WIN 45)
33. Get More Help (WIN 47)
34. Search Windows 7 Help & How-to Online (WIN 48)
35. Add a Page to Favorites (WIN 50)
36. Delete a Link from Favorites (WIN 52)
37. Log Off the Computer (WIN 54)
38. Turn Off the Computer (WIN 56)

Learn It Online

Test your knowledge of chapter content and key terms.

Instructions: To complete the Learn It Online exercises, start your browser, click the Address bar, and then enter the Web address scsite.com/win7/learn. When the Windows 7 Learn It Online page is displayed, click the link for the exercise you want to complete and then read the instructions.

Chapter Reinforcement TF, MC, and SA
A series of true/false, multiple-choice, and short-answer questions that test your knowledge of the chapter content.

Flash Cards
An interactive learning environment where you identify chapter key terms associated with displayed definitions.

Practice Test
A series of multiple-choice questions that test your knowledge of chapter content and key terms.

Who Wants To Be a Computer Genius?
An interactive game that challenges your knowledge of chapter content in the style of a television quiz show.

Wheel of Terms
An interactive game that challenges your knowledge of chapter key terms in the style of the television show *Wheel of Fortune*.

Crossword Puzzle Challenge
A crossword puzzle that challenges your knowledge of key terms presented in the chapter.

Apply Your Knowledge

Reinforce the skills and apply the concepts you learned in this chapter.

What's New in Windows 7?

Instructions: Use Windows Help and Support to perform the following tasks.

Part 1: Launching Windows Help and Support
1. Click the Start button and then click Help and Support on the Start menu.
2. Click the What's new in Windows 7 link in the 'More on the Windows website' area in the Windows Help and Support window.

Part 2: Exploring What's new in Windows 7
1. In the Windows 7 simplifies everyday tasks area, click the HomeGroup link to display the 'Windows 7 features - HomeGroup' page (Figure 1–79), and then click the Play button to watch the video. As you watch the video, answer the following questions:
   a. What is HomeGroup?

   _____

   b. How does HomeGroup protect privacy?

   _____

   c. How do you share files with other computers?

   _____

2. Click the Close button to close the Internet Explorer Window.
3. If necessary, click the Windows Help and Support button on the taskbar to make it the active window.

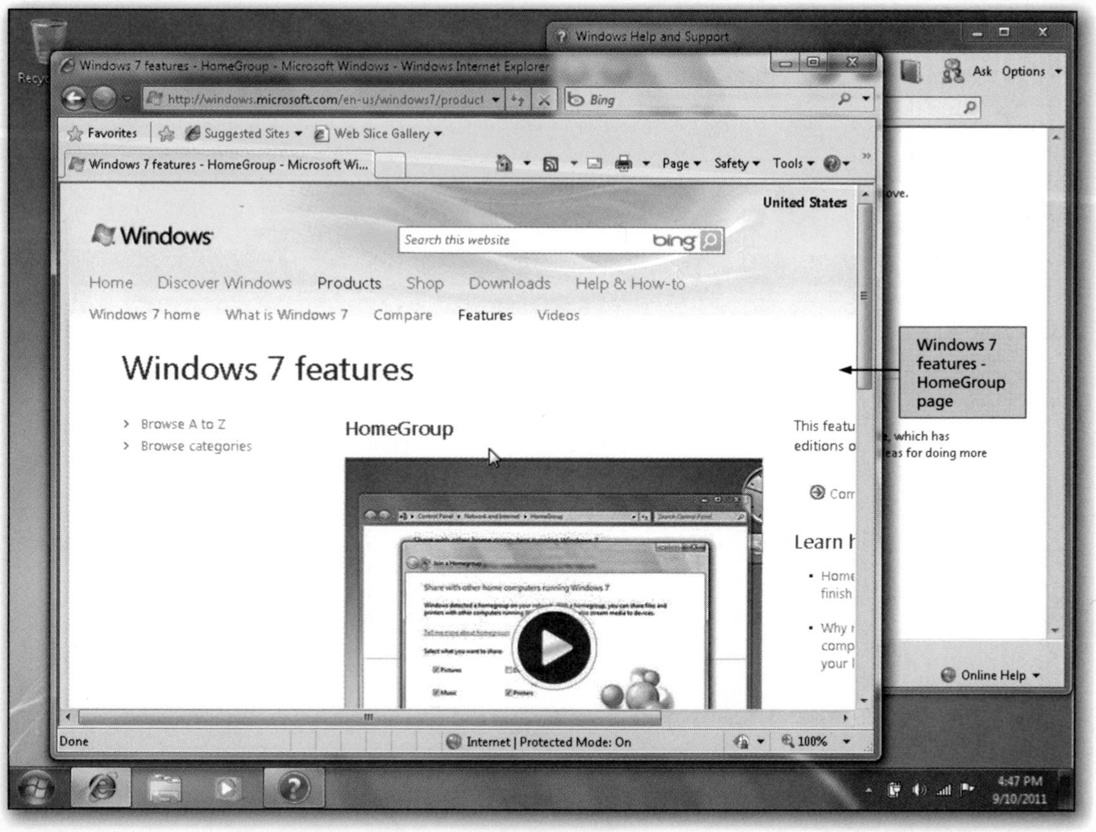

Figure 1–79

Part 3: What's New in Security?

1. In the 'Not sure where to start?' area, click the Browse Help topics link.
2. Click the 'Security and privacy' link to open the 'Security and privacy' page.
3. Click the Action Center link in the Categories area to open the Action Center page.
4. Click the What is Action Center? link to open the What is Action Center page.
5. Read the page, and then scroll down until you see the Click to open Action Center link.
6. Click the Click to open Action Center link to open the Action Center (Figure 1–80 on the next page). Answer the following questions:

    a. What are the main areas shown in the Action Center?

    _____

    b. Are there any issues in the Action Center that you need to review?

    _____

    c. What link should you click if you need to restore your computer to an earlier time?

    _____

7. Close the Action Center and return to the Windows Help and Support window. Click the Back button two times to return to the All Help > Security and privacy page.
8. Browse the topics and look for information about firewalls. What does a firewall do?
9. Click the Back button as necessary to return to the 'Security and privacy' page.

Continued >

Apply Your Knowledge *continued*

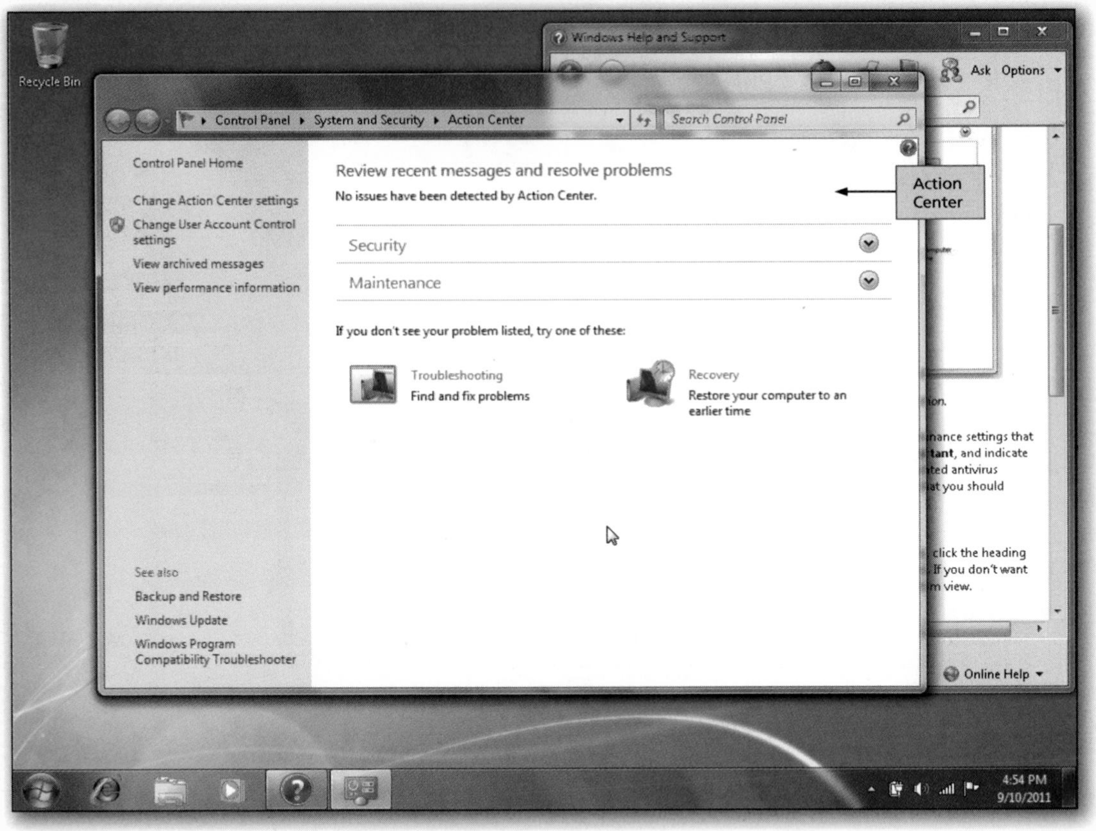

Figure 1–80

Part 4: What are Parental Controls?

1. Scroll down to view and click the Parental Controls link.

2. On the Parental Controls page, click the What can I control with Parental Controls link. Answer the following questions:

   a. What can you do with Parental Controls?

   _____

   _____

   b. After setting up Parental Controls, how can a parent keep a record of a child's computer activity?

   _____

3. Click the Back button as necessary to return to the Contents page in the Windows Help and Support window.

Part 5: What's New in the Picture Area?

1. Click the 'Pictures, CDs, DVDs, TV, music, and sound' link on the Contents page.

2. In the Categories area, click the Pictures link.

3. Click the 'Working with digital pictures' link, and answer the following question:

   a. What are the two main ways to import pictures?

   _____

4. Click the Back button as necessary to return to the Contents page in the Windows Help and Support window.

Part 6: What's New in Mobile PC Features Area?

1. Click the Laptops link to open the Laptops page.

2. Click the 'Using Windows Mobility Center' link, and answer the following question:

   a. How do you open the Mobility Center?

   _____

   _____

3. Click the Close button in the Windows Help and Support window.

Extend Your Knowledge

Extend the skills you learned in this chapter and experiment with new skills. You might need to use Help to complete the assignment.

Using Windows Help and Support to Obtain Help

Instructions: Use Windows Help and Support to perform the following tasks.

1. Find Help about Windows keyboard shortcuts by typing `shortcuts` in the Search Help text box and then clicking the Search Help button (Figure 1–81). Click the result titled Keyboard shortcuts.

   a. What general keyboard shortcut is used to display the Start menu?

   b. What general keyboard shortcut is used to display the shortcut menu for an active window?

   c. What general keyboard shortcut is used to view the properties for a selected item?

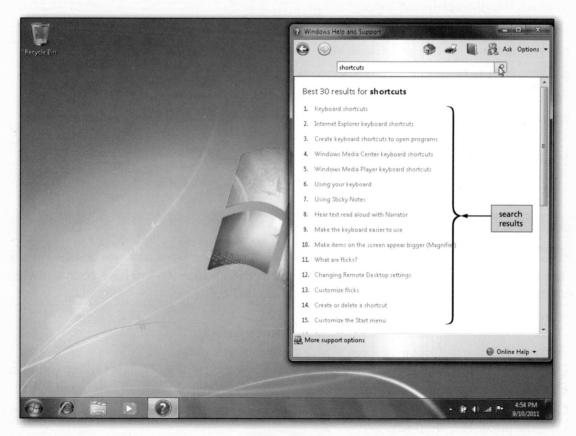

Figure 1–81

Continued >

    d. What dialog box keyboard shortcut is used to move backward through options?

    e. What dialog box keyboard shortcut is used to display Help?

    f. What keyboard shortcut is used to open the Computer folder window?

2. Use the Help and Support Content page to answer the following questions.

    a. How do you reduce computer screen flicker?

    b. What dialog box do you use to change the appearance of the mouse pointer?

    c. How do you minimize all windows?

    d. What is a server?

3. Use the Search Help text box in Windows Help and Support to answer the following questions:

    a. How can you reduce all open windows on the desktop to taskbar buttons?

    b. How do you launch a program using the Run command?

    c. What are the steps to add a toolbar to the taskbar?

    d. What wizard do you use to remove unwanted desktop icons?

4. The tools to solve a problem while using Windows 7 are called **troubleshooters**. Use Windows Help and Support to find the list of troubleshooters, and answer the following questions.

    a. What problems does the HomeGroup troubleshooter allow you to resolve?

    b. List five Windows 7 troubleshooters.

5. Use Windows Help and Support to obtain information about software licensing and product activation, and answer the following questions. To get the most current information, you will need to search Windows Help and Support online.

    a. What is software piracy?

    b. What are the five types of software piracy?

    c. Why should I be concerned about software piracy?

    d. What is a EULA (End-User License Agreement)?

    e. Can you legally make a second copy of Windows 7 for use at home, work, or on a portable computer?

    f. What is Windows Product Activation?

6. Close the Windows Help and Support window.

In the Lab

Use the guidelines, concepts, and skills presented in this chapter to increase your knowledge of Windows 7. Labs are listed in order of increasing difficulty.

Lab 1: Improving Your Mouse Skills with Windows Gadgets

Instructions: Perform the following steps to play a game using a gadget.

1. Open the Start menu and then open All Programs. Click the Desktop Gadget Gallery command. Double-click the Picture Puzzle to add it to the desktop. Close the Gadget Gallery window.

2. Click the Show picture button on the Picture Puzzle to see what the picture will look like once you solve the puzzle (Figure 1–82).

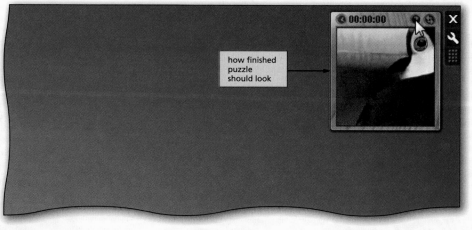

Figure 1–82

3. Play the Picture Puzzle game, by moving the puzzle tiles around by clicking on them when they are near the empty slot. Continue to rearrange the tiles until you have completed the picture (you can show the picture at any time to determine if you are close to the solution). Record your time here: _____

4. Click the Close button on the gadget to remove the gadget from the desktop.

In the Lab

Lab 2: Switching through Open Windows

Instructions: Perform the following steps to launch multiple programs using the Start menu and then use different methods to switch through the open windows (Figure 1–83 on the next page).

Part 1: Launching the Getting Started Window, WordPad, and Internet Explorer
1. Click the Start button, click the All Programs command, and then click the Internet Explorer command to launch Internet Explorer.

2. Click the Start button, click the All Programs command, click the Accessories folder, and then click the Getting Started command to display the Getting Started window.

3. Click the Start button, click the All Programs command, click the Accessories folder, and then click WordPad to launch WordPad.

Part 2: Switching through the Windows
1. Press ALT+TAB to switch to the next open window.

2. While holding the WINDOWS key, press the TAB key two times to switch to the next open window.

3. Press CTRL+ALT+TAB to view the open programs. Press TAB. Click the WordPad window to switch to WordPad.

4. Press CTRL+WINDOWS+TAB to view the open programs. Press TAB. Click the Internet Explorer window to switch to Internet Explorer.

Part 3: Report your Findings
1. What is the difference between pressing ALT+TAB and pressing WINDOWS+TAB? _____

_____

2. What is the difference between pressing ALT+TAB and CTRL+ALT+TAB? _____

_____

Continued >

In the Lab *continued*

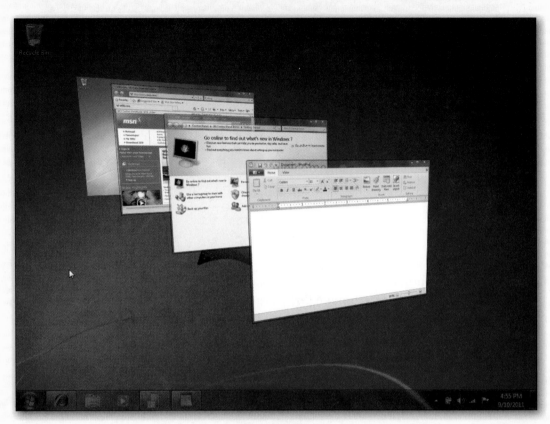

Figure 1–83

3. What is your favorite method of switching between windows? _____

_____

4. Besides using the keyboard shortcuts, what other ways can you switch between open windows?

Part 4: Closing the open Windows
1. Close WordPad.
2. Close Internet Explorer.
3. Close the Getting Started window.

In the Lab

Lab 3: Launching and Using Internet Explorer

Instructions: Perform the following steps to Internet Explorer to explore a selection of Web sites.

Part 1: Launching Internet Explorer
1. If necessary, connect to the Internet.
2. Click the Internet Explorer button on the taskbar. Maximize the Windows Internet Explorer window.

Part 2: Exploring CNN's Web Site
1. Click the Web address in the Address bar to select it.
2. Type www.cnn.com in the Address bar and then press the ENTER key.

3. Answer the following questions:

  a. What Web address displays in the Address bar? _____

  _____

  b. What window title displays on the title bar? _____

  _____

4. If necessary, scroll the Web page to view the contents of the Web page. List five links shown on this Web page. _____

5. Click any link on the Web page. What link did you click? _____

  _____

6. Describe the Web page that displayed when you clicked the link. _____

  _____

7. If requested by your instructor, click the Print button to print the Web page.

Part 3: Exploring Universal Studios: Orlando's Web Site

1. Click the Web address in the Address bar to select it.

2. Type www.universalorlando.com in the Address bar and then press the ENTER key.

3. What title displays on the title bar? _____

  _____

4. Scroll the Web page to view the contents of the Web page. Do any graphic images display on the Web page? _____

5. Pointing to an image on a Web page and having the mouse pointer change to a hand indicates the image is a link. Does the Web page include an image that is a link? _____

  _____

  If so, describe the image. _____

  _____

6. Click the image to display another Web page. What window title displays on the title bar?

7. If requested by your instructor, click the Print button to print the Web page.

Part 4: Displaying Previously Displayed Web Pages

1. Click the Back button. What Web page displays? _____

2. Click the Back button twice. What Web page displays? _____

3. Click the Forward button. What Web page displays? _____

Part 5: Exploring the Shelly Cashman Series Web Site

1. Click the Web address in the Address bar to select it.

2. Type www.scsite.com in the Address bar and then press the ENTER key.

3. Scroll the Web page to display the Operating Systems link, and then click the Operating Systems link.

4. Click the Microsoft Windows 7 link, and then click the title of your Windows 7 textbook.

5. Click any links that are of interest to you. Which link did you like the best? _____

  _____

6. Use the Back button or Forward button to display the Web site you like the best.

7. Click the Print button to print the Web page, if requested by your instructor.

8. Click the Close button on the Internet Explorer title bar to close Internet Explorer.

Cases and Places

Apply your creative thinking and problem-solving skills to design and implement a solution.

• Easier   •• More Difficult

• 1: Researching Technical Support

Technical support is an important consideration when installing and using an operating system or a program. The ability to obtain a valid answer to a question at the moment you have the question can be the difference between a frustrating incident and a positive experience. Using Windows Help and Support, the Internet, or another research facility, write a brief report on the options that are available for obtaining help and technical support while using Windows 7.

• 2: Assessing Windows 7 Compatibility

The Windows 7 operating system can be installed only on computers found in the Windows 7 hardware compatibility list. Locate three older personal computers. Look for them in your school's computer lab, at a local business, or in your house. Use the Windows Web site on the Internet to locate the Windows 7 Compatibility Center. Check each computer against the list and write a brief report summarizing your results.

•• 3: Researching Multiple Operating Systems

Using the Internet, a library, or other research facility, write a brief report on the Windows, Mac OS, and Linux operating systems. Describe the systems, pointing out their similarities and differences. Discuss the advantages and disadvantages of each. Finally, tell which operating system you would purchase and explain why.

•• 4: Sharing Your Pictures

Make it Personal

Using Windows Help and Support and the keywords, digital pictures, locate the "Working with Digital Pictures" article. In a brief report, summarize the steps required to send a photo in an e-mail message as well as the different ways to get photos from your camera. Next, research Windows Live Essentials and include a description of how to organize and find your pictures.

•• 5: Researching Operating Systems in Use

Working Together

Because of the many important tasks an operating system performs, most businesses put a great deal of thought into choosing an operating system. Each team member should interview a person at a local business about the operating system he or she uses with his or her computers. Based on the interview, write a brief report on why the businesses chose that operating system, how satisfied it is with it, and under what circumstances it might consider switching to a different operating system.

2 | Working with the Windows 7 Desktop

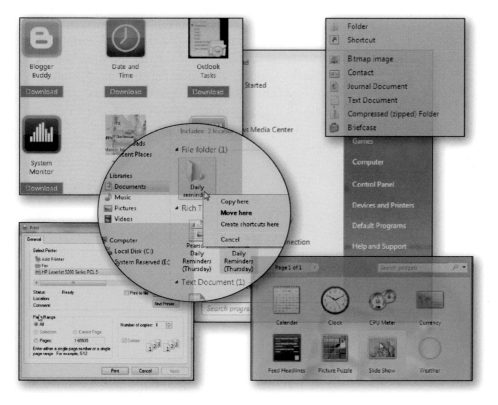

Objectives

You will have mastered the material in this chapter when you can:

- Create, name, and save a document directly in the Documents library

- Change the view and arrange objects in groups in the Documents library

- Create and name a folder in the Documents library

- Move documents into a folder

- Add and remove a shortcut on the Start menu

- Open a document using a shortcut on the Start menu

- Open a folder using a desktop shortcut

- Open, modify, and print multiple documents in a folder

- Store files on a USB flash drive

- Delete multiple files and folders

- Work with the Recycle Bin

- Work with gadgets

2 | Working with the Windows 7 Desktop

Introduction

In Chapter 2, you will learn about the Windows 7 desktop. With thousands of hardware devices and software products available for desktop and notebook computers, users need to manage these resources quickly and easily. One of Windows 7's impressive features is the ease with which users can create and access documents and files. You will organize the lives of two computer users by developing and updating their daily reminders lists. You will create folders, use shortcuts, open and modify multiple documents, and work with gadgets.

Mastering the desktop will help you to take advantage of user-interface enhancements and innovations that make computing faster, easier, and more reliable, and that offer seamless integration with the Internet. Working with the Windows 7 desktop in this chapter, you will find out how these features can save time, reduce computer clutter, and ultimately help you work more efficiently.

Overview

As you read this chapter, you will learn how to work with Windows 7 to create the documents shown in Figure 2–1 and how to perform these general tasks:

- Creating and editing a WordPad document
- Moving and renaming a file
- Creating and moving a folder
- Storing documents on a USB flash drive
- Deleting and restoring shortcuts, files, and folders using the Recycle Bin
- Customizing and rearranging gadgets

Plan Ahead

Working with the Windows 7 Desktop
Working with the Windows 7 desktop requires a basic knowledge of how to use the desktop, insert a USB flash drive, access the Internet, and use a printer.

1. **Be aware that there might be different levels of access on the computer you will be using.** A user account might be restricted to a certain level of access to the computer. Depending on the level of access that has been set for your account, you might or might not be able to perform certain operations.

2. **Identify how to connect a USB flash drive to your computer.** Depending on the setup of the computer you are using, there might be several ways to connect a USB flash drive to your computer. You should know which USB ports you can use to connect a USB flash drive to your computer.

3. **Determine how to access the Internet.** Many gadgets can be found online, free of charge. You will want to know if your computer has Internet access and how to access it.

4. **Ascertain how to access a printer.** To print, you must know which printer you can use and where it is located.

Creating a Document in WordPad

As introduced in Chapter 1, a program is a set of computer instructions that carries out a task on the computer. For example, you create written documents with a word-processing program, spreadsheets and charts with a spreadsheet program, and presentations with a presentation program.

To learn how to work with the Windows 7 desktop, you will create two daily reminders lists, one for Mr. Sanchez and one for Ms. Pearson. Because they will be reviewing their lists throughout the day, you will need to update the lists with new reminders as necessary. You decide to use WordPad, a popular word-processing program available with Windows 7, to create the daily reminders lists. The finished documents are shown in Figure 2–1.

Sanchez Daily Reminders (Thursday)

1. Update E-Bay bid on HP Laptop with Windows 7

2. Add Blog entry for Thursday

3. E-mail Elma Patterson - update Myspace entry - put me back at top of list!

4. Download and Install new marble game Gadget

5. Register for next semester's classes

6. Notify Sales - NetMeeting at 3:00 p.m.

7. Dinner with Art Perez - 7:00 p.m., The Crab House

```
Pearson Daily Reminders (Thursday)

1. Teleconference Ron Klein - Authentication Problem
2. E-mail Susie Yang - Groove presentation for board meeting
Tuesday
3. Lunch with Sam - Noon, Cyber Cafe
4. Call Dan - Birthday party for Carol
```

Figure 2–1

To Launch a Program and Create a Document

You will first create the daily reminders document for Mr. Sanchez using WordPad, by launching the WordPad application program, typing the reminders, and then saving the document in your My Documents folder using the Documents library. The Documents library acts as a central location for managing documents and folders. In computing terminology, this method of opening an application program and then creating a document is known as the **application-centric approach**. The steps on the following page launch WordPad and create a daily reminders document for Mr. Sanchez.

1

- Display the Start menu.

- Type wordpad in the Search box to prompt Windows 7 to search for the WordPad program.

- Press the ENTER key to launch WordPad and display the Document - WordPad window (Figure 2–2).

Q&A

Do I have to type the entire word before I press the ENTER key?

No. As soon as you see the result you are looking for at the top of the list in the Programs area above the Start menu Search box, you can press the ENTER key.

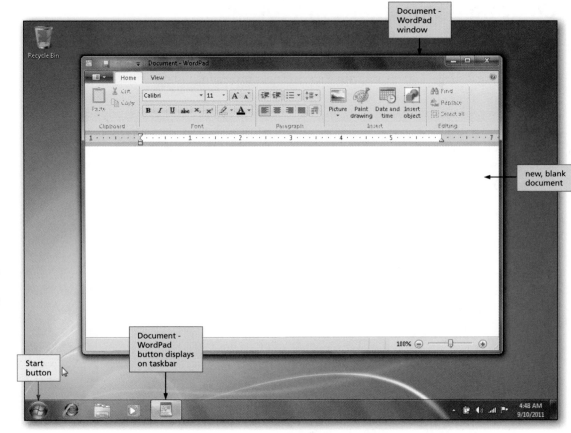

Figure 2–2

2

- Type Sanchez Daily Reminders (Thursday) and then press the ENTER key two times.

- Type 1. Update eBay bid on HP Laptop with Windows 7 and then press the ENTER key.

- Type 2. Add blog entry for Thursday and then press the ENTER key.

- Type 3. E-mail Elma Patterson – update Myspace entry – put me back at top of list! and then press the ENTER key.

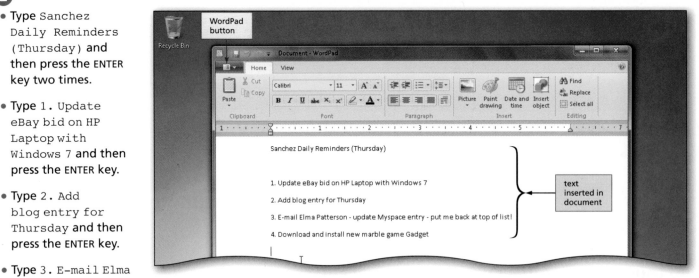

Figure 2–3

- Type 4. Download and install new marble game Gadget and then press the ENTER key (Figure 2–3).

Other Ways
1. Open Start menu, type wordpad in Search box, click WordPad	2. Open Start menu, click All Programs, click Accessories, click WordPad

Saving Documents

When you create a document using a program such as WordPad, the document is stored in the main memory (RAM) of the computer. If you close the program without saving the document or if the computer accidentally loses electrical power, the document will be lost. To protect against the accidental loss of a document and to allow you to modify the document easily in the future, you should save your document. Although you can save a file on the desktop, it is recommended that you save the document in a different location to keep the desktop free from clutter. For example, you can save files to the Documents library or to a USB flash drive.

The **Documents library** displays links to the user's documents as well as any public documents. The files and folders are not stored in the library; instead, the library links to files and folders regardless of where they are stored. You can add items to the Documents library as if you were working in the My Documents folder. A document saved to the Documents library will be easier to find when searching. The **My Documents** folder contains a particular user's documents and folders. The Documents library will show the links, although the actual folders and files will be stored in the My Documents folder. By default, the Documents library shows all files and folders in the My Documents folder.

When you save a document, you are creating a file. A **file** refers to a group of meaningful data that is identified by a name. For example, a WordPad document is a file; an Excel spreadsheet is a file; a picture made using Paint is a file; and a saved e-mail message is a file. When you create a file, you must assign a file name to the file. All files are identified by a file name. A file name should be descriptive of the saved file.

To associate a file with a program, Windows 7 assigns an extension to the file name, consisting of a period followed by three or more characters. Most documents created using the WordPad program are saved as Rich Text Format documents with the .rtf extension, but they also can be saved as plain text with the .txt extension. A Rich Text Format document allows for formatting text and inserting graphics, which is not supported in plain text files.

Many computer users can tell at least one horror story of working on their computers for a long period of time and then losing all of their work because of a power failure or software problem. Consider this a warning: Save often to protect your work.

BTW

File Names
A file name can contain up to 255 characters, including spaces. Any uppercase or lowercase character is valid when creating a file name, except a backslash (\), slash (/), colon (:), asterisk (*), question mark (?), quotation mark (''), less-than sign (<), greater-than sign (>), or vertical bar (|) because these symbols have special meaning for the operating system. Similarly, file names cannot be CON, AUX, COM1, COM2, COM3, COM4, LPT1, LPT2, LPT3, PRN, or NUL because those are names reserved by the operating system.

To Save a Document to the Documents Library

The steps on the following pages save the document you created using WordPad to the Documents library using the file name, Sanchez Reminders (Thursday).

1

- Click the WordPad button to display the WordPad menu (Figure 2–4).

Q&A

Why is there an arrow following the Save as command?

The arrow indicates that there are several preset ways to save the file, which can be accessed by clicking the arrow.

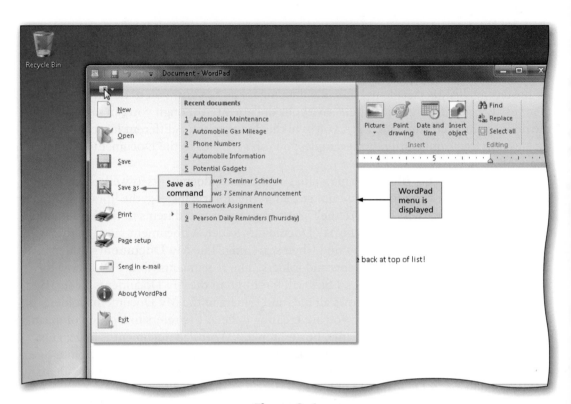

Figure 2–4

2

- Click the Save as command to display the Save As dialog box (Figure 2–5).

- Type `Sanchez Daily Reminders (Thursday)` in the File name text box.

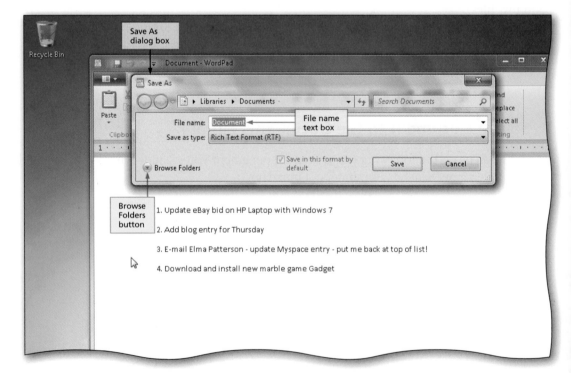

Figure 2–5

3
- Click the Browse Folders button to expand the folders list (Figure 2–6).

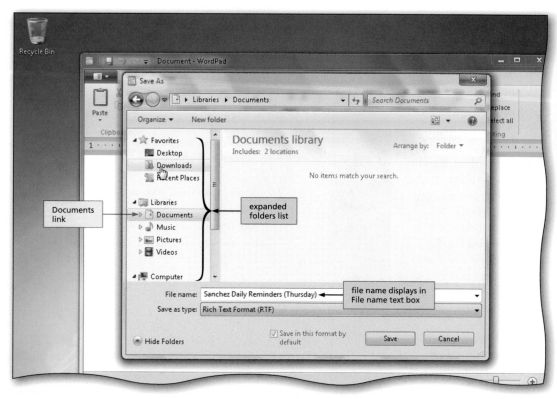

Figure 2–6

4
- Click the Documents link to select the Documents library (Figure 2–7).

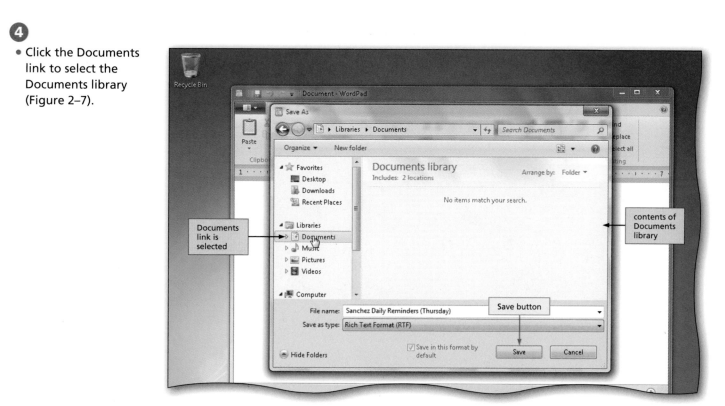

Figure 2–7

5

• Click the Save button to save the document and close the Save As dialog box (Figure 2–8).

Q&A Why did the title bar of WordPad change?

Now that you have saved the document with a file name, the file name will display on the title bar. To display a preview of the Sanchez Daily Reminders (Thursday) - WordPad window, point to the WordPad button on the taskbar.

Q&A Will I have to use the Save as command every time to save?

Now that you have saved the document, you can use the Save command to save changes to the document

WordPad button

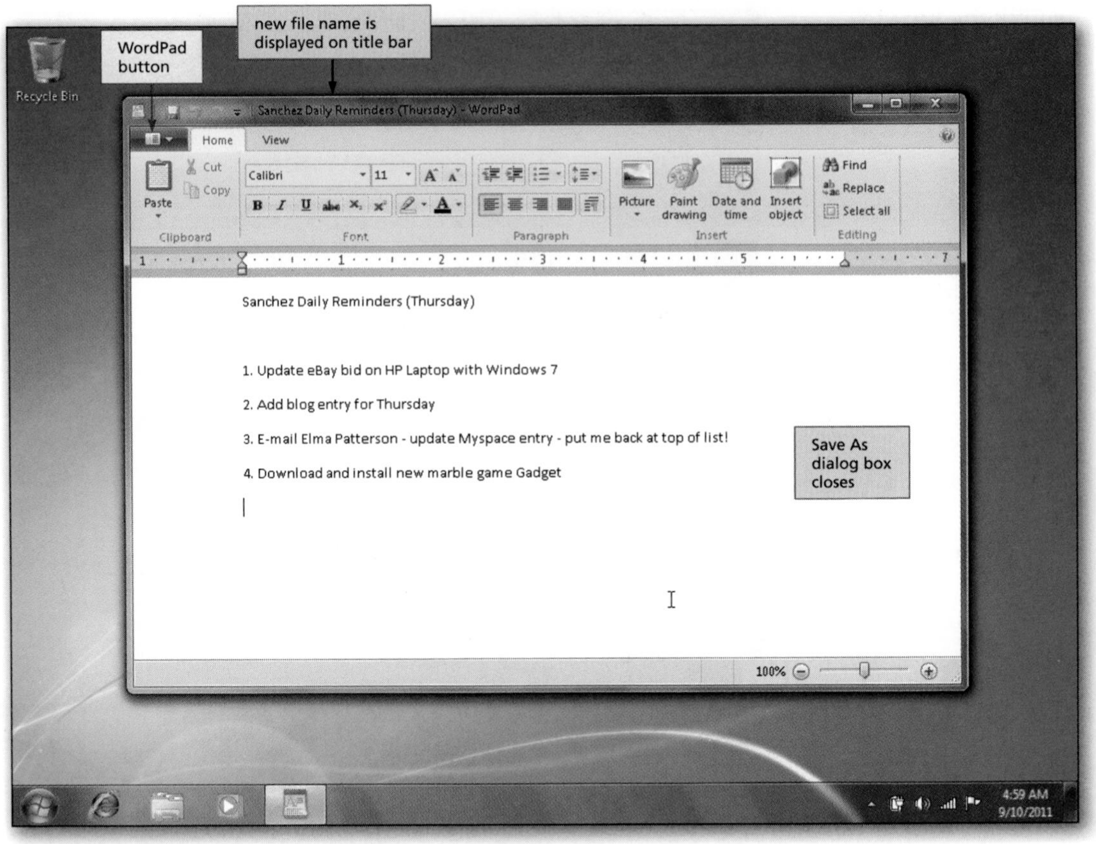

new file name is displayed on title bar

Sanchez Daily Reminders (Thursday) - WordPad

Sanchez Daily Reminders (Thursday)

1. Update eBay bid on HP Laptop with Windows 7

2. Add blog entry for Thursday

3. E-mail Elma Patterson - update Myspace entry - put me back at top of list!

4. Download and install new marble game Gadget

Save As dialog box closes

100%

Figure 2–8

without having to type a new name or select a new storage location. If you want to save the file with a different name or to a different location, you would use the Save as command. By changing the location using the Address bar, you can save a file in a different folder, library, or drive.

To Open the Print Dialog Box from a Program

Paper printouts are and will remain an important form of output for electronic documents. However, many sophisticated programs are expanding their printing capabilities to include sending e-mail messages and posting documents to Web pages on the World Wide Web. One method of printing a document is to print it directly from a program. The following steps open the Print dialog box in WordPad.

1

- Click the WordPad button to display the WordPad menu.

2

- Click the Print command to display the Print dialog box (Figure 2–9).

Q&A

What do the four options in the Page Range area represent?

The option buttons give you the choice of printing all pages of a document (All), selected parts of a document (Selection), current page (Current Page), or selected pages of a document (Pages). The selected All option button indicates all pages of a document will print.

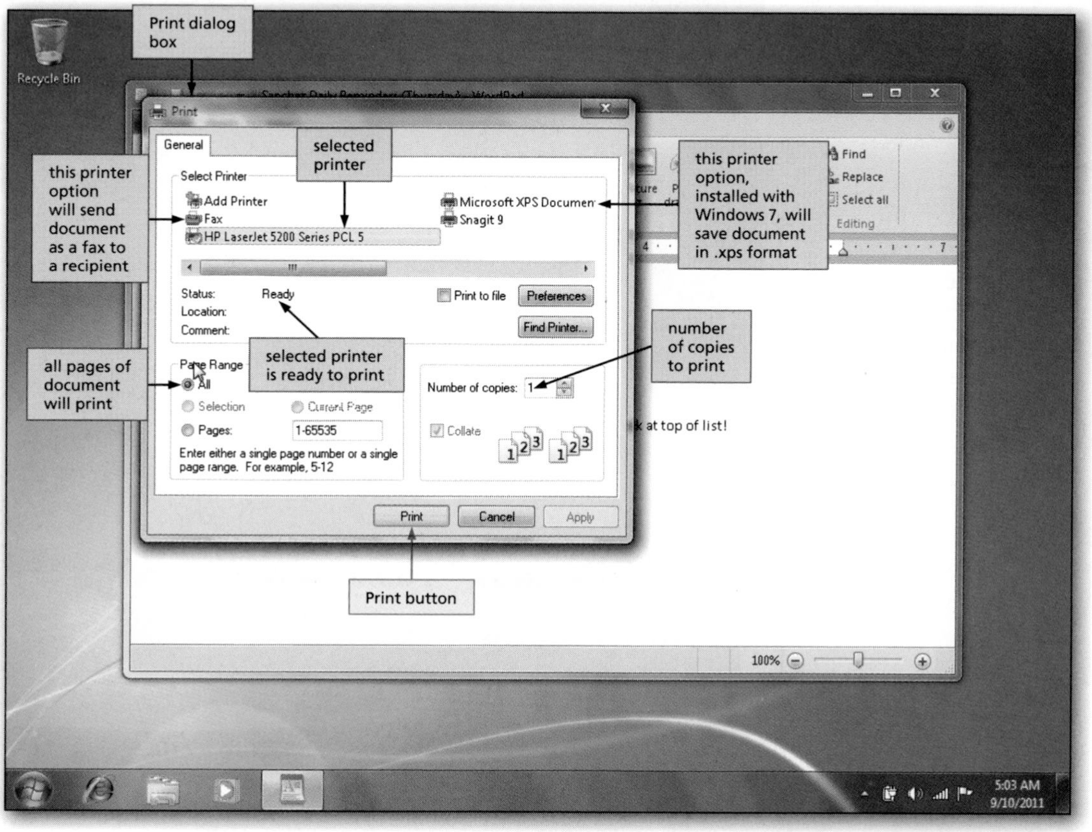

Figure 2–9

Other Ways
1. Press ALT+F, press P

To Print a Document

The following step prints the Sanchez Daily Reminders (Thursday) document.

1

- Ready the printer according to the printer's instructions.

- If necessary, click the appropriate printer to select your printer.

- Click the Print button to print the document and return to the Sanchez Daily Reminders (Thursday) - WordPad window (Figure 2–10).

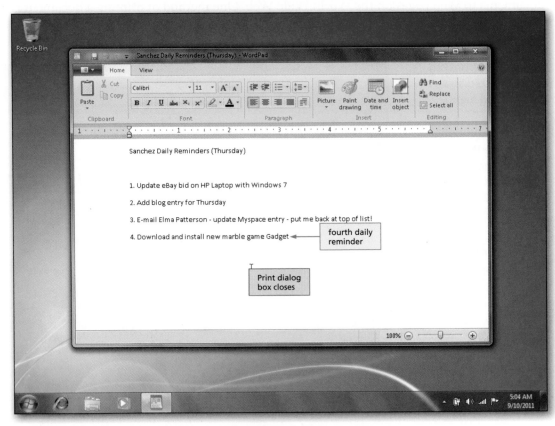

Figure 2–10

Other Ways

1. Click appropriate printer, press ENTER

To Edit a Document

Undoubtedly, you will want to make changes to a document after you have created it and saved it. For any document, your edits can be as simple as correcting a spelling mistake or as complex as rewriting the entire document. The following step edits the Sanchez Daily Reminders (Thursday) document by adding a new reminder.

1

- Click directly after the fourth daily reminder and then press the ENTER key.

- Type 5. Register for next semester's classes and then press the ENTER key (Figure 2–11).

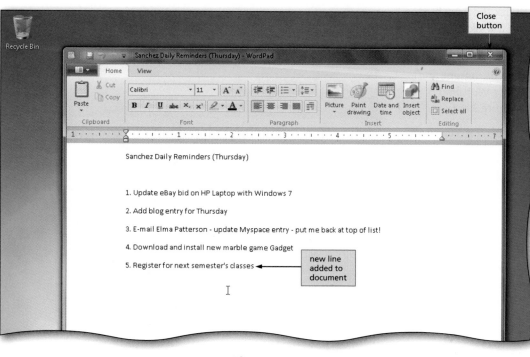

Figure 2–11

To Save and Close a Document

If you forget to save a document after you have edited it, a dialog box will display asking if you want to save your changes. This is how many programs help protect you from losing your work. If you choose to not save your changes, then all edits you made since the last time you saved will be lost. If you click the Cancel button, your changes are not saved, but the document remains open and you can continue working. The following steps close and save the Sanchez Daily Reminders (Thursday) document.

1

- Click the Close button on the title bar to display the WordPad dialog box (Figure 2–12).

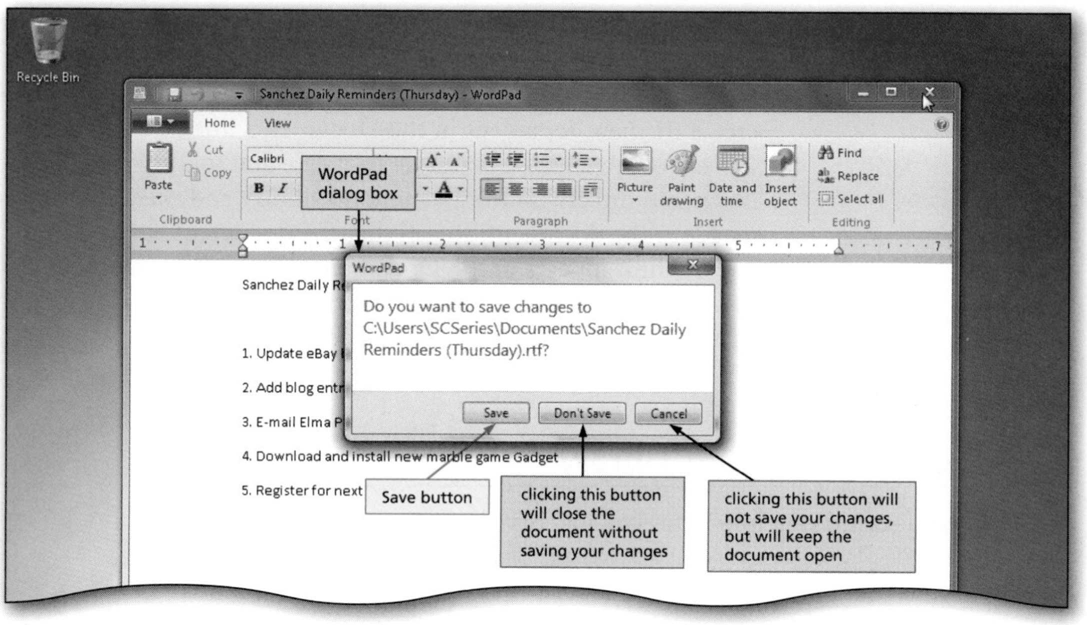

Figure 2–12

2
- Click the Save button in the WordPad dialog box to save your changes to the document and close WordPad (Figure 2–13).

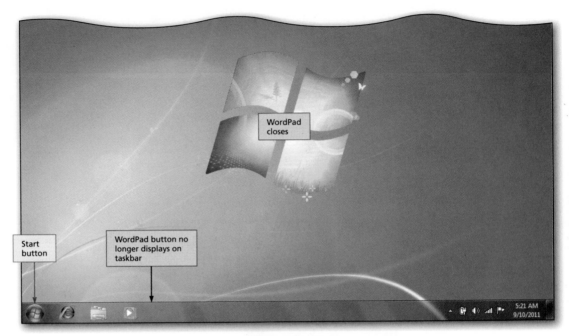

WordPad closes

Start button

WordPad button no longer displays on taskbar

5:21 AM
9/10/2011

Figure 2–13

Other Ways

1. On title bar double-click WordPad icon, click Save
2. On title bar click WordPad icon, click Close, click Save
3. On WordPad menu click Exit, click Save
4. Press ALT+F, press X; or press ALT+F4, press ENTER

Creating a Document in the Documents Library

After completing the reminders list for Mr. Sanchez, the next step is to create a similar list for Ms. Pearson. Opening a program and then creating a document (the application-centric approach) was the method used to create the first document. Although the same method could be used to create the document for Ms. Pearson, another method is to create the new document in the Documents library without first starting a program. Instead of launching a program to create and modify a document, you first create a blank document directly in the Documents library and then use the WordPad program to enter data into the document. Recall that the document is saved in the My Documents folder, and the link appears in the Documents library. This method, called the **document-centric approach**, will be used to create the document that contains the reminders for Ms. Pearson.

To Open the Documents Library

The following step opens the Documents library.

● Display the Start menu.

● Click the Documents command to display the Documents library window (Figure 2–14).

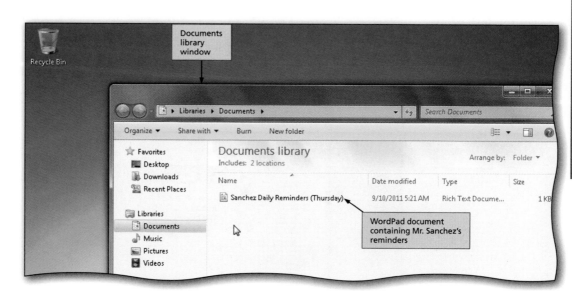

Figure 2–14

To Create a Blank Document in the Documents Library

The phrase, creating a document in the Documents library, might be confusing. The document you actually create contains no data; it is blank. You can think of it as placing a blank piece of paper with a name inside the Documents library. The document has little value until you add text or other data to it. The following steps create a blank document in the Documents library to contain the daily reminders for Ms. Pearson.

● Right-click an open area of the Documents library to display the shortcut menu.

● Point to the New command on the shortcut menu to display the New submenu (Figure 2–15).

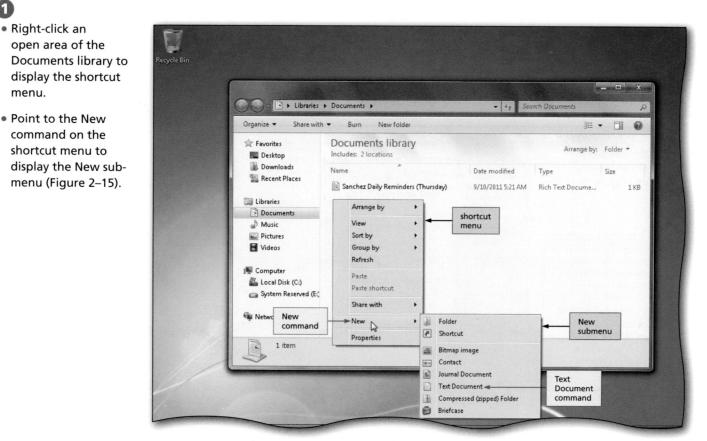

Figure 2–15

2

- Click the Text Document command to display an entry for a new text document in the Documents library window (Figure 2–16).

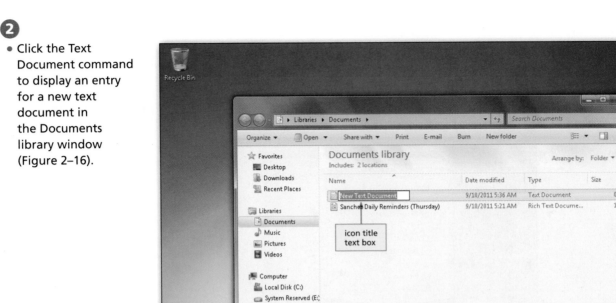

Figure 2–16

To Name a Document in the Documents Library

After you create a blank document, you need to name the document so that it is easily identifiable. In Figure 2–16, the default file name (New Text Document) is highlighted and the insertion point is blinking, indicating that you can type a new file name. The following step assigns the file name, Pearson Daily Reminders (Thursday), to the blank document you just created.

1

- Type `Pearson Daily Reminders (Thursday)` in the icon title text box, and then press the ENTER key to assign a name to the new file in the Documents library (Figure 2–17).

Other Ways

1. Right-click icon, click Rename on shortcut menu, type `Pearson Daily Reminders (Thursday)`, press ENTER

2. Click icon to select icon, press F2, type `Pearson Daily Reminders (Thursday)`, press ENTER

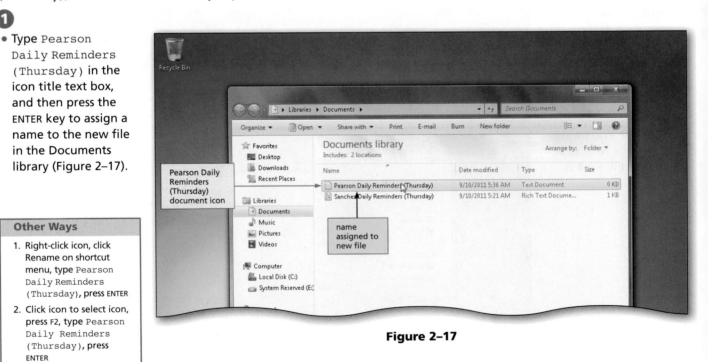

Figure 2–17

To Open a Document with WordPad

Although you have created the Pearson Daily Reminders (Thursday) document, the document contains no text. To add text to the blank document, you must open the document. Because text files open with Notepad by default, you need to use the shortcut menu to open the file using WordPad. The following steps open a document in WordPad.

1

- Right-click the Pearson Daily Reminders (Thursday) document icon to display the shortcut menu.

- Point to the Open with command on the shortcut menu to display the Open with submenu (Figure 2–18).

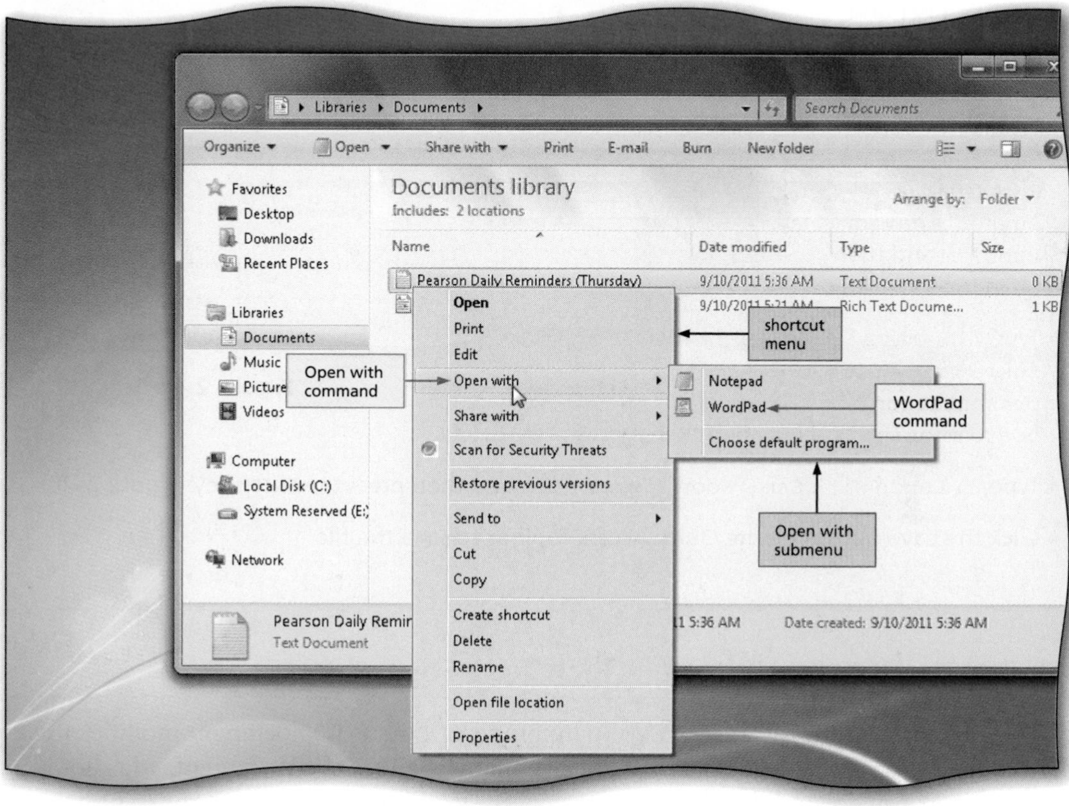

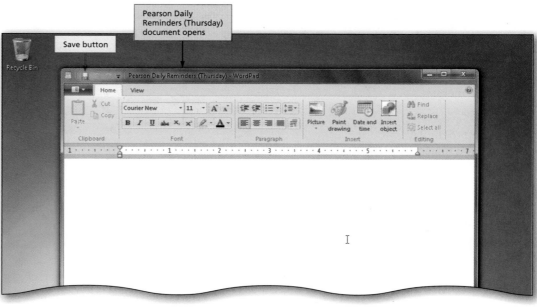

Figure 2–18

2

- Click the WordPad command on the Open with submenu to open the Pearson Daily Reminders (Thursday) document in WordPad (Figure 2–19).

Figure 2–19

To Add Text to a Blank Document

After the document is open, you can add text by typing in the document. The following step adds text to the Pearson Daily Reminders (Thursday) document, and then saves the document.

1

- **Type** Pearson Daily Reminders (Thursday) **and then press the** ENTER **key twice.**

- **Type** 1. Teleconference Ron Klein – Authentication Problem **and then press the** ENTER **key.**

- **Type** 2. E-mail Susie Yang – Groove presentation for board meeting Tuesday **and then press the** ENTER **key.**

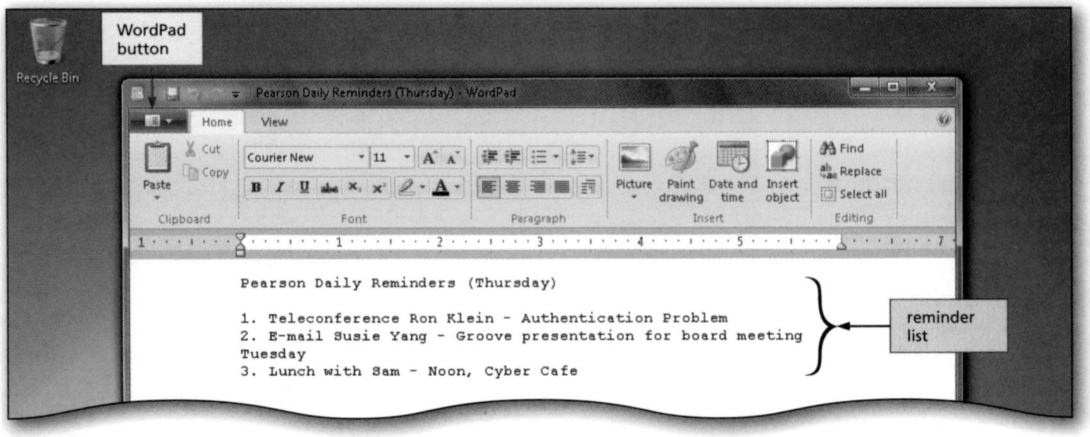

- **Type** 3. Lunch with Sam – Noon, Cyber Cafe **and then press the** ENTER **key (Figure 2–20).**

- **Click the Save button on the Quick Access Toolbar to save the file.**

Figure 2–20

To Save a Text Document in Rich Text Format (RTF)

Typing text into the Pearson Daily Reminders (Thursday) document modifies the document, which results in the need to save the document. If you make many changes to a document, you should save the document as you work. When you created the blank text document, Windows 7 assigned it the .txt file name extension, so you will need to use the Save as command to save it in Rich Text Format, which is WordPad's default format. Using the Rich Text Format will allow you to use all of WordPad's features, including formatting options. The following steps save the document in Rich Text Format.

1

- **Click the WordPad button to display the WordPad menu.**

- **Click the Save as command to display the Save As dialog box.**

- **Click the 'Save as type' list box arrow to display the 'Save as type' list (Figure 2–21).**

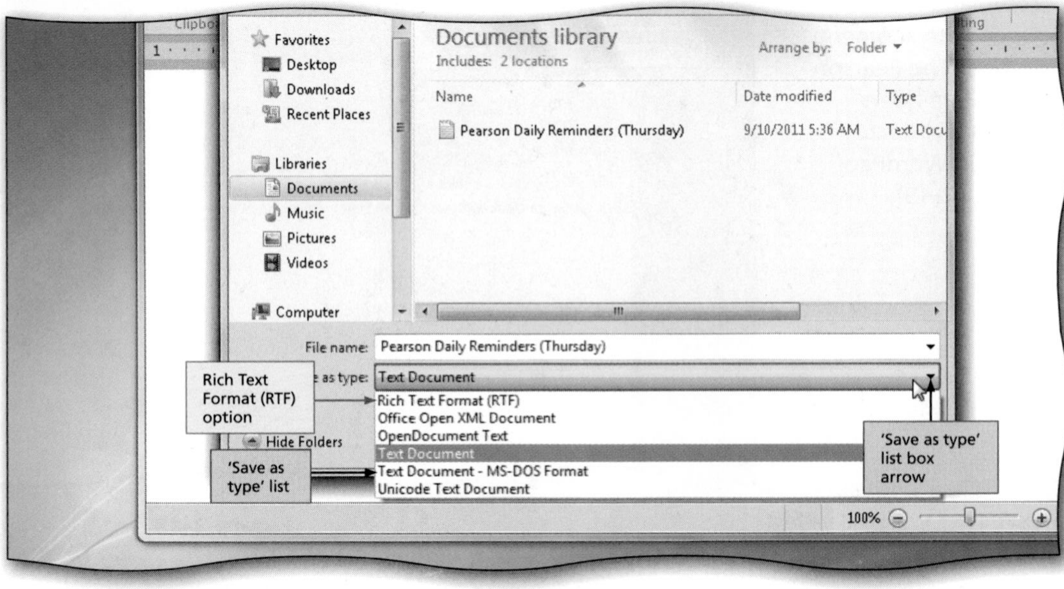

Figure 2–21

2
- Click the Rich Text Format (RTF) option to change the file type to Rich Text Format.

- Type Pearson Daily Reminders (Thursday).rtf in the File name text box to change the file name (Figure 2–22).

- Click the Save button to save the document in Rich Text Format.

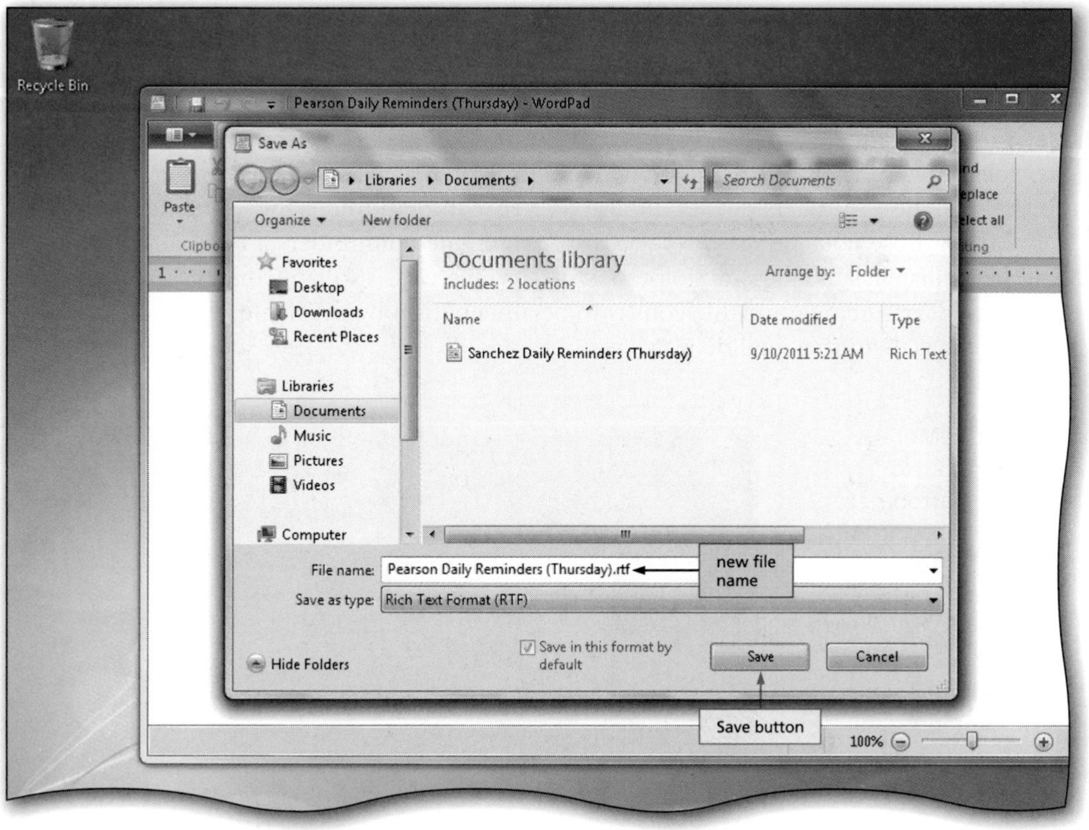

Figure 2–22

To Close the Document

You have saved your changes to Pearson Daily Reminders (Thursday), and now you can close the document.

1 Click Exit on the WordPad menu to close the Document and exit WordPad.

Working with the Documents Library

Once you create documents in the Documents library using either the application-centric or document-centric approach, you can continue to modify and save the documents, print the documents, or create a folder to contain the documents and then move the documents to the folder. Having a single storage location for documents makes it easy to create a copy of the documents so that they are not accidentally lost or damaged.

BTW

The Documents Library
Windows 7 creates a unique Documents library for each computer user. When you have multiple users on a single computer, having a unique central storage area for each user makes it easier to back up important files and folders.

To Change the View to Small Icons

The default view in the Documents library (shown in Figure 2–23) is Details view. Details view shows a list of files and folders, in addition to common properties such as Date Modified and Type. You can use the Change your view button to change to other views. The Small icons, Medium icons, Large icons, and Extra large icons views display the icons in increasingly larger sizes. When Medium, Large, or Extra large icon views are selected, Windows 7 provides a live preview option. With live preview, the icons display images that more closely reflect the actual contents of the files or folders. For example, a folder icon for a folder that contains text documents would show sample pages from those documents. List view displays the files and folders as a list of file names without any extra details. Tiles view displays the files and folders as tiles, which consist of an icon and icon description. With all of these views, the default arrangement for the icons is to be alphabetical by file name. The following steps change the view from the Details view to the Small icons view.

1

- Click the More options button arrow button next to the 'Change your view' button on the toolbar of the Documents library window to display the 'Change your view' menu (Figure 2–23).

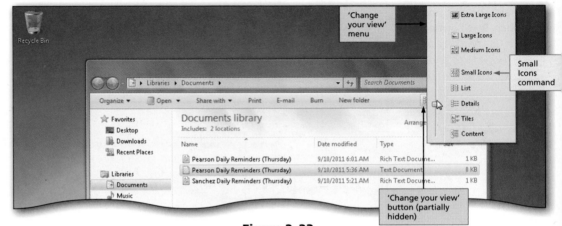

Figure 2–23

2

- Click the Small Icons command to display the files and folders as small icons (Figure 2–24).

Experiment

- Select each of the options from the 'Change your view' menu to see the various ways that Windows can display folder contents. After you have finished, be sure to select the Small Icons command from the 'Change your view' menu.

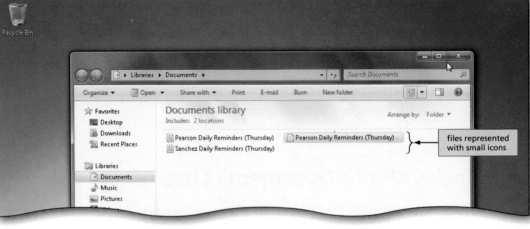

Figure 2–24

Other Ways

1. Right-click open space in Documents library, point to View, click Small icons

To Arrange Items in Groups by File Type

There are other methods of arranging the icons in the Documents library. One practical arrangement is to display the icons in groups based upon file type. This arrangement places files of the same type (File Folder, Text Documents, Microsoft Word, Microsoft Excel, and so on) in separate groups. When a window contains many files and folders, this layout makes it easier to find a particular file or folder quickly. The following steps group the icons in the Documents library by file type.

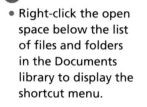

- Right-click the open space below the list of files and folders in the Documents library to display the shortcut menu.

- Point to the Group by command to display the Group by submenu (Figure 2–25).

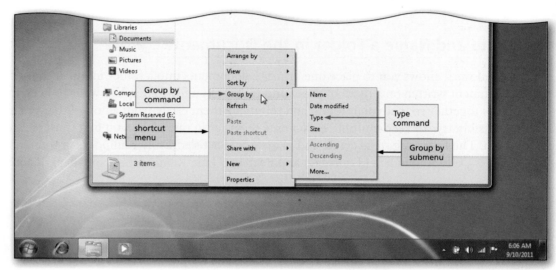

Figure 2–25

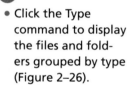

- Click the Type command to display the files and folders grouped by type (Figure 2–26).

Q&A

Can I group the files and folders in other ways?

You can group the files by any of the options on the Group by submenu. This includes Name, Date modified, Type, and Size. To remove the groupings, select (None) on the Group by submenu. The Ascending and Descending options change the order of the groups from alphabetical order to reverse alphabetical order.

Figure 2–26

Other Ways
1. Press ALT+V, press P, press T

To Change to Medium Icons View

Small icons view is not the best view when creating folders, so you will change the view to Medium icons.

1 Click the More options button arrow button next to the 'Change your view' button on the toolbar and then click the Medium Icons command to change to Medium icons view.

To Create and Name a Folder in the Documents Library

Windows 7 allows you to place one or more documents into a folder in much the same manner as you might take a document written on a piece of paper and place it in a file folder. You want to keep the Sanchez and Pearson documents together so that you can find and reference them easily from among other documents stored in the Documents library. To keep multiple documents together in one place, you first must create a folder in which to store them. The following steps create and name a folder titled Daily reminders in the Documents library to store the Sanchez Daily Reminders (Thursday) and Pearson Daily Reminders (Thursday) documents.

1

• Click the New folder button on the toolbar to create a new folder (Figure 2–27).

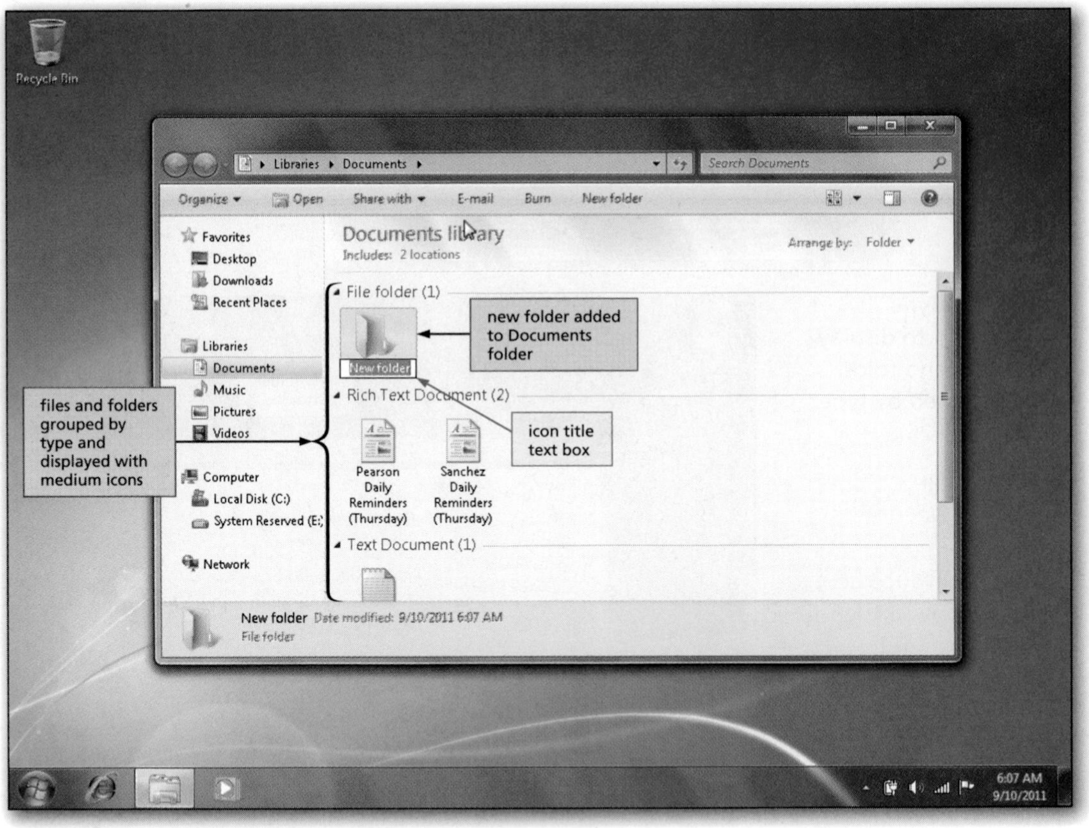

Figure 2–27

2

- Type `Daily reminders` in the icon title text box and then press the ENTER key to name the folder and sort the folder in the Documents library (Figure 2–28).

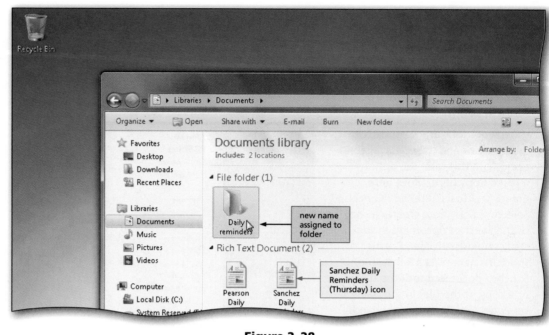

Figure 2–28

Other Ways

1. Right-click open space in Documents library, click New, click Folder, type file name, press ENTER
2. Press ALT+F, press W, press F, type file name, press ENTER

To Move a Document into a Folder

The ability to organize documents and files within folders allows you to keep the Documents library organized when using Windows 7. After you create a folder in the Documents library, the next step is to move documents into the folder. The following steps move the Sanchez Daily Reminders (Thursday) and the Pearson Daily Reminders (Thursday) documents into the Daily reminders folder.

1

- Right-click and drag (also known as right-drag) the Sanchez Daily Reminders (Thursday) icon onto the Daily reminders folder icon to display the shortcut menu (Figure 2–29).

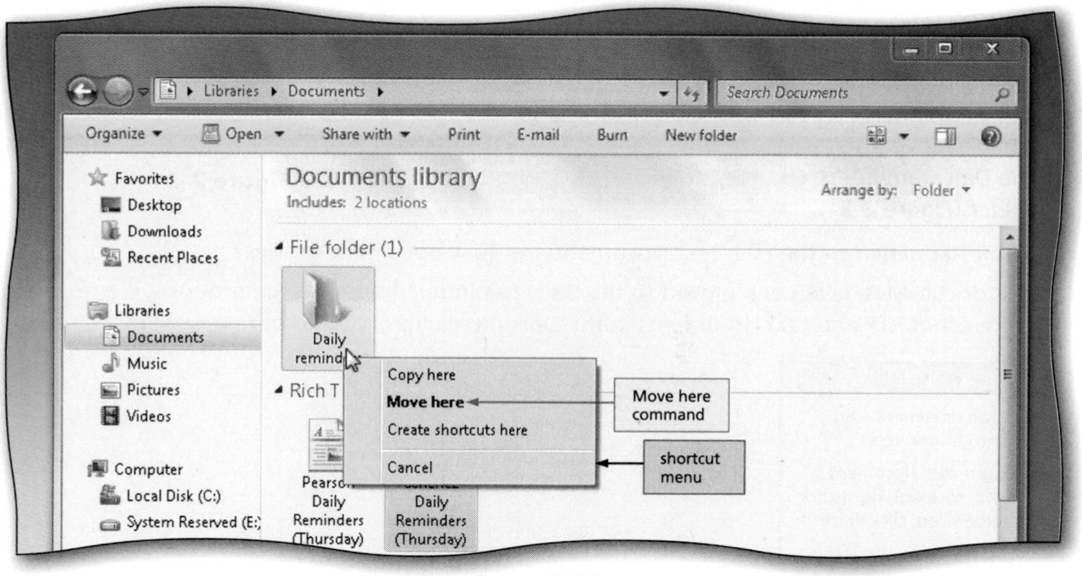

Figure 2–29

2

- Click the Move here command on the shortcut menu to move the Sanchez Daily Reminders (Thursday) icon to the Daily reminders folder (Figure 2–30).

Q&A

What are the other options in the shortcut menu?

When you right-drag, a shortcut menu opens and lists the available options. In this case, the options include Copy here, Move here, Create shortcuts here, and Cancel. Selecting Copy here creates a copy of the Sanchez document in the Daily reminders folder, Create shortcuts here puts a link to the Sanchez document (not the file or a copy of the file) in the Daily reminders folder and Cancel ends the right-drag process. The options in the shortcut menu might change, depending on the type of file and where you are dragging it.

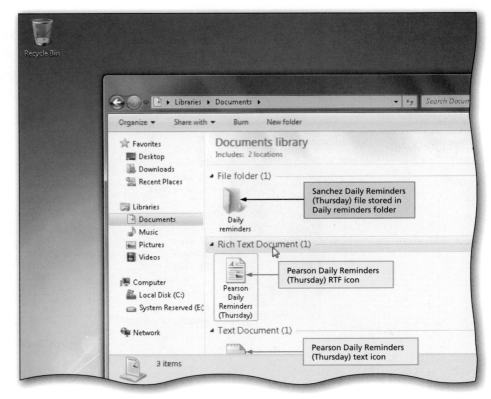

Figure 2–30

3

- Right-drag the Pearson Daily Reminders (Thursday) RTF icon onto the Daily reminders icon to move it to the Daily reminders folder.

- Right-drag the Pearson Daily Reminders (Thursday) text icon onto the Daily reminders icon to move it to the Daily reminders folder (Figure 2–31).

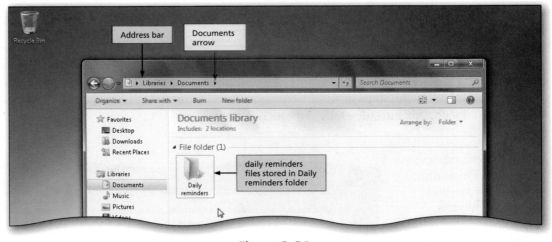

Figure 2–31

Q&A

What happened to the Rich Text Document and Text Document groups?

The documents have been moved to the Daily reminders folder, so the groups were no longer needed. Only if there were other RTF and text documents in the Documents library would the groupings remain.

Other Ways

1. Drag document icon onto folder icon
2. Right-click document icon, click Cut, right-click folder icon, click Paste

To Change Location Using the Address Bar

If you would like to navigate to the folder to see if your files are there, there are several ways to do this. One way in Windows 7 is to use the Address bar. The Address bar appears at the top of the Documents library window and displays your current location as a series of links separated by arrows. By clicking the arrows, you can change your location. The Forward and Back buttons can be used to navigate through the locations you have visited just like the Forward and Back buttons in a Web browser. The following steps change your location to the Daily reminders folder.

1
- Click the Documents arrow on the Address bar to display a location menu that contains a list of folders in the Documents library (Figure 2–32).

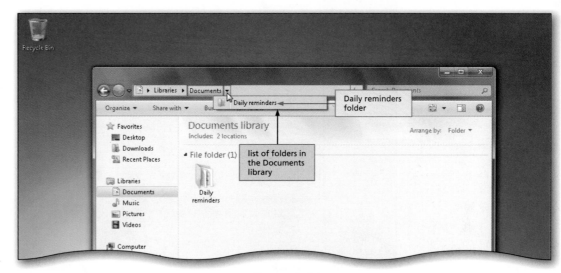

Figure 2–32

2
- Click the Daily reminders folder on the location menu to move to the Daily reminders folder (Figure 2–33).

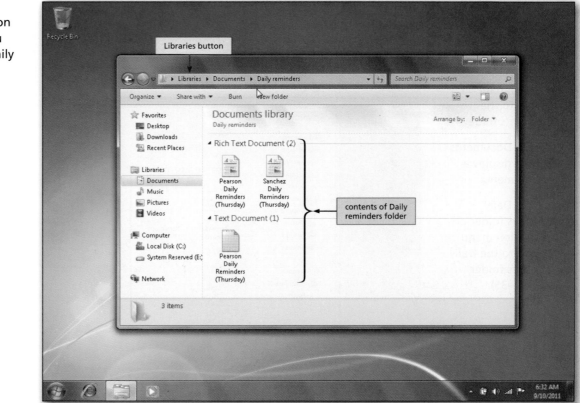

Figure 2–33

3

- Click the Libraries button on the Address bar to switch to the Libraries window (Figure 2–34).

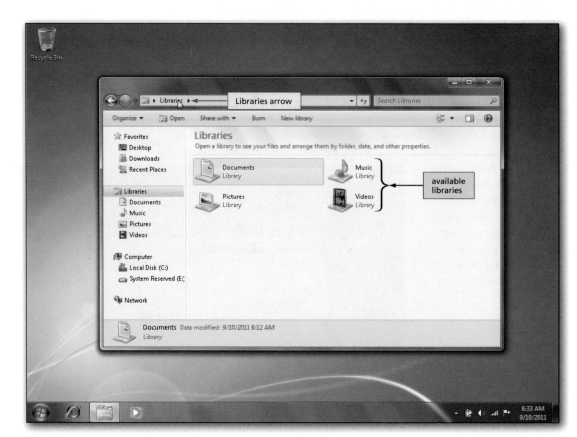

Figure 2–34

4

- Click the Libraries arrow to display a location menu.

- Click Documents on the location menu to move to the Documents folder.

- Click the Documents arrow to display a location menu.

- Click the Daily reminders folder on the location menu to move to the Daily reminders folder (Figure 2–35).

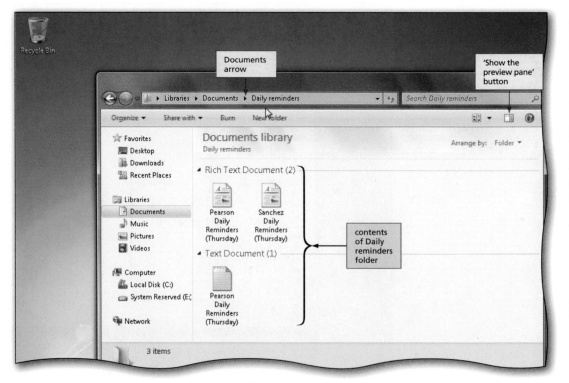

Figure 2–35

To Display and Use the Preview Pane

Now that you are viewing the contents of the Daily reminders folder, you can add a Preview pane to the layout, which will provide you with an enhanced live preview of your documents. When you select a document, the Preview pane displays a live view of the document to the right of the list of files in the folder window. The following steps add the Preview pane to the layout of the Daily reminders folder and then display a live preview of the Sanchez document.

1

- Click the 'Show the preview pane' button on the toolbar to display the Preview pane (Figure 2–36).

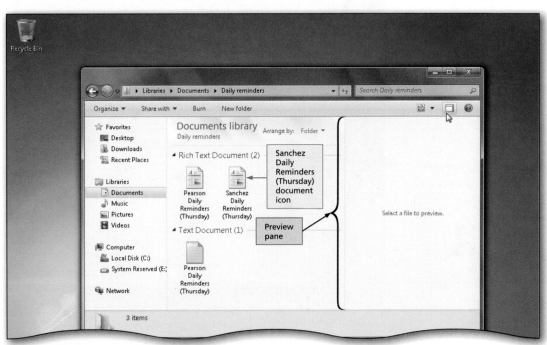

Figure 2–36

2

- Click the Sanchez Daily Reminders (Thursday) document icon on the right to display a preview of the document in the Preview pane (Figure 2–37).

Experiment

- Select different documents to display their preview in the Preview pane.

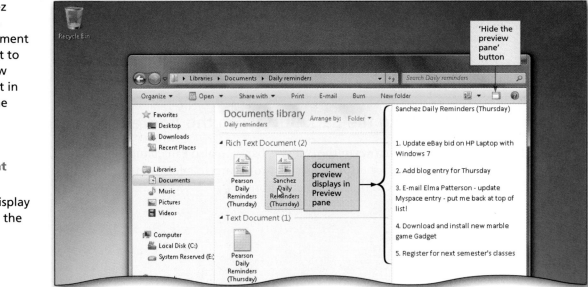

Figure 2–37

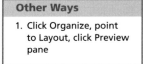

Other Ways
1. Click Organize, point to Layout, click Preview pane

To Close the Preview Pane

After verifying that your files are in the Daily reminders folder, you can close the Preview pane and then use the Address bar to return to the Documents library. The following step closes the Preview pane.

1

- Click the 'Hide the preview pane' button on the toolbar to close the Preview pane (Figure 2–38).

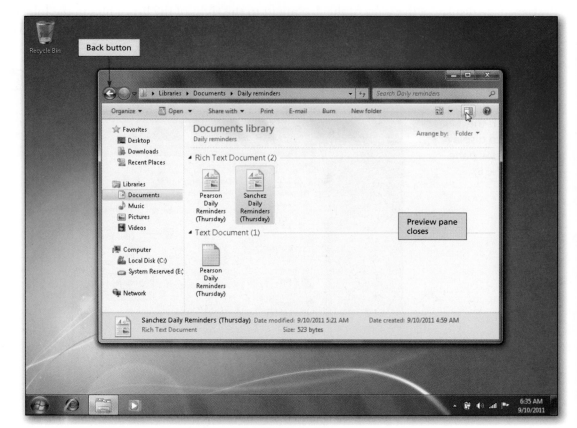

Figure 2–38

Other Ways

1. Click Organize, point to Layout, click Preview pane

To Change Location Using the Back Button on the Address Bar

In addition to clicking the arrows in the Address bar, you also can change locations by using the Back and Forward buttons. Clicking the Back button allows you to return to a location that you already have visited. The following step changes your location to the Documents library.

1
• Click the Back button on the Address bar once to return to the Documents library (Figure 2–39).

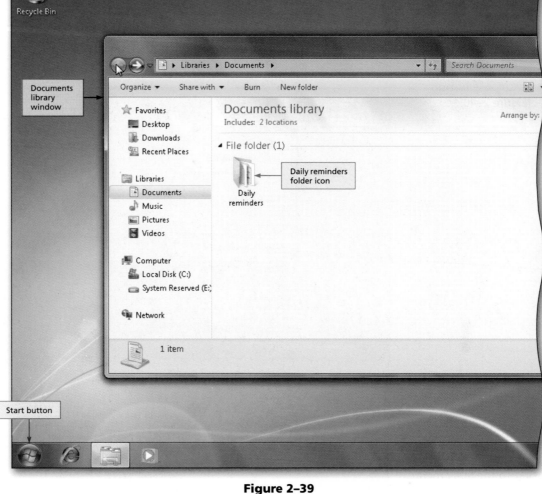

Figure 2–39

Creating Folder Shortcuts

One way to customize Windows 7 is to use shortcuts to launch programs and open files or folders. A shortcut is a link to any object on the computer or on a network, such as a program, file, folder, Web page, printer, or another computer. Placing a shortcut to a folder on the Start menu or on the desktop can make it easier to locate and open the folder.

A shortcut icon is not the actual document or program. You do not actually place the folder on the menu; instead, you place a shortcut icon that links to the folder on the menu. When you delete a shortcut, you delete the shortcut icon but do not delete the actual document or program; they remain on the hard disk.

To Add a Shortcut on the Start Menu

The steps on the following pages place the Daily reminders folder shortcut on the Start menu.

1

- Drag the Daily reminders folder icon onto the Start button to begin to add the icon to the Start menu. Do not release the left mouse button (Figure 2–40).

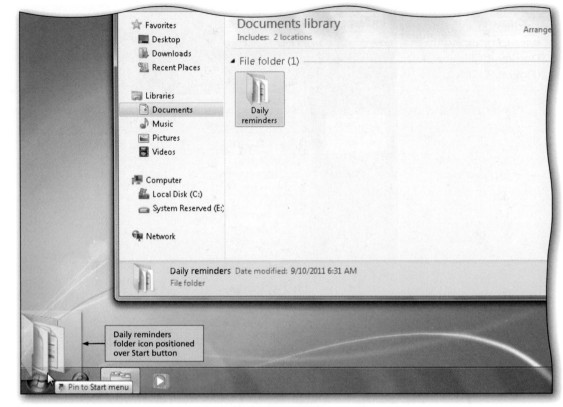

Daily reminders folder icon positioned over Start button

Figure 2–40

2

- Release the left mouse button to add the Daily reminders shortcut to the Start menu (Figure 2–41).

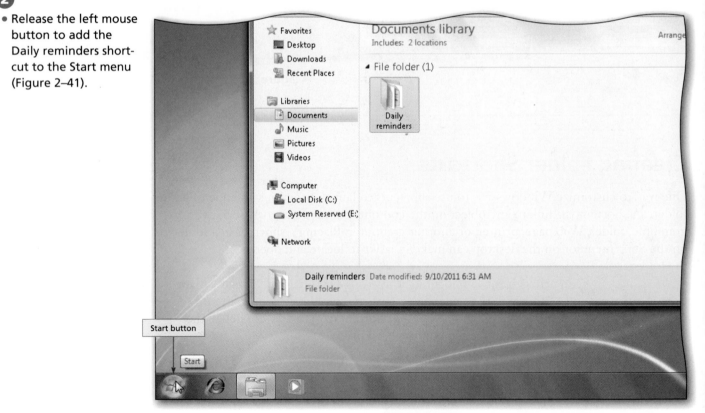

Start button

Figure 2–41

3

- Display the Start menu to see the Daily reminders icon pinned to the Start menu (Figure 2–42).

Q&A

Can I add other shortcuts to the Start menu?

In addition to placing a folder shortcut on the Start menu, you also can place a shortcut to other objects (programs, files, USB flash drives, Web pages, printers, or other computers) on the Start menu in a similar manner. First display the object's icon and then drag the icon onto the Start button.

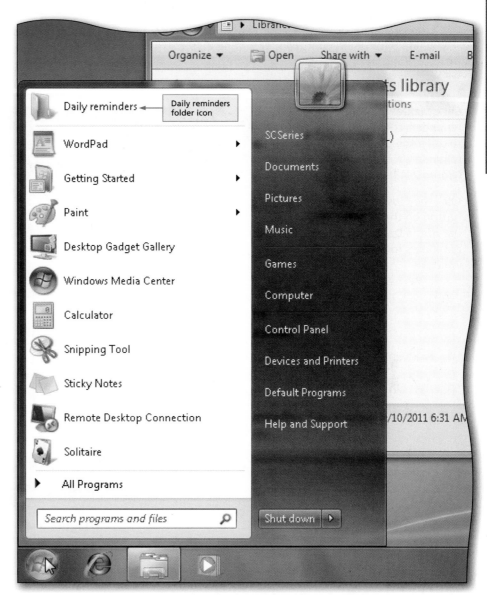

Figure 2–42

Other Ways
1. Right-drag folder icon onto Start button

To Open a Folder Using a Shortcut on the Start Menu

After placing a shortcut to the Daily reminders folder on the Start menu, you can open the Daily reminders folder by clicking the Start button and then clicking the Daily reminders command. The following step opens the Daily reminders folder window from the Start menu, and then closes the window.

1

- Click the Daily reminders command to open the Daily reminders folder (Figure 2–43).

- Click the Close button on the title bar of the Daily reminders folder window.

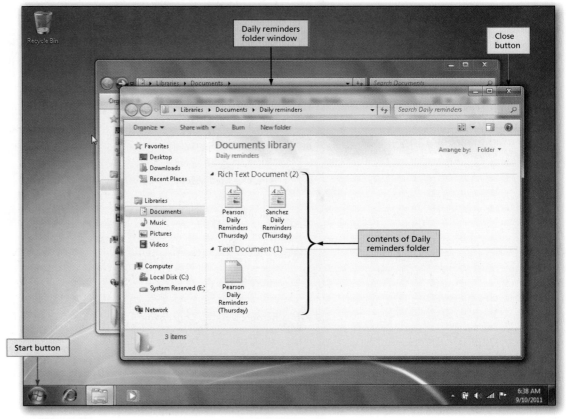

Figure 2–43

To Remove a Shortcut from the Start Menu

The capability of adding shortcuts to and removing them from the Start menu provides great flexibility when customizing Windows 7. Just as you can add shortcuts to the Start menu, you also can remove them. The following steps remove the Daily reminders shortcut from the Start menu.

1

- Display the Start menu.

- Right-click the Daily reminders command on the Start menu to display the shortcut menu (Figure 2–44).

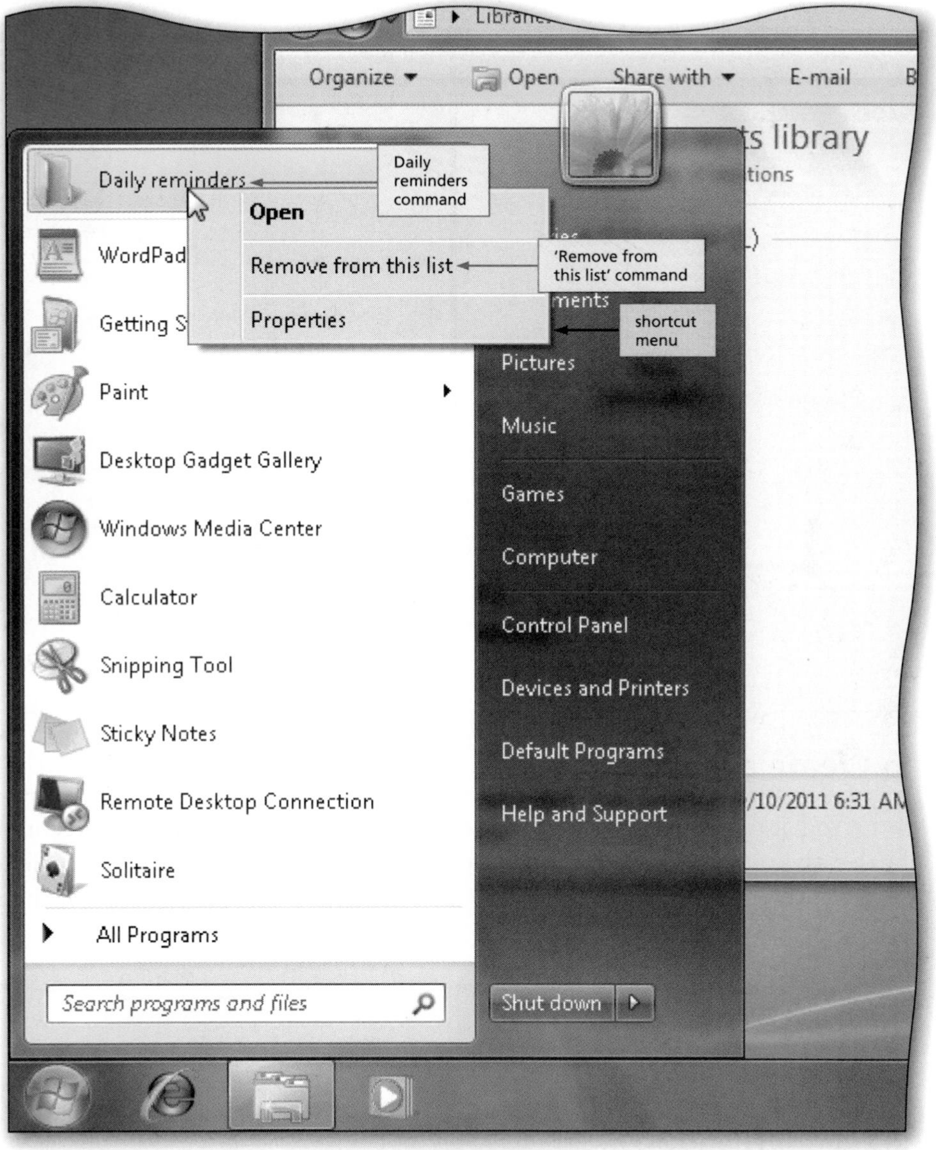

Figure 2–44

2

- Click the 'Remove from this list' command to remove the Daily reminders shortcut from the Start menu (Figure 2–45).

- Close the Start menu.

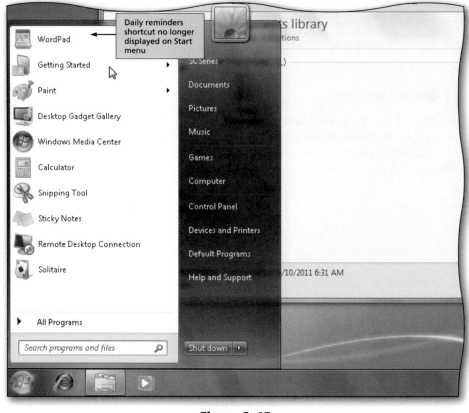

Figure 2–45

To Create a Shortcut on the Desktop

You also can create shortcuts directly on the desktop. Windows 7 recommends that only shortcuts be placed on the desktop rather than actual folders and files. This is to maximize the efficiency of file and folder searching, which will be covered in a later chapter. The following steps create a shortcut for the Daily reminders folder on the desktop.

1

- Right-click the Daily reminders folder to display the shortcut menu.

2

- Point to the Send to command to display the Send to submenu (Figure 2–46).

3

- Click the Desktop (create shortcut) command to create a shortcut on the desktop.

4

- Close the Documents library.

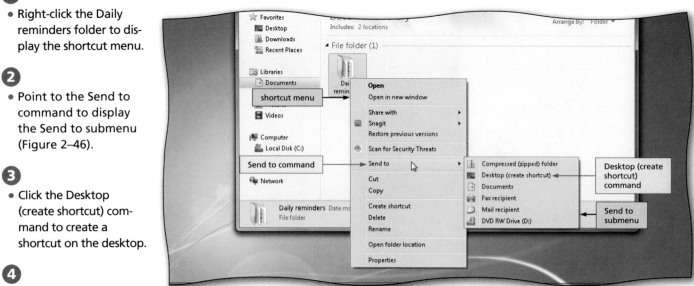

Figure 2–46

Opening and Modifying Documents within a Folder

When editing a document, you can open the document directly instead of first opening the program and then opening the document. You have received new information to add to Mr. Sanchez's daily reminders. An Internet meeting with the Sales Department in the western United States has been scheduled for 3:00 p.m. and the Sales Department must be notified of the meeting. To add this new item to the Daily reminders document, you first must open the Daily reminders folder that contains the document.

To Open a Folder Using a Shortcut on the Desktop

You have created a shortcut on the desktop for the Daily reminders folder, so you can use the shortcut icon to open the Daily reminders folder the same way you opened the Documents library using a shortcut in Chapter 1.

 Double-click the Daily reminders shortcut on the desktop to open the Daily reminders folder.

To Move the Pearson Daily Reminders (Thursday) Text File to the Recycle Bin

You will not be using the Pearson Daily Reminders (Thursday) text file, so you will move it to the Recycle Bin.

 If necessary, click the Restore Down button so that the Daily reminders folder is not maximized and the Recycle Bin icon is visible.

 Drag the Pearson Daily Reminders (Thursday) text icon to the Recycle Bin.

To Open and Modify a Document in a Folder

Now you will edit the remaining document in the Daily reminders folder. The following steps open the Sanchez Daily Reminders (Thursday) document and add new text about the Internet meeting.

1

- Open the Sanchez Daily Reminders (Thursday) document in WordPad.

2

- Move the insertion point to the blank line below item 5 in the document.

- Type 6. Notify Sales – NetMeeting at 3:00 p.m. and then press the ENTER key to modify the Sanchez Daily Reminders (Thursday) document (Figure 2–47).

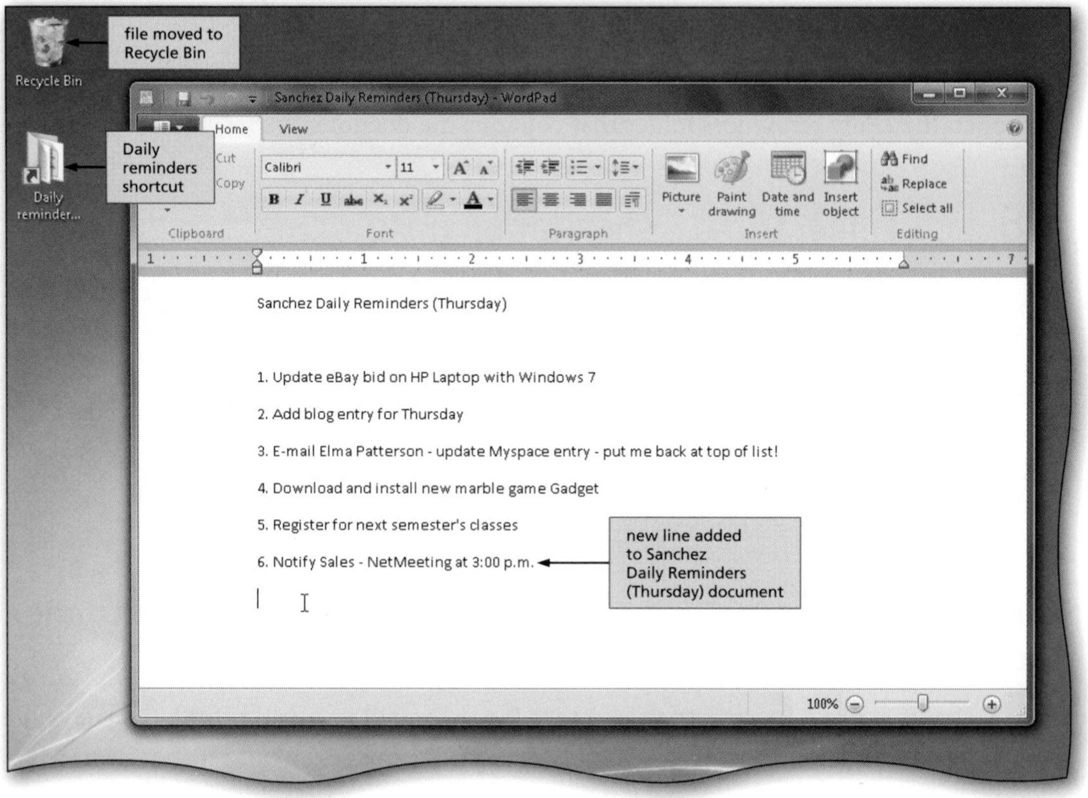

Figure 2–47

To Open and Modify Multiple Documents

Windows 7 allows you to have more than one document and program open at the same time so that you can work on multiple documents. The concept of multiple programs running at the same time is called **multitasking.** To illustrate how you can work with multiple windows open at the same time, you now will edit the Pearson Daily Reminders (Thursday) document to include a reminder to talk to Dan about Carol's birthday party. You will not have to close the Sanchez Daily Reminders (Thursday) document. The following steps open the Pearson Daily Reminders (Thursday) document and add the new reminder.

1

- Open the Pearson Daily Reminders (Thursday) document in WordPad.

Q&A | Why does the font look different in the two documents?

Because the Pearson Daily Reminders (Thursday) document was created as a text file, its font will appear different from that of the Sanchez Daily Reminders (Thursday) document. Remember, Rich Text Format documents allow for more formatting than plain text files.

Q&A | Why did the WordPad icon on the taskbar change?

When only one document is open in WordPad, the WordPad icon appears like a single button. If multiple documents are open, the icon changes to appear as a stacked button to indicate there is more than one document open.

2

- Move the insertion point to the end of the document in the WordPad window.

- Type 4. Call Dan – Birthday party for Carol and then press the ENTER key (Figure 2–48).

Opening Windows
In addition to clicking the taskbar button of an inactive window to make that window the active window, you can click any open area of the window. For example, many people click the title bar of a window to activate the window.

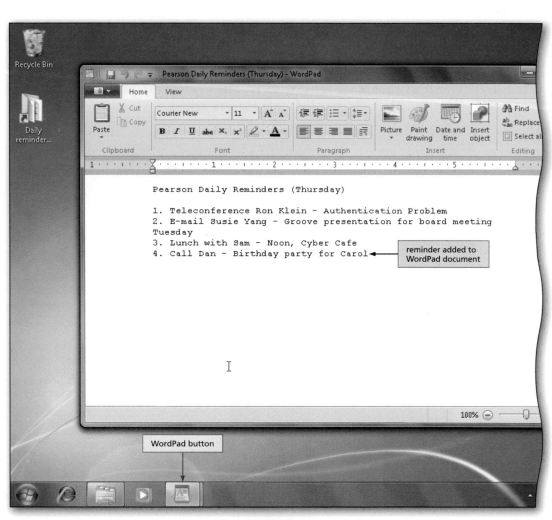

Figure 2–48

To Display an Inactive Window

After you have modified the Pearson Daily Reminders (Thursday) document, you receive information that a dinner meeting with Art Perez has been scheduled for Mr. Sanchez for 7:00 p.m. at The Crab House. You are directed to add this entry to Mr. Sanchez's reminders. To do this, you must make the Sanchez Daily Reminders (Thursday) - WordPad window the active window. The following steps make the Sanchez Daily Reminders (Thursday) - WordPad window active and enter the new reminder.

1

- Point to the WordPad button on the taskbar to display a live preview of the two documents (Figure 2–49).

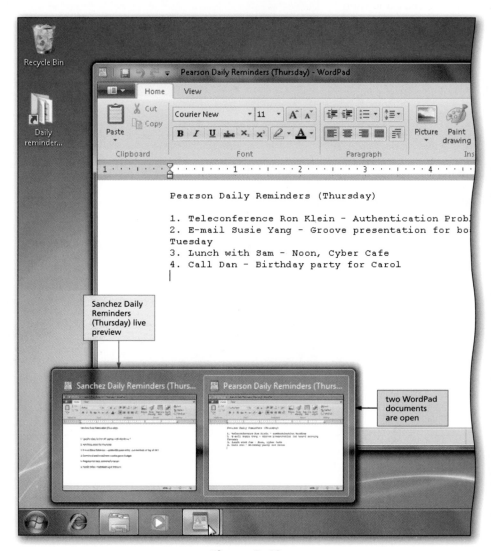

Figure 2–49

2
- Click the Sanchez Daily Reminders (Thursday) live preview to make it the active window (Figure 2–50).

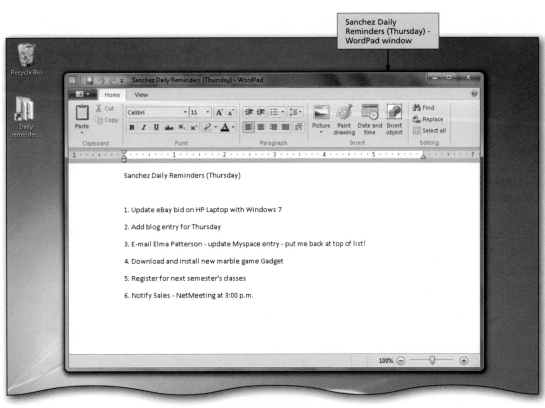

Figure 2–50

3
- When the window opens, type
7. Dinner with Art Perez – 7:00 p.m., The Crab House
and then press the ENTER key to update the document (Figure 2–51).

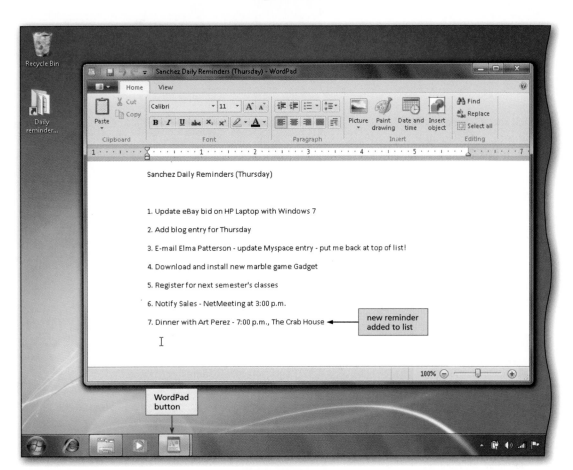

Figure 2–51

To Close Multiple Open Windows and Save Changes Using the Taskbar

When you have finished working with multiple windows, you should close them. If the windows are open on the desktop, you can click the Close button on the title bar of each open window to close them. Regardless of whether the windows are open on the desktop or are minimized using the Show desktop button, you can close the windows using the buttons on the taskbar. The following steps close the Sanchez Daily Reminders (Thursday) - WordPad and Pearson Daily Reminders (Thursday) - WordPad windows using the taskbar.

1

- Right-click the WordPad button on the taskbar to display a shortcut menu (Figure 2–52).

Q&A

Why are there multiple instances of the documents in the Recent list?

The list shows the files you recently have edited, and does not remove duplicate listings. As a result, a document might appear in the list multiple times.

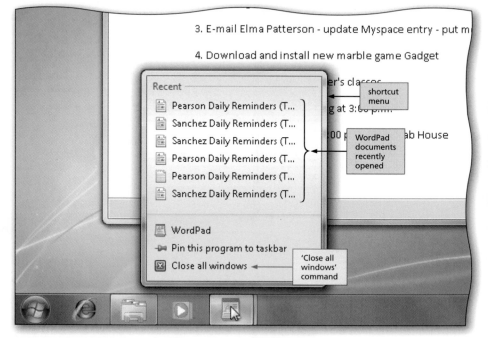

Figure 2–52

2

- Click the 'Close all windows' command to display the WordPad dialog box (Figure 2–53).

- Click the Save button in the WordPad dialog box to save the changes and close the Sanchez Daily Reminders (Thursday) document.

- Click the Save button in the WordPad dialog box to save the changes and close the Pearson Daily Reminders (Thursday) document.

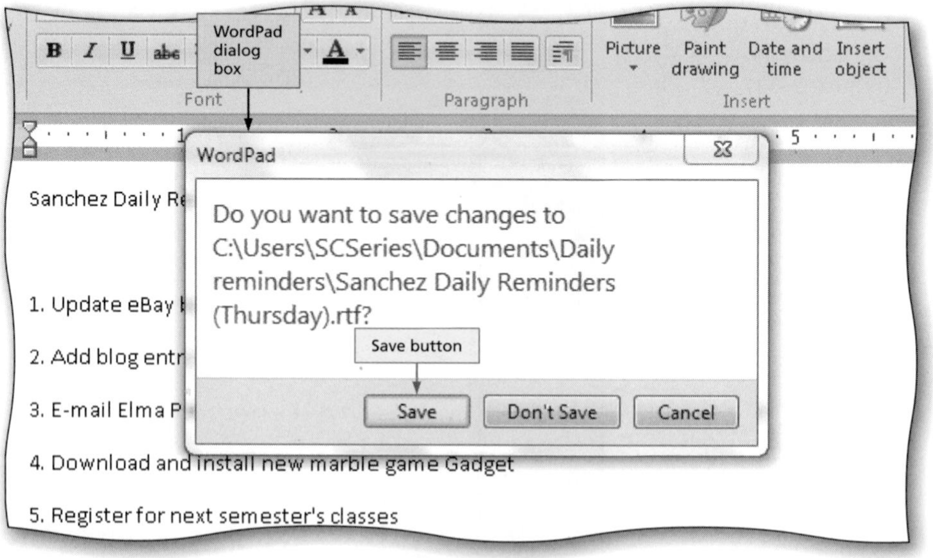

Other Ways

1. Click taskbar, select document, on WordPad menu click Save, click Close

2. Click taskbar, select document, on title bar click Close, click Save

3. Click taskbar, select document, on WordPad menu click Exit, click Save

Figure 2–53

To Print Multiple Documents from within a Folder

After you modify and save documents on the desktop, you might want to print them so that you have an updated hard copy of the documents. Earlier in this chapter, you used the Print command on the WordPad menu to print an open document. You also can print multiple documents from within a folder without actually opening the documents.

Before you can print them, you must select both of them. There are several different ways to select multiple items. You can select the first item, then while holding down the CTRL key, you can select the other items, or you can select the first item, then while holding down the SHIFT key, you can select the other items. The first method works when the items you want to select are not adjacent, whereas the second method (using the SHIFT key) only works if all of the items are next to each other. The following steps print both the Sanchez Daily Reminders (Thursday) and the Pearson Daily Reminders (Thursday) documents from the Daily reminders folder.

1
- Make the Daily reminders folder window the active window.
- Click the Pearson Daily Reminders (Thursday) icon in the Daily reminders folder to select the icon.
- Press and hold the SHIFT key, click the Sanchez Daily Reminders (Thursday) icon, and then release the SHIFT key to select both items in the Daily reminders folder (Figure 2–54).

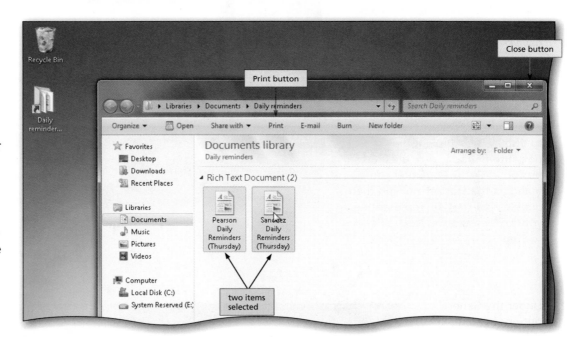

Figure 2–54

2
- Click the Print button on the toolbar to print the two files.

3
- Click the Close button in the Daily reminders window to close the Daily reminders window.

Copying a Folder onto a USB Flash Drive

A shortcut on the desktop is useful when you frequently use one or more documents within the folder. It is a good policy to make a copy of a folder and the documents within the folder so that if the folder or its contents are accidentally lost or damaged, you do not lose your work. This is referred to as making a backup of the files and folders. Another reason to make copies of files and folders is so that you can take the files and folders from one computer to another, for instance if you need to take a file or folder from a work computer to your home computer. A USB flash drive is a handy device for physically moving copies of files and folders between computers.

BTW

Backups
Copying a file or folder to a USB flash drive is one way to create a backup, but backing up files often is a much more elaborate process. Most backup systems use tape or portable hard disks that contain hundreds of gigabytes (billions of characters) or even terabytes (thousands of gigabytes).

To Copy a Folder onto a USB Flash Drive

You want to be able to use the files you have created on another computer. To do so, you will need to copy the files to your USB flash drive. The following steps copy the Daily reminders folder on to a USB flash drive.

1

• Insert a USB flash drive into an open USB port to display the AutoPlay dialog box (Figure 2–55).

Q&A Why does my USB flash drive have a different letter?

Depending on how many devices you have connected to your computer, your USB flash drive might have been assigned a different letter such as E or G.

Q&A What happens if the AutoPlay dialog box does not appear?

If your computer is not configured to display the AutoPlay dialog box automatically, click the Start button, click the Computer command on the Start menu, and then double-click the icon representing your USB flash drive. Next, skip to Step 3.

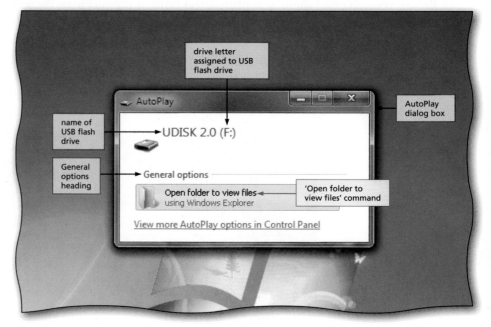

Figure 2–55

2

• Under the General options heading in the AutoPlay dialog box, click the 'Open folder to view files' command to open a folder window that displays the contents of your USB flash drive (Figure 2–56).

Figure 2–56

3

- Click the Documents link in the left pane to display the contents of the Documents library.

- Right-click the Daily reminders folder to display the shortcut menu.

- Point to the Send to command to display the Send to submenu (Figure 2–57).

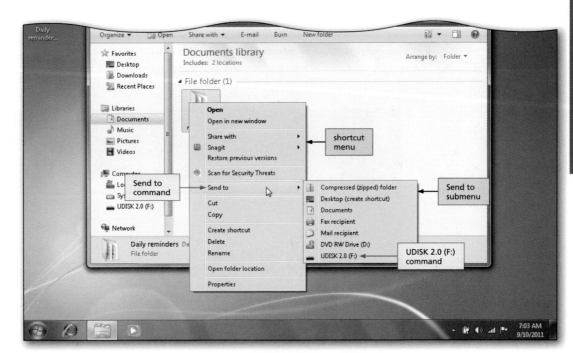

Figure 2–57

4

- Click the UDISK 2.0 (F:) command (or the name and drive letter representing your USB flash drive) to copy the folder to the USB flash drive (Figure 2–58).

Q&A

Can I back up the entire Documents library?

Yes. It is important to regularly back up the entire contents of your Documents library. To back up the Documents library, display the Start menu, right-click the Documents command, click Send to on the shortcut menu, and then click the location of the backup drive.

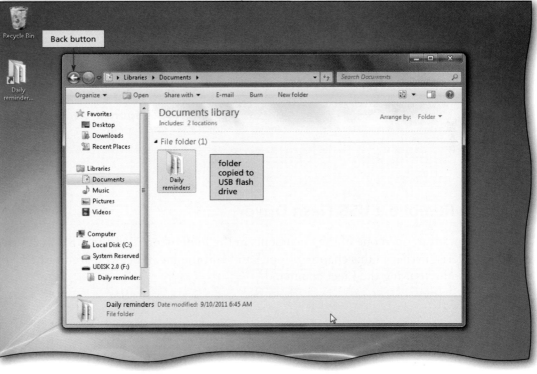

Figure 2–58

Other Ways

1. Press ALT+F, point to Send to, click UDISK 2.0 (F:)

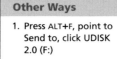

To Open a Folder Stored on a USB Flash Drive

After copying a folder onto a USB flash drive, in order to verify that the folder has been copied properly, you can open the folder from the USB flash drive and view its contents. The following steps open a folder stored on a USB flash drive.

1
- Click the Back button on the Address bar of the Documents library to return to the USB flash drive window (Figure 2–59).

2
- Double-click the Daily reminders icon to open the folder and verify the files are in the Daily reminders folder.

3
- Close the Daily reminders folder window.

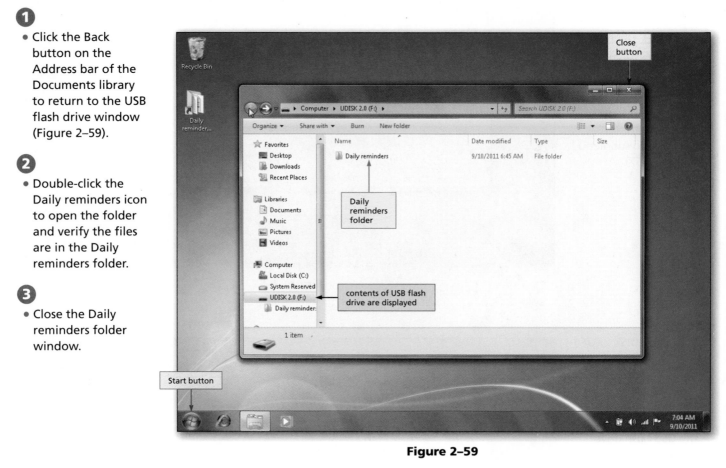

Figure 2–59

To Safely Remove a USB Flash Drive

If you want to open one of the documents in the folder stored on the USB flash drive, you can use one of the methods covered earlier in this chapter to open and edit the file. Once you are finished, you should safely remove the USB flash drive using the Eject command.

1
- Display the Start menu and then click the Computer command to open the Computer folder window (Figure 2–60).

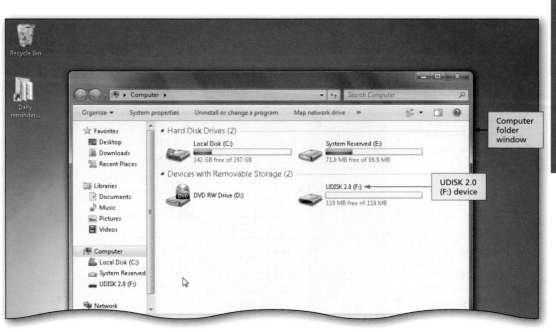

Figure 2–60

2
- Right-click the UDISK 2.0 (F:) device to display the shortcut menu (Figure 2–61).

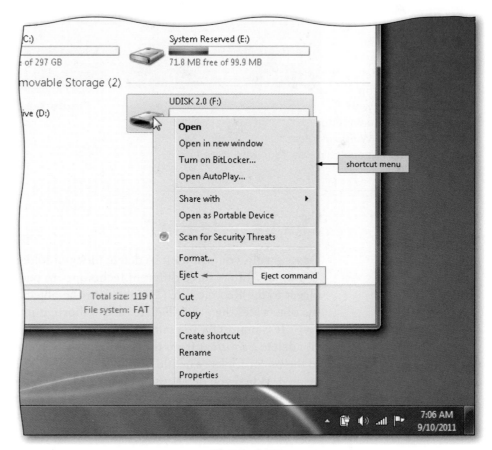

Figure 2–61

3

- Click the Eject command on the shortcut menu to close the USB flash drive and display the Safe To Remove Hardware message in the notification area (Figure 2–62).

- Remove the USB flash drive from the USB port.

- Close the Computer folder window.

Q&A

Why do I need to safely remove the USB flash drive?

Even though you might not have anything open on the USB flash drive, Windows 7 still might be accessing it in the background. Safely removing the USB flash drive tells Windows 7 to stop communicating with the device. If you were to remove it while Windows 7 was still accessing it, you could lose your data stored on it.

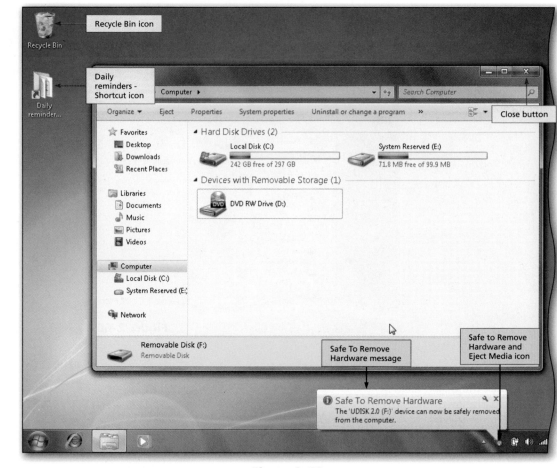

Figure 2–62

The Recycle Bin

Occasionally, you will want to delete files and folders from the Documents library. Windows 7 offers three different techniques to perform this operation: (1) Drag the object to the Recycle Bin; (2) right-drag the object to the Recycle Bin; and (3) right-click the object and then click Delete on the shortcut menu.

It is important to realize what you are doing when you delete a file or folder. When you delete a shortcut from the desktop, you only delete the shortcut icon and its reference to the file or folder. The file or folder itself is stored elsewhere on the hard disk and is not deleted. When you delete the icon for a file or folder (not a shortcut), the actual file or folder is deleted. A shortcut icon includes an arrow to indicate that it is a shortcut, whereas a file or folder does not have the arrow as part of its icon.

When you delete a file or folder, Windows 7 places these items in the Recycle Bin, which is an area on the hard disk that contains all the items you have deleted. If you are running low on hard disk space, one way to gain additional space is to empty the Recycle Bin. Up until the time you empty the Recycle Bin, you can recover deleted files. Even though you have this safety net, you should be careful whenever you delete anything from your computer.

To Delete a Shortcut from the Desktop

The following step removes a shortcut from the desktop.

1 Drag the Daily reminders - Shortcut icon onto the Recycle Bin icon on the desktop to move the shortcut to the Recycle Bin.

To Restore an Item from the Recycle Bin

At some point, you might discover that you accidentally deleted a shortcut, file, or folder that you did not want to delete. As long as you have not emptied the Recycle Bin, you can restore them. The following steps restore the Daily reminders - Shortcut icon to the desktop.

1
- Double-click the Recycle Bin icon to open the Recycle Bin.
- Click the Daily reminders - Shortcut icon to select it (Figure 2–63).

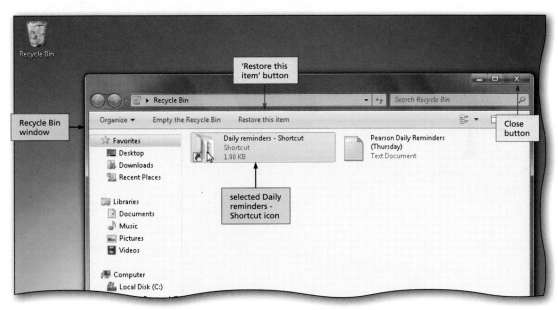

Figure 2–63

2
- Click the 'Restore this item' button to restore the Daily reminders - Shortcut icon to its previous location. In this case, the icon is restored to the desktop (Figure 2–64).
- Close the Recycle Bin window.

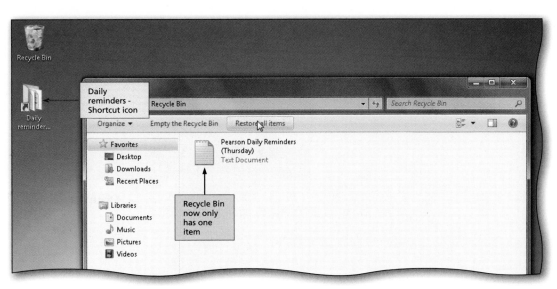

Figure 2–64

To Delete a Shortcut from the Desktop

Now you should delete the Daily reminders shortcut icon again so that you can leave the desktop how you found it.

1 Drag the Daily reminders - Shortcut icon onto the Recycle Bin icon.

To Delete Multiple Files from a Folder

You can delete several files at one time. The following steps delete both the Sanchez Daily Reminders (Thursday) and the Pearson Daily Reminders (Thursday) documents.

1

- Open the Documents library.

- Open the Daily reminders folder.

- Click the Sanchez Daily Reminders (Thursday) document to select it.

- Press and hold the CTRL key, and then click the Pearson Daily Reminders (Thursday) document.

- Right-click the documents to display the shortcut menu (Figure 2–65).

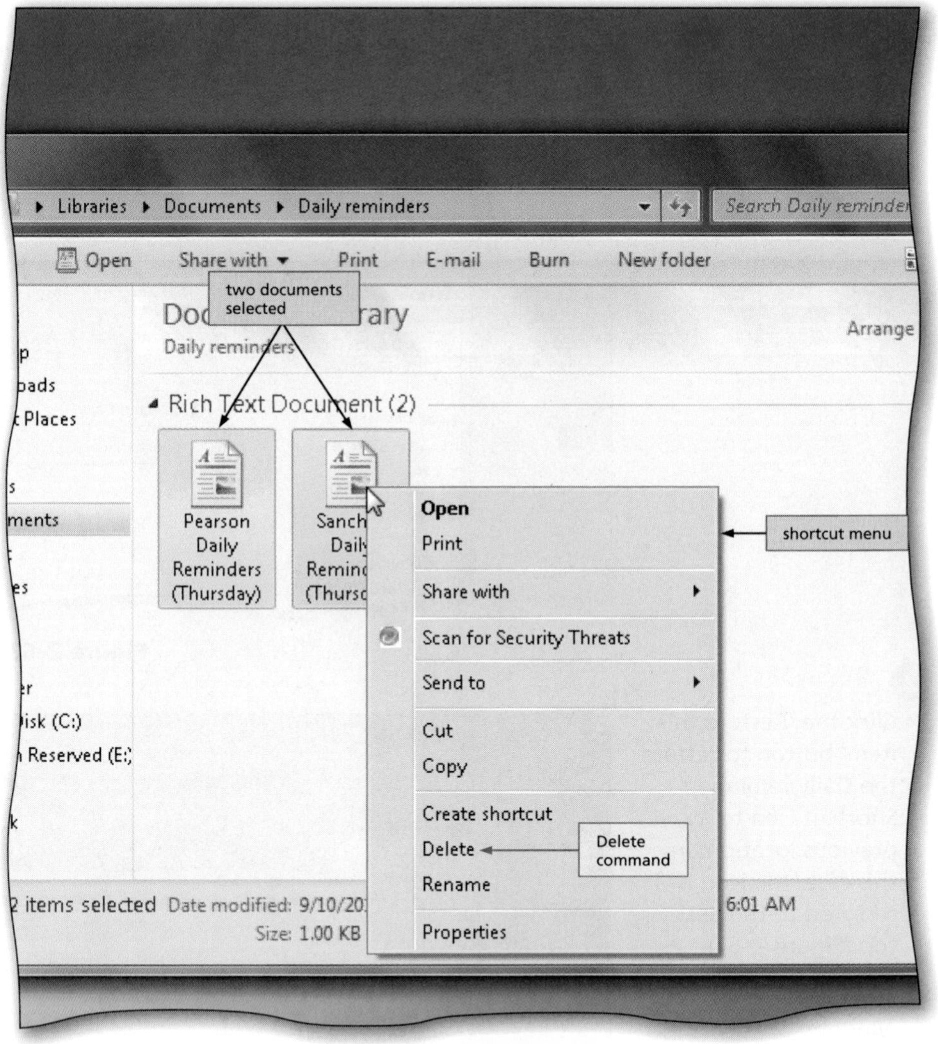

Figure 2–65

2

- Click the Delete command to display the Delete Multiple Items dialog box (Figure 2–66).

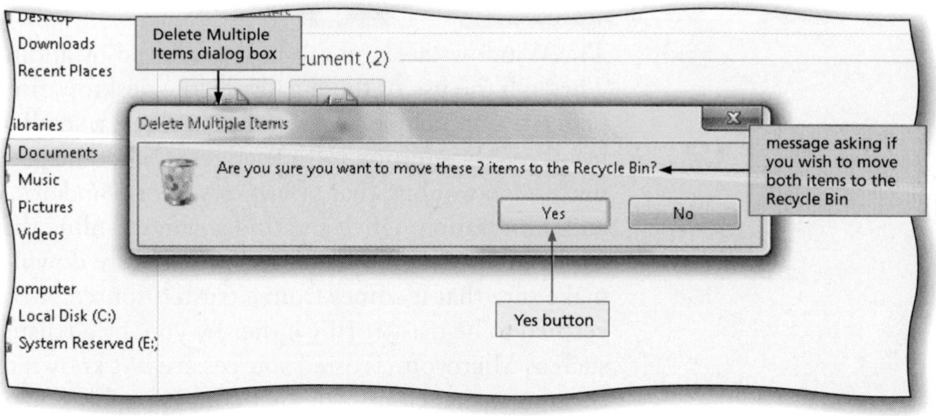

Figure 2–66

3

- Click the Yes button to move the files to the Recycle Bin (Figure 2–67).

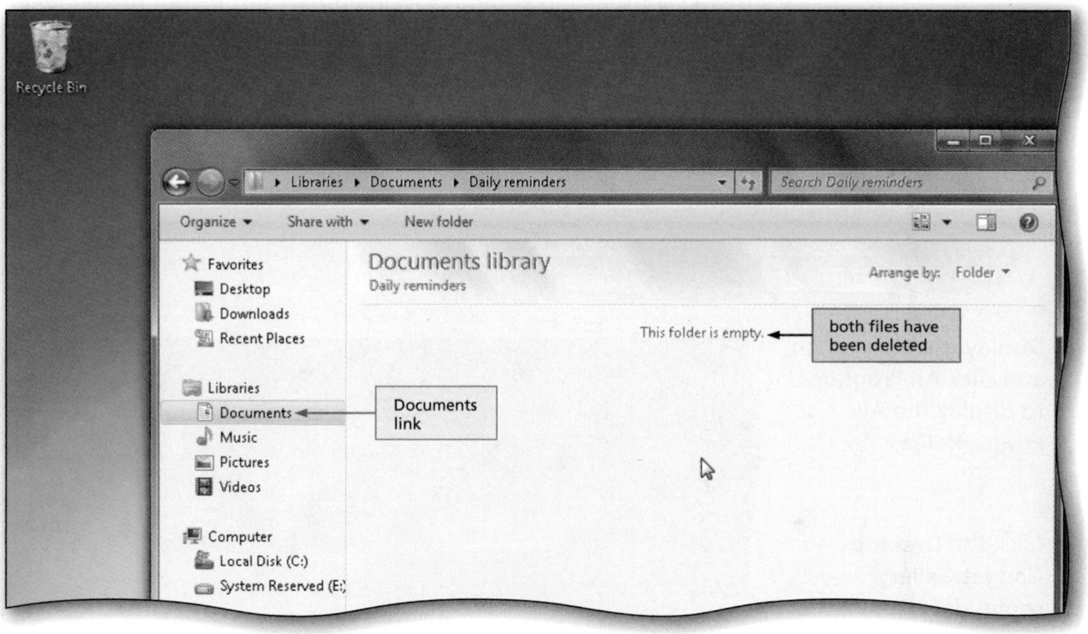

Figure 2–67

To Delete a Folder from the Documents Library and Empty the Recycle Bin

You also can delete folders from the Documents library using the same method.

1 Click the Documents link in the navigation pane.

2 Delete the Daily reminders folder.

3 Close the Documents library.

4 Right-click the Recycle Bin to display the shortcut menu.

5 Click the Empty Recycle Bin command.

6 Click the Yes button in the Delete Multiple Items dialog box to permanently delete the contents of the Recycle Bin.

Desktop Gadgets

The Windows desktop can be customized by adding miniprograms called gadgets. Through the use of these gadgets, the desktop can display useful tools and information. Gadgets can include items such as a clock, a small calendar, the current weather, and news headlines. In addition to the gadgets that come preinstalled with Windows 7, you also can find gadgets online that offer news, sports updates, entertainment, or other useful tools and information. Once you find a gadget online that you are interested in, you can download and install it on your computer. Before downloading and installing a gadget, first make sure that it comes from a trusted source. A **trusted source** is a source that has been verified to be trustworthy either by you, by a trusted friend, or by a trusted organization such as Microsoft. Trusted sources are not known to offer gadgets that contain offensive content or malicious code that could possibly damage your computer or do any other type of harm. If you download from a trusted source, you can feel secure about what you are installing on your computer. If the developer of the gadget you want to download is not a trusted source, you should not download and install the gadget.

To Add Multiple Gadgets to the Desktop

As you learned in Chapter 1, you can add gadgets to the Windows desktop. You also can customize the existing gadgets. Depending on the gadget, different options are available to you for customizing the gadget. You decide to add the Clock and the Slide Show gadgets to the desktop.

1
- Display the Start menu, and click All Programs to display the All Programs list.

2
- Click the Desktop Gadget Gallery command to open the Gadget Gallery.

3
- Double-click the Clock gadget in the Gadget Gallery to add the gadget to the desktop.

4
- Double-click the Slide Show gadget in the Gadget Gallery to add the gadget to the desktop (Figure 2–68).

5
- Close the Gadget Gallery window.

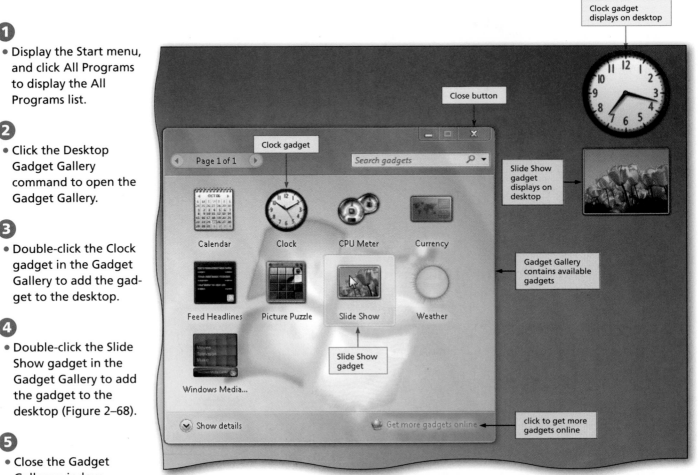

Figure 2–68

To Customize the Clock Gadget

You decide to experiment with the Clock gadget as you would like to see a different clock design, and you would like to add your name to it. The following steps customize and personalize the Clock gadget.

1

• Right-click the Clock gadget on the desktop to display the shortcut menu (Figure 2–69).

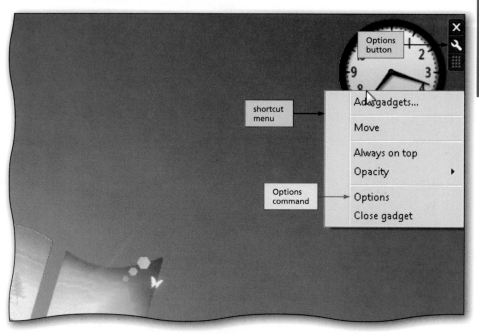

Figure 2–69

2

• Click the Options command to display the Clock dialog box (Figure 2–70).

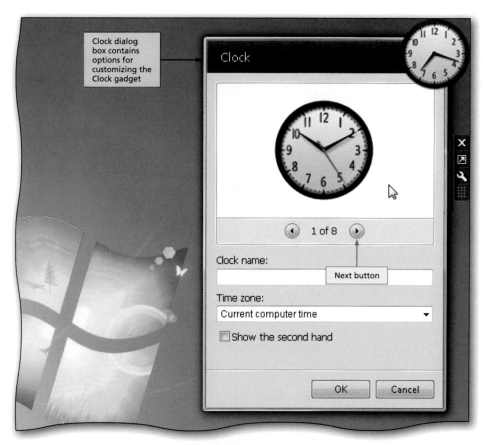

Figure 2–70

3
- Click the Next button three times to display the neon light clock (Figure 2–71).

Figure 2–71

4
- Click the Clock name text box to select it.

- Type Steve's (or your own name) in the Clock name text box (Figure 2–72).

Figure 2–72

5

- Click the OK button to apply your changes and close the Clock dialog box (Figure 2–73).

Q&A Do all gadgets have the same options?

Every gadget has different options. For example, the Calendar gadget can be customized to show a week or a month, instead of just the current day.

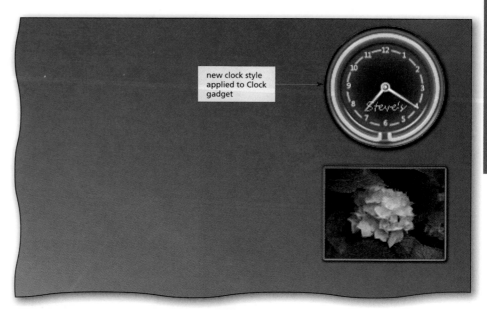

new clock style applied to Clock gadget

Figure 2–73

To Undo the Changes to the Clock Gadget

Although you like the new look for the Clock gadget, you decide that the original style was easier to read. You, therefore, want to undo the changes you have made. The following steps undo the changes to the Clock gadget.

1

- Point to the Clock gadget to display the icons associated with the gadget.

- Click the Options button to display the Clock dialog box (Figure 2–74).

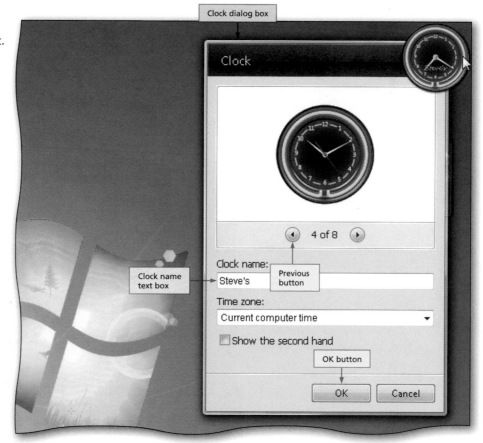

Clock dialog box

Clock

4 of 8

Clock name:
Steve's

Previous button

Clock name text box

Time zone:
Current computer time

☐ Show the second hand

OK button

OK   Cancel

Figure 2–74

2

- Click the Previous button three times to display the original clock.

- Delete the text from the Clock name text box (Figure 2–75).

- Click the OK button to apply your changes and close the Clock dialog box.

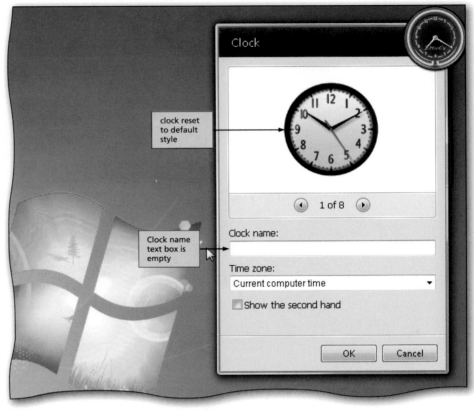

Figure 2–75

To Rearrange Gadgets on the Desktop

In addition to customizing the gadgets, you also can rearrange the gadgets on the desktop. Rearranging gadgets is as simple as dragging them to the desired location. You decide to see how the gadgets would look in another arrangement. The following steps rearrange the gadgets on the desktop.

1

- Point to the Drag gadget button located to the right of the Clock gadget (Figure 2–76).

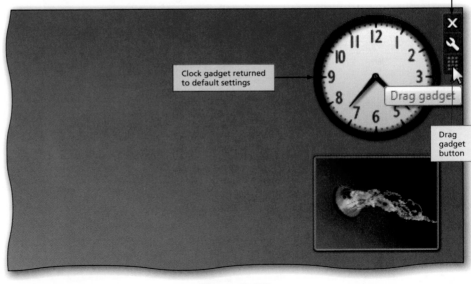

Figure 2–76

• Click the Drag gadget button and drag the Clock gadget below the Recycle Bin to reposition it on the desktop (Figure 2–77).

Figure 2–77

To Search for Gadgets Online

Now you decide to browse the Internet for new gadgets, although you are not going to download and install any new gadgets at this time. You want to become familiar with what types of gadgets are available. In fact, because you have been so busy, you want to find some gadgets to provide quick relief from work, without the gadgets becoming too distracting or time consuming. The following steps search for gadgets online.

1

• Display the Start menu, and click All Programs to display the All Programs list.

• Click the Desktop Gadget Gallery command to open the Gadget Gallery (Figure 2–78).

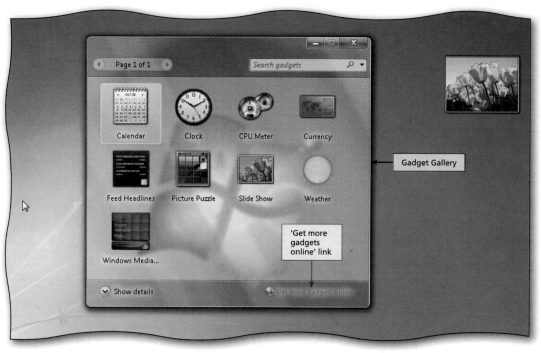

Figure 2–78

2

• Click the 'Get more gadgets online' link to open Windows Internet Explorer and display the Personalization Gallery Web page (Figure 2–79).

Q&A

Why do I see different gadgets on my computer?

The Personalization Gallery Web site is frequently updated. Each time you search for gadgets online, different gadgets might display.

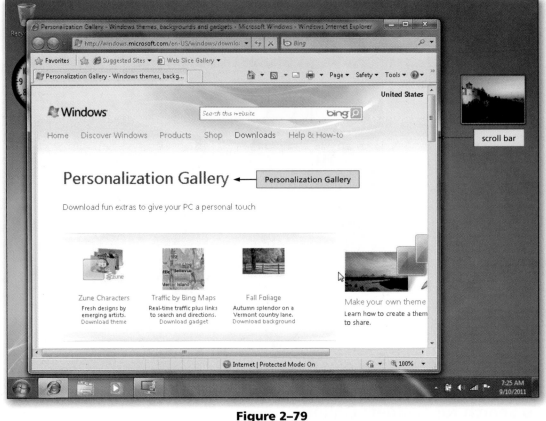

Figure 2–79

3

• Scroll down to view the Desktop gadgets tab.

• Click the Desktop gadgets tab to display the available Desktop gadgets (Figure 2–80).

🔎 **Experiment**

• Click the 'Get more desktop gadgets' link, located below the featured gadgets, to see what gadgets other developers have created. Review the various categories and available gadgets.

Figure 2–80

To Close the Internet Explorer and Gadget Gallery Windows

After having reviewed some of the gadgets available online, you decide to close Internet Explorer. You do not want to download gadgets yet; you want to wait until you have verified that the gadgets you want are from trusted sources. The following steps close Internet Explorer and the Gadget Gallery windows.

1 Click the Close button to close Internet Explorer.

2 Click the Close button in the Gadget Gallery to close the window.

To Remove Gadgets from the Desktop

Not only can you place gadgets on the desktop, you can remove them. The following steps remove the gadgets you added.

1 Point to the Clock gadget and click the Close button to remove the Clock gadget from the desktop.

2 Point to the Slide Show gadget and click the Close button to remove the Slide Show gadget from the desktop.

To Log Off from the Computer

After removing the gadgets from the desktop, you decide to log off the computer. The following steps log off the computer.

1 Display the Start menu.

2 Point to the arrow to the right of the Shut down button to display the Shut Down options menu.

3 Click the Log off command, and then wait for Windows 7 to prompt you to save any unsaved data, if any, and log off.

To Turn Off the Computer

The following step turns off the computer. If you are not sure whether you should turn off the computer, read the following step without actually performing it.

1 Click the Shut down button to turn off the computer.

Chapter Summary

In this chapter, you learned to create text documents using both the application-centric approach and document-centric approach. You moved these documents to the Documents library, and then modified and printed them. You created a new folder in the Documents library, placed documents in the folder, and copied the new folder onto a USB flash drive. You worked with multiple documents open at the same time. You placed a folder shortcut on both the Start menu and on the desktop. Using various methods, you deleted shortcuts, documents, and a folder. Finally, you learned how to customize a gadget, rearrange gadgets on the desktop, search for new gadgets online, and remove gadgets from the desktop. The items listed below include all the new Windows 7 skills you have learned in this chapter.

1. To Launch a Program and Create a Document (WIN 69)
2. Save a Document to the Documents Library (WIN 71)
3. Open the Print Dialog Box from a Program (WIN 75)
4. Print a Document (WIN 76)
5. Edit a Document (WIN 76)
6. Save and Close a Document (WIN 77)
7. Open the Documents Library (WIN 78)
8. Create a Blank Document in the Documents Library (WIN 79)
9. Name a Document in the Documents Library (WIN 80)
10. Open a Document with WordPad (WIN 81)
11. Add Text to a Blank Document (WIN 82)
12. Save a Text Document in Rich Text Format (RTF) (WIN 82)
13. Change the View to Small Icons (WIN 84)
14. Arrange Items in Groups by File Type (WIN 85)
15. Create and Name a Folder in the Documents Library (WIN 86)
16. Move a Document into a Folder (WIN 87)
17. Change Location Using the Address Bar (WIN 89)
18. Display and Use the Preview Pane (WIN 91)
19. Close the Preview Pane (WIN 92)
20. Change Location Using the Back Button on the Address Bar (WIN 92)
21. Add a Shortcut on the Start Menu (WIN 93)
22. Open a Folder Using a Shortcut on the Start Menu (WIN 96)
23. Remove a Shortcut from the Start Menu (WIN 97)
24. Create a Shortcut on the Desktop (WIN 98)
25. Open and Modify a Document in a Folder (WIN 100)
26. Open and Modify Multiple Documents (WIN 100)
27. Display an Inactive Window (WIN 102)
28. Close Multiple Open Windows and Save Changes Using the Taskbar (WIN 104)
29. Print Multiple Documents from within a Folder (WIN 105)
30. Copy a Folder onto a USB Flash Drive (WIN 106)
31. Open a Folder Stored on a USB Flash Drive (WIN 108)
32. Safely Remove a USB Flash Drive (WIN 108)
33. Restore an Item from the Recycle Bin (WIN 111)
34. Delete Multiple Files from a Folder (WIN 112)
35. Add Multiple Gadgets to the Desktop (WIN 114)
36. Customize the Clock Gadget (WIN 115)
37. Undo the Changes to the Clock Gadget (WIN 117)
38. Rearrange Gadgets on the Desktop (WIN 118)
39. Search for Gadgets Online (WIN 119)

Learn It Online

Test your knowledge of chapter content and key terms.

Instructions: To complete the Learn It Online exercises, start your browser, click the Address bar, and then enter the Web address `scsite.com/win7/learn`. When the Windows 7 Learn It Online page is displayed, click the link for the exercise you want to complete and then read the instructions.

Chapter Reinforcement TF, MC, and SA
A series of true/false, multiple-choice, and short-answer questions that test your knowledge of the chapter content.

Flash Cards
An interactive learning environment where you identify chapter key terms associated with displayed definitions.

Practice Test
A series of multiple-choice questions that test your knowledge of chapter content and key terms.

Who Wants To Be a Computer Genius?
An interactive game that challenges your knowledge of chapter content in the style of a television quiz show.

Wheel of Terms
An interactive game that challenges your knowledge of chapter key terms in the style of the television show *Wheel of Fortune*.

Crossword Puzzle Challenge
A crossword puzzle that challenges your knowledge of key terms presented in the chapter.

Apply Your Knowledge

Reinforce the skills and apply the concepts you learned in this chapter.

Creating a Document with WordPad
Instructions: Use WordPad to create the homework list shown in Figure 2–81.

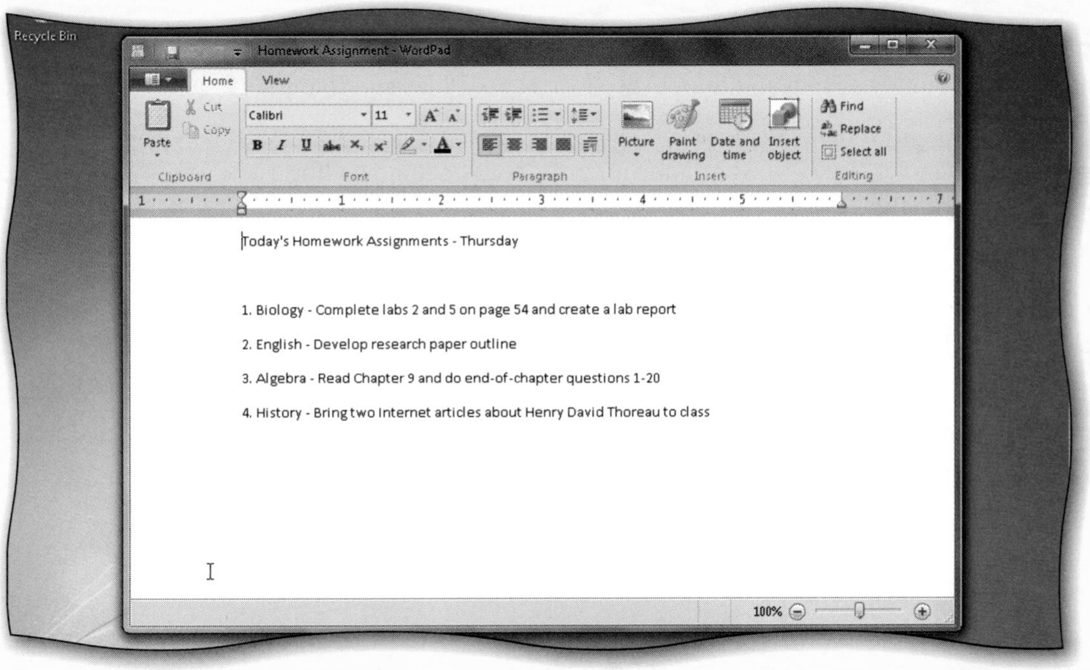

Figure 2–81

Continued >

Apply Your Knowledge *continued*

Part 1: Launching WordPad
1. Click the Start button.
2. Launch WordPad.

Part 2: Creating a Document Using WordPad
1. Type Today's Homework Assignments - Thursday and then press the ENTER key twice.
2. Type 1. Biology - Complete labs 2 and 5 on page 54 and create a lab report and then press the ENTER key.
3. Type 2. English - Develop research paper outline and then press the ENTER key.
4. Type 3. Algebra - Read Chapter 9 and do end-of-chapter questions 1-20 and then press the ENTER key.
5. Type 4. History - Bring two Internet articles about Henry David Thoreau to class and then press the ENTER key.

Part 3: Printing the Today's Homework Document
1. Click the WordPad button and then click Print to display the Print dialog box. Click the Print button to print the document.

Part 4: Saving and Closing the WordPad Window
1. Insert a USB flash drive.
2. Save your document as Homework Assignment to the USB flash drive.
3. Close WordPad and any open windows.

Extend Your Knowledge

Extend the skills you learned in this chapter and experiment with new skills. You might need to use Help to complete the assignment.

Finding File and Folder Help
Instructions: Use Windows Help and Support to learn about files and folders.

Part 1: Creating a Document in the Documents Library
1. Start WordPad and create a WordPad document in the Documents library. Save the document as Working with Files and Folders.
2. Maximize the Working with Files and Folders - WordPad window.

Part 2: Launching Windows Help and Support
1. Click the Start button on the taskbar.
2. Click Help and Support on the Start menu.
3. Click Learn about Windows Basics in the 'Not sure where to start?' area.
4. Scroll down to the Programs, files, and folders area.
5. Click 'Working with files and folders'. The 'Working with files and folders' page displays (Figure 2–82).

STUDENT ASSIGNMENTS

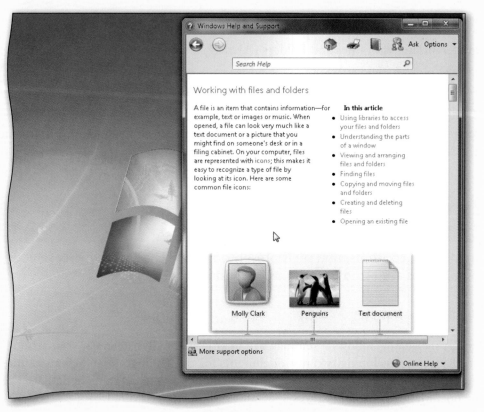

Figure 2–82

Part 3: Copying Selected Text to the WordPad Window

1. Click the 'Creating and deleting files' link.

2. Click and drag from the 'Creating and deleting files' heading through the paragraphs below to highlight them.

3. Right-click the highlighted text to display a shortcut menu.

4. Click Copy on the shortcut menu.

5. Click the Working with Files and Folders button in the taskbar button area to display the Working with Files and Folders - WordPad window.

6. Right-click the text area of the WordPad window to display a shortcut menu.

7. Click Paste. The Creating and deleting files text displays in the window.

8. Click the WordPad button to display the WordPad menu, and then click the Save button to save the document.

9. Click the Windows Help and Support button in the taskbar button area to display the Windows Help and Support window.

Part 4: Copying Additional Text to the WordPad Window

1. Using the method shown in Part 3, scroll up, and copy and paste the following headings and paragraphs to the WordPad window: 'Using libraries to access your files and folders', 'Understanding the parts of a window', and 'Finding files'.

2. Click the WordPad button to display the WordPad menu, and then click the Save button to save the document.

3. Click the WordPad button to display the WordPad menu, click Print on the WordPad menu, and then click the Print button to print the document.

Continued >

Extend Your Knowledge *continued*

4. Close the Working with Files and Folders - WordPad window.

5. Close the Windows Help and Support window.

6. Insert a USB flash drive and copy the Working with Files and Folders document in the Documents library to the USB flash drive.

7. Delete the Working with Files and Folders document from the Documents library and empty the Recycle Bin.

In the Lab

Use the guidelines, concepts, and skills presented in this chapter to increase your knowledge of Windows 7. Labs are listed in order of increasing difficulty.

Lab 1: Windows 7 Seminar Announcement and Schedule

Instructions: A two-day Windows 7 seminar will be offered to all teachers at your school. You have been put in charge of developing two text documents for the seminar. One document announces the seminar and will be sent to all teachers. The other document contains the schedule for the seminar. You prepare the documents shown in Figures 2–83 and 2–84 using WordPad.

Part 1: Creating the Windows 7 Seminar Announcement Document

1. Open a new WordPad document. Save the document as Windows 7 Seminar Announcement on the desktop.

2. Enter the text shown in Figure 2–83.

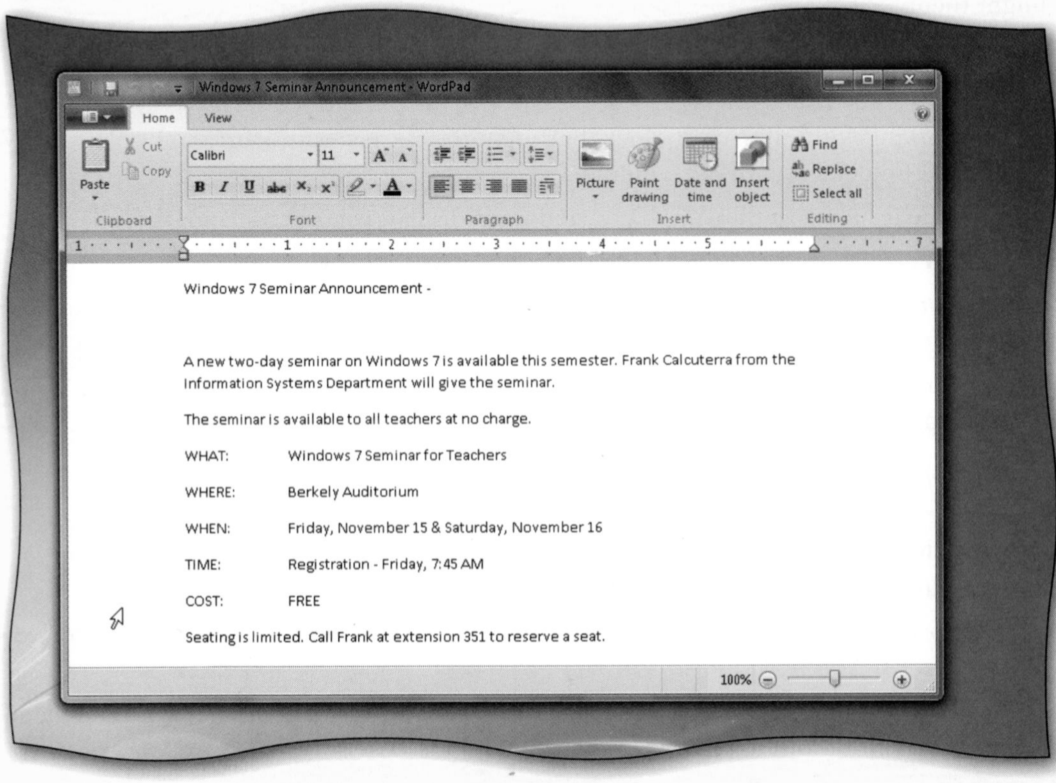

Figure 2–83

3. Save the document.

4. Print the document.

5. Close the document.

6. Move the document to the Documents library.

7. Create a folder in the Documents library called Windows 7 Seminar Documents.

8. Place the Windows 7 Seminar Announcement document in the Windows 7 Seminar Documents folder.

Part 2: Creating the Windows 7 Seminar Schedule Document

1. Open a new WordPad document. Save the document as Windows 7 Seminar Schedule on the desktop.

2. Enter the text shown in Figure 2–84.

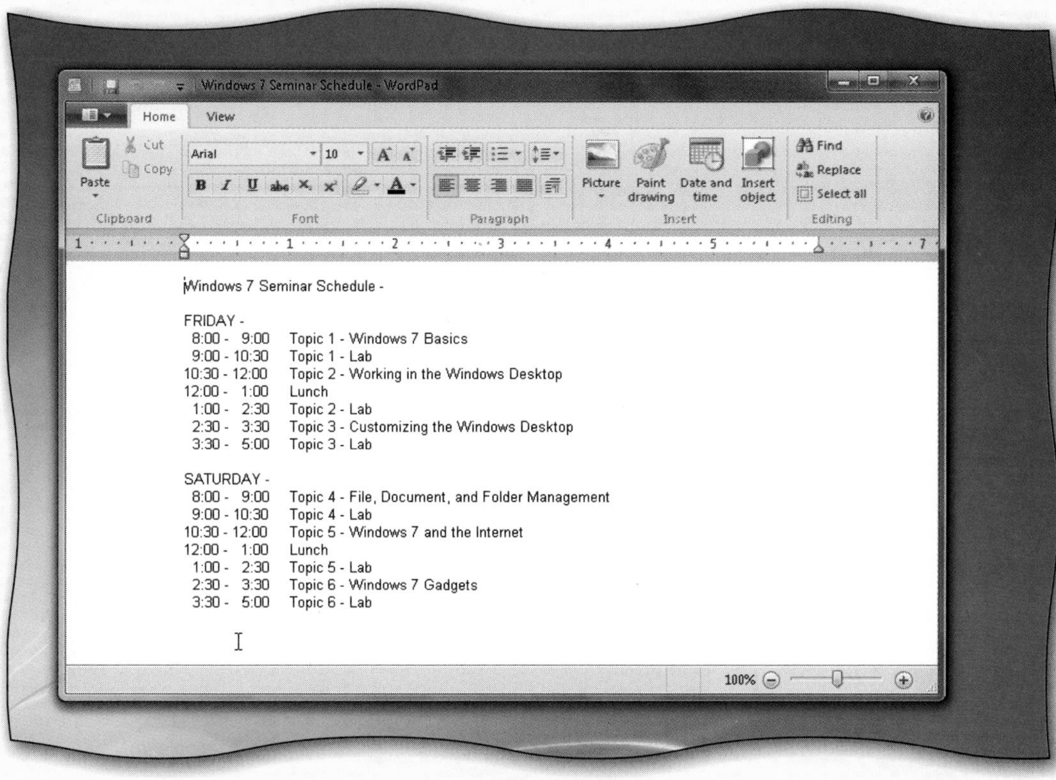

Figure 2–84

3. Save the document.

4. Print the document.

5. Close the document.

6. Move the Windows 7 Seminar Schedule document to the Documents library.

7. Place the Windows 7 Seminar Schedule document in the Windows 7 Seminar Documents folder.

8. Move the Windows 7 Seminar Documents folder to your USB flash drive.

In the Lab

Lab 2: Researching Online Gadgets

Instructions: You are asked to create a list of gadgets that your company might find useful. Using the Personalization Gallery Web site, you will create a gadget list that lists the gadgets and the categories in which they are located. Your boss is interested in four main categories. Create the headings shown in Figure 2–85 using the application-centric approach and WordPad. Then follow the steps to find some potentially useful gadgets online.

Perform the following tasks:

1. Start WordPad.
2. Enter the text shown in Figure 2–85.

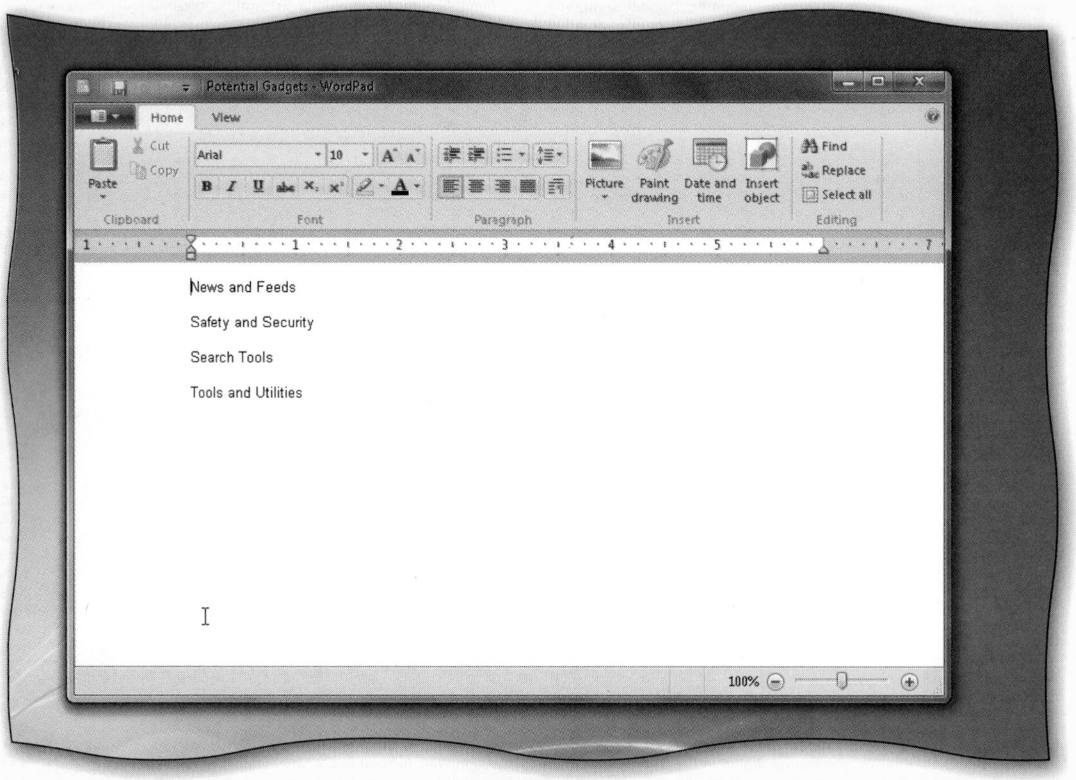

Figure 2–85

3. Use Save as to save the document in the Documents library with the file name Potential Gadgets.
4. Right-click an empty area of the desktop and then click the Gadgets command on the shortcut menu to display the Gadget Gallery.
5. Click the 'Get more gadgets online' link to open the Personalization Gallery Web page.
6. Scroll down to display the Desktop gadgets tab. Click the tab to display the Desktop gadgets area. Click the 'Get more desktop gadgets' link.

7. Click the 'News and feeds' link.

8. Find at least three news gadgets that you think a business might use. Write down the name of each gadget you selected and who developed it in the following space.

_____

_____

_____

9. In WordPad, under the News and Feeds heading, enter a numbered list stating the names of the three gadgets and who developed them.

10. In Internet Explorer, click the All categories link. Click on the 'Safety and security' link.

11. Find at least three safety and security gadgets that you think a business might use. Write down the name of each gadget, who developed it, and why it might be of use to a business.

_____

_____

_____

12. In WordPad, under the Safety and Security heading, enter a numbered list that includes the names of the gadgets, who developed them, and why they might be of use to a business.

13. In Internet Explorer, click All categories. Click the Search tools link.

14. Find at least three search tool gadgets that you think a business might use. In WordPad, under the Search Tools heading, enter a numbered list stating the names of the three gadgets and who developed them.

15. In Internet Explorer, return to the main list of gadgets. Click the 'Tools and utilities' link.

16. Find at least three tools or utilities gadgets that you think a business might use. In WordPad, under the Tools and Utilities heading, enter a numbered list stating the names of the three gadgets and who developed them.

17. Save the document.

18. Print the document from WordPad.

19. Close WordPad.

20. Insert a USB flash drive in an open USB port.

21. Right-click the Potential Gadgets icon in the Documents library, click Send to, and then click the USB flash drive.

22. Close the Documents library.

23. Safely remove the USB flash drive.

24. Close the Gadget Gallery.

25. Close Internet Explorer.

In the Lab

Lab 3: Creating, Saving, and Printing Automobile Information Documents

Instruction: For eight months, you have accumulated data about your 2008 Chevy Malibu automobile. Some of the information is written on pieces of paper, while the rest is in the form of receipts. You have decided to organize this information using your computer. You create the documents shown in Figures 2–86 and 2–87 using the application-centric approach and WordPad.

Part 1: Creating the Automobile Information Document

1. Create a new WordPad document. Save the document on the desktop with the file name Automobile Information.
2. Enter the text shown in Figure 2–86.

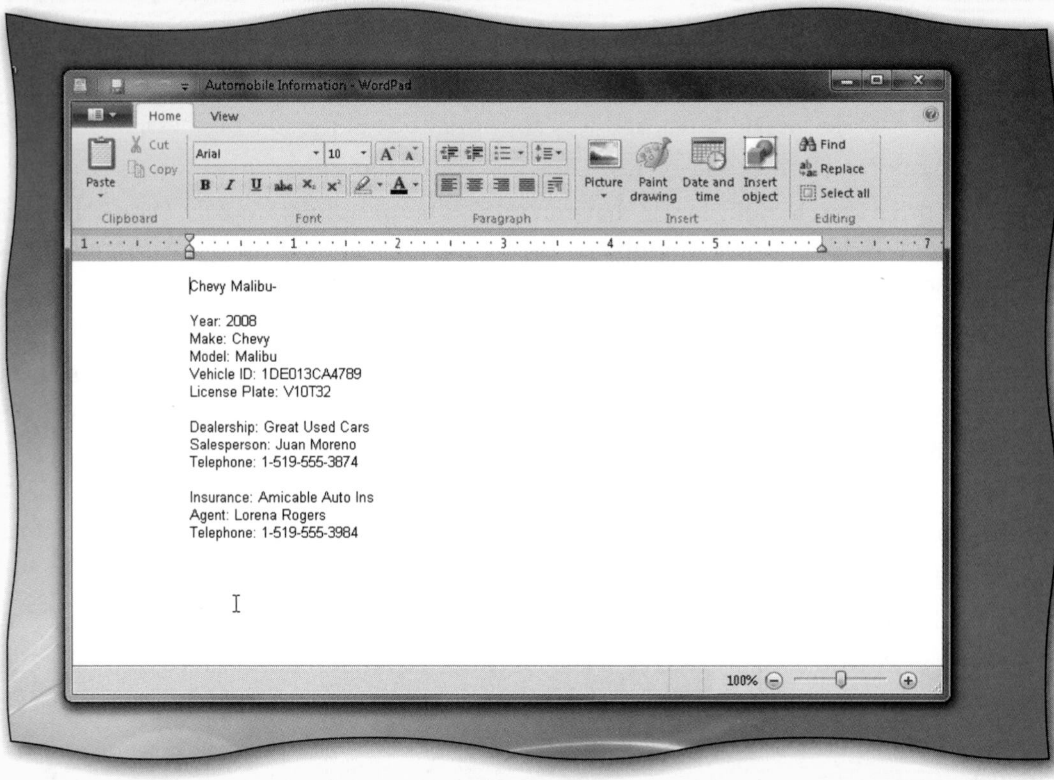

Figure 2–86

3. Save the document.
4. Print the document.
5. Create a folder in the Documents library called Automobile Documents.
6. Place the Automobile Information document in the Automobile Documents folder.

Part 2: Other Automobile Documents

1. Create the Phone Numbers document (Figure 2–87a), the Automobile Gas Mileage document (Figure 2–87b), and the Automobile Maintenance document on the desktop (Figure 2–87c).
2. Move each document into the Documents library.

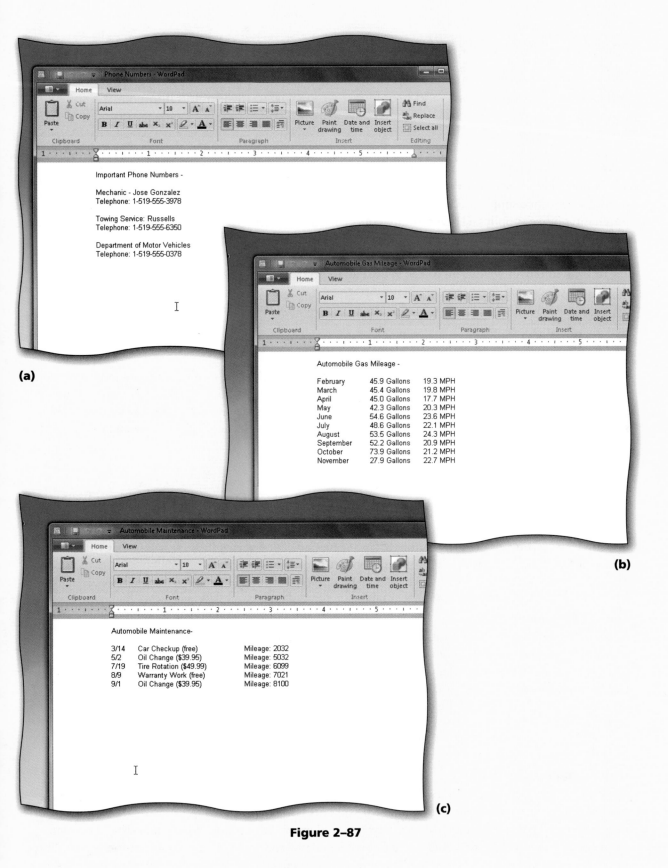

(a)

Phone Numbers - WordPad

Important Phone Numbers -

Mechanic - Jose Gonzalez
Telephone: 1-519-555-3978

Towing Service: Russells
Telephone: 1-519-555-6350

Department of Motor Vehicles
Telephone: 1-519-555-0378

(b)

Automobile Gas Mileage - WordPad

Automobile Gas Mileage -

February	45.9 Gallons	19.3 MPH
March	45.4 Gallons	19.8 MPH
April	45.0 Gallons	17.7 MPH
May	42.3 Gallons	20.3 MPH
June	54.6 Gallons	23.6 MPH
July	48.6 Gallons	22.1 MPH
August	53.5 Gallons	24.3 MPH
September	52.2 Gallons	20.9 MPH
October	73.9 Gallons	21.2 MPH
November	27.9 Gallons	22.7 MPH

(c)

Automobile Maintenance - WordPad

Automobile Maintenance-

3/14	Car Checkup (free)	Mileage: 2032
5/2	Oil Change ($39.95)	Mileage: 5032
7/19	Tire Rotation ($49.99)	Mileage: 6099
8/9	Warranty Work (free)	Mileage: 7021
9/1	Oil Change ($39.95)	Mileage: 8100

Figure 2–87

3. Print each document.

4. Place each document in the Automobile Documents folder.

5. Move the Automobile Documents folder to a USB flash drive.

Cases and Places

Apply your creative thinking and problem solving skills to design and implement a solution.

• EASIER   •• MORE DIFFICULT

• 1 Creating an Employer Request List

Your employer is concerned that some people in the company are not thoroughly researching purchases of office supplies. She has prepared a list of steps she would like everyone to follow when purchasing office supplies: (1) Determine your department's need for office supplies, (2) identify at least two Internet sites that sell the office supplies you need, and (3) obtain prices for the office supplies from their Web sites.

Your employer wants you to use WordPad to prepare a copy of this list to post in every department. Save and print the document. After you have printed one copy of the document, try experimenting with different WordPad features to make the list more eye-catching. Save and print a revised copy of the document.

• 2 Locating Gadgets Online

As you have learned, you can add useful gadgets to your desktop. You would like to find out more about gadgets and install one for yourself. Visit the Windows 7 Personalization Gallery Web site and locate gadgets that will provide up-to-date weather. Download one and try it out. Write a brief report about what you found online and what you think about weather gadgets. Include the name and developer of the gadget you installed.

•• 3 Researching Retraining Costs

Retraining employees can be an expensive task for a business of any size. Many Windows 7 users believe that the Windows 7 operating system is an intuitive, easy-to-learn operating system that can reduce retraining costs. Using the Internet, current computer magazines, or other resources, research this topic and write a brief report summarizing your findings. Explain those features that you think make the Windows 7 operating system an easy-to-use operating system.

•• 4 Research Gadgets for Personal Use

Make It Personal

Just like for business, there are lots of useful gadgets for you to find and use. Look online for a multimedia gadget that will let you play a radio station, monitor your Facebook account, or watch a television show. Select a few that you find interesting. Download and install them. Write a brief report comparing and contrasting them. Which one is the easiest to use? Which one is the worst? If you decide you do not like any of the ones you downloaded, try more until you find one you like. Include in your report how likely you will or will not download more gadgets to use in the future.

•• 5 Researching Course Registration Procedures

Working Together

Registering for classes can be a daunting task for incoming college freshmen. As someone who has gone through the process, prepare a guide for students who are about to register for the first time next semester. Working with classmates, research and create your guide. Your guide should contain two or more documents, including a schedule of key dates and times, a description of the registration procedure, and suggestions for a smooth registration process. Give the documents suitable names and save them in a folder in the Documents library. Print each document.

3 | File and Folder Management

Objectives

You will have mastered the material in this chapter when you can:

- View the contents of a drive and folder using the Computer folder window
- View the properties of files and folders
- Find files and folders from a folder window
- Cascade, stack, and view windows side by side on the desktop
- View the contents of the Pictures library
- Open and use the Windows Photo Viewer

- View pictures as a slide show
- View the contents of the Music library
- View information about an audio file
- Play an audio file using Windows Media Player
- Create a backup on a USB flash drive and an optical disc
- Restore a folder from a backup on a USB flash drive

3 | File and Folder Management

Introduction

In Chapter 2, you used Windows 7 to create documents on the desktop and work with documents and folders in the Documents library. Windows 7 also allows you to examine the files and folders on the computer in a variety of other ways, enabling you to choose the easiest and most accessible manner when working with the computer. The Computer folder window and the Documents library provide two ways for you to work with files and folders. In addition, the Pictures library allows you to organize and share picture files, and the Music library allows you to organize and share your music files. This chapter illustrates how to work with files in the Computer folder, as well as the Documents, Pictures, and Music libraries.

Overview

As you read this chapter, you will learn how to work with the Computer folder window, as well as the Pictures and Music libraries, by performing these general tasks:

- Opening and using the Computer folder window
- Searching for files and folders
- Managing open windows
- Opening and using the Pictures library
- Using Windows Photo Viewer
- Opening and using the Music library
- Playing a music file in Windows Media Player
- Backing up and restoring a folder

Plan Ahead

Working with Files and Folders
Working with files and folders requires a basic knowledge of how to use the Windows 7 desktop.

1. **Be aware that there might be different levels of access on the computer you will be using.** A user account can be restricted to a certain level of access to the computer. Depending on the level of access that has been set for your account, you might or might not be able to perform certain operations.

2. **Identify how to connect a USB flash drive to your computer.** Depending upon the setup of your computer, there might be several ways to connect a USB flash drive to your computer. You should know which USB ports you can use to connect a USB flash drive to your computer.

3. **Determine if your computer has speakers.** Some computer labs do not provide speakers. If you are going to be using a computer in a lab, you need to know if the computer has speakers or if you will need to bring earbuds.

(continued)

(continued)

4. **Determine whether you have access to the sample files installed with Windows 7.** To complete the steps in this chapter, you will need access to the sample pictures, videos, and sounds installed with Windows 7.

5. **Determine if your computer has an optical disc burner.** Some labs do not provide optical disc burners. If you are going to be using a computer in a lab, you should know whether you have access to an optical disc burner to back up your files.

6. **Understand copyright issues.** When working with multimedia files, you should be aware that most pictures, movies, and music files are protected by copyright. Before you use these files, you should make sure that you are aware of any copyright restrictions. Although you can download a picture or music file from the Internet, it does not mean you have permission to use it.

The Computer Folder Window

As noted in previous chapters, the Start menu displays the Computer command. Clicking the Computer command displays a window that contains the storage devices that are installed on the computer. The Computer folder window looks very similar to the Documents library that you worked with in the previous chapter. This is because Windows 7 uses folder windows to display the contents of the computer. A **folder window** consists of an Address bar at the top, a toolbar containing various options, a Navigation pane on the left below the toolbar, a headings bar and list area on the right below the toolbar, and a Details pane at the bottom of the window. Depending upon which folder or library you are viewing—Computer, Documents, Pictures, and so on—the folder window will display the toolbar options that are most appropriate for working with the contents.

BTW

Managing Windows
Having multiple windows open on the desktop can intimidate some users. Consider working in a maximized window, and when you want to switch to another open window, click its button on the taskbar and then maximize it. Many people find it easier to work with maximized windows.

To Open and Maximize the Computer Folder Window

The list area of the Computer folder window groups objects based upon the different types of devices connected to your computer. The Hard Disk Drives group contains the Local Disk (C:) icon that represents the hard disk on the computer. The **hard disk** is where you can store files, documents, and folders. Storing data on a hard disk is more convenient than storing data on a USB flash drive because the hard disk is more convenient and generally has more available storage space. A computer always will have at least one hard disk, which normally is designated as drive C. On the computer represented by the Computer folder window in Figure 3–1, the icon consists of an image of a hard disk and a **disk label**, or title, Local Disk, and a drive letter (C:). The label text can change, and may differ depending upon the name assigned to the hard disk. For example, some people label their drives based upon usage; therefore, it could be called PRIMARY (C:), where PRIMARY is the label given to the hard disk as it is the drive that houses the operating system and main programs.

The steps on the following page open and maximize the Computer folder window so that you can view its contents.

1
- Display the Start menu.

2
- Click the Computer command to open the Computer folder window. If necessary, maximize the Computer folder window.

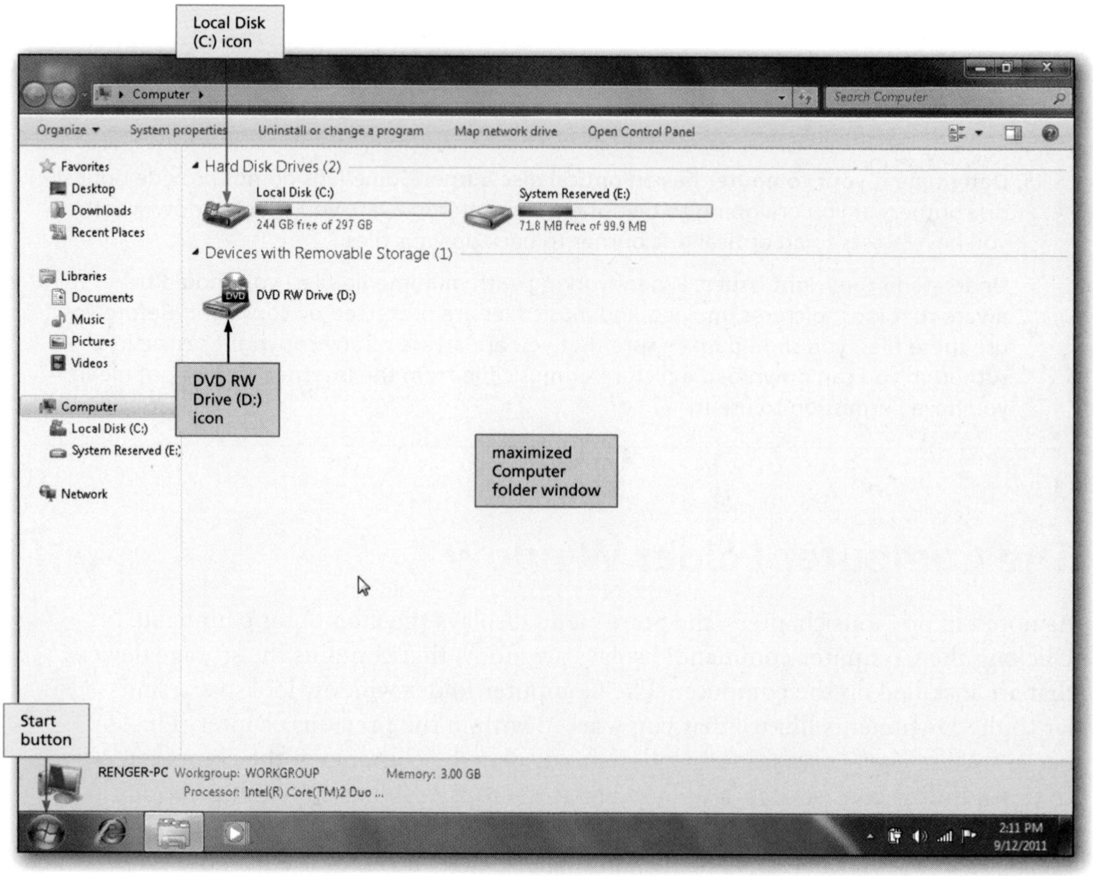

Q&A
What does the Devices with Removable Storage group contain?

The Devices with Removable Storage group contains the DVD RW Drive (D:) icon, indicating that there is a DVD burner attached to your computer. If the icon displayed a CD RW Drive (D:), it would indicate that your computer has a CD burner instead of a DVD burner. If your computer has a CD or DVD drive that cannot burn to the discs, you would not see the RW. **RW** is an abbreviation for rewritable, which means that the drive can write data onto read/writable optical discs.

Figure 3–1

Q&A
Why do the icons on my computer differ from the figure?

It is possible that some icons might appear that you do not recognize. Software vendors develop hundreds of icons to represent their products. Each icon is supposed to be unique, meaningful, and eye-catching. You can purchase thousands of icons on a CD or DVD that you can use to represent documents you create.

To Display Properties for the Local Disk (C:) Drive in the Details Pane

The Details pane of a folder window displays the properties of devices, programs, files, and folders, which all are considered to be objects by Windows 7. Every object in Windows 7 has properties that describe the object. A **property** is a characteristic of an object such as the amount of storage space on a storage device or the number of items in a folder. The properties of each object will differ, and in some cases, you can change the properties of an object. For example, in the Local Disk (C:) properties, you could check the Space free property to determine how much space is available on the C drive. To determine the drive's capacity, you would view the Total size property. The following step displays the properties for the Local Disk (C:) in the Details pane of the Computer folder window.

①

- Click the Local Disk (C:) icon to select the hard disk and display the properties in the Details pane (Figure 3–2).

Experiment

- See what properties display for the other disks and devices shown. Click each one and note what properties display in the Details pane. Return to the Local Disk (C:) when you are done.

Q&A Why do the properties of my Local Disk differ from those in the figure?

The size and contents of your disk will be different from the one in the figure. As a result, the properties of the disk also will be different. Depending upon what has been installed on the disk and how it is formatted, the Space used, File system, Space free, and Total size properties will vary.

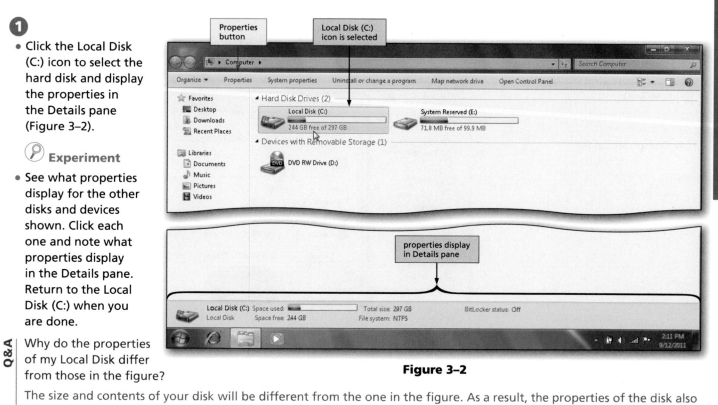

Figure 3–2

To Display the Local Disk (C:) Properties Dialog Box

The properties shown in the Details pane are just a few of the properties of the C drive. In fact, the Details pane is used to highlight the most popular properties of a hard disk: the size of the disk, how much space is free, how much space is used, and how the disk is formatted. However, you can display more detailed information about the hard disk.

The Local Disk (C:) Properties dialog box includes tabs that contain advanced features for working with the hard disk. The Tools sheet, accessible by clicking the Tools tab, allows you to check for errors on the hard disk, defragment the hard disk, or back up the hard disk. The Hardware sheet allows you to view a list of all disk drives, troubleshoot disk drives that are not working properly, and display the properties for each disk drive. The Sharing sheet allows you to share the contents of a hard disk with other computer users. However, to protect a computer from unauthorized access, sharing the hard disk is not recommended. The Security sheet displays the security settings for the drive, such as user permissions. The Previous Versions sheet allows you to work with copies of your hard disk that are created when using backup utilities or from automatic saves. Finally, the Quota sheet can be used to see how much space is being used by various user accounts. Other tabs might display in the Local Disk (C:) Properties dialog box on your computer.

The step on the following page displays the Properties dialog box for the Local Disk (C:) drive.

1

- Click the Properties button on the toolbar to display the Local Disk (C:) Properties dialog box (Figure 3–3).

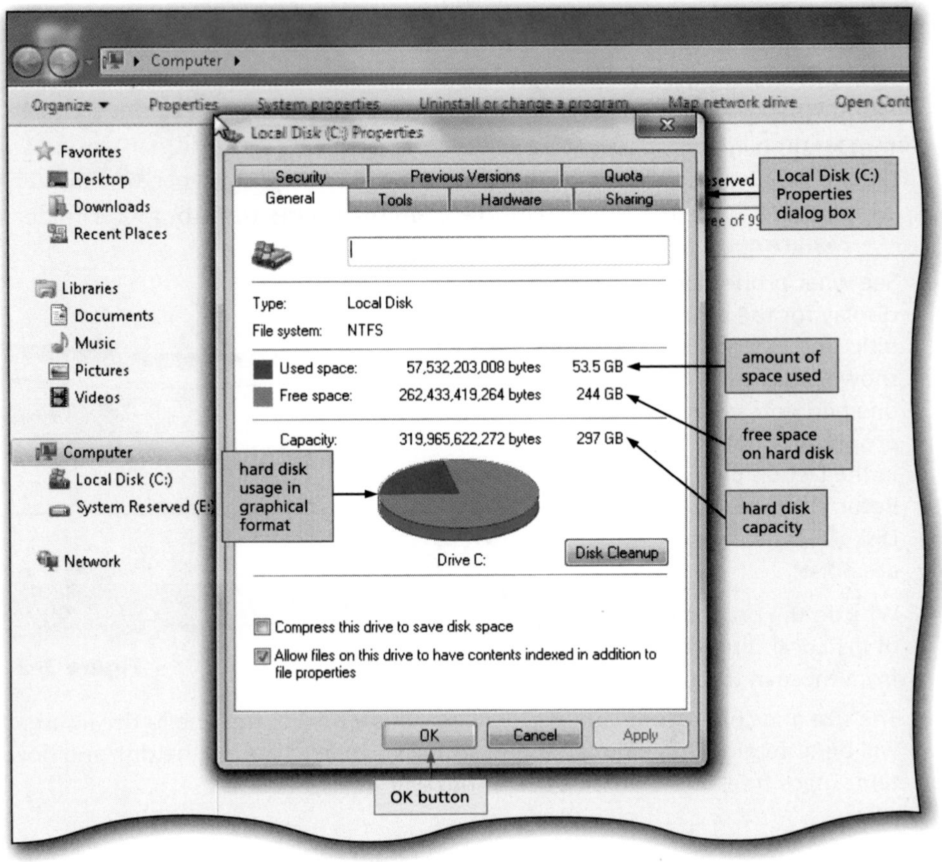

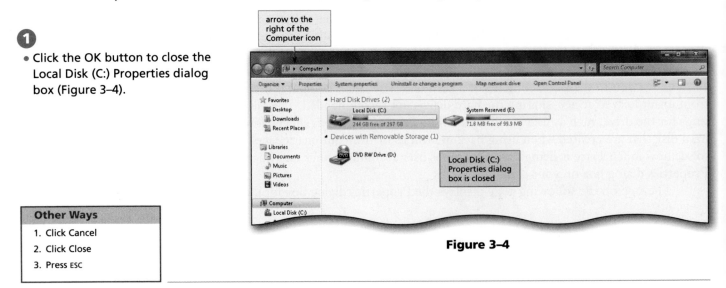

Other Ways

1. Right click Local Disk (C:) icon, click Properties
2. Click disk icon, press ALT, on File menu click Properties
3. Select drive icon, press ALT+ENTER

Figure 3–3

To Close the Local Disk (C:) Properties Dialog Box

Now that you have reviewed the Local Disk (C:) Properties dialog box, you should close it.

1

- Click the OK button to close the Local Disk (C:) Properties dialog box (Figure 3–4).

Other Ways

1. Click Cancel
2. Click Close
3. Press ESC

Figure 3–4

To Switch Folders Using the Address Bar

Found in all folder windows, the Address bar lets you know which folder you are viewing. A useful feature of the Address bar is its capability to allow you to switch to different folder windows by clicking the arrows preceding or following the folder names. Clicking the arrow to the right of the computer icon, for example, displays a command menu containing options for showing the desktop in a folder window, switching to the Computer folder, the Recycle Bin, the Control Panel, and other locations and folders that can vary from computer to computer. The following steps change the folder window from displaying the Computer folder to displaying the desktop and then return to the Computer folder.

1

• Click the arrow to the right of the computer icon on the Address bar to display a menu that contains folder switching commands (Figure 3–5). Depending upon your computer's configuration, the list of commands might differ.

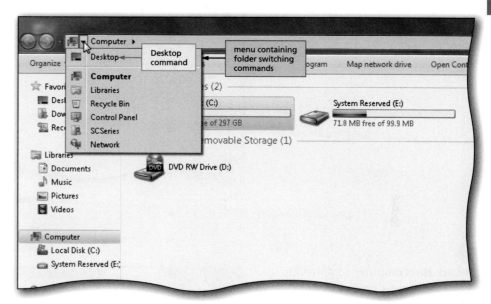

Figure 3–5

2

• Click the Desktop command to switch to viewing the contents of the desktop in the folder window (Figure 3–6).

Q&A

Why do icons appear in this folder window that do not display on the desktop?

Although these icons do not display on the desktop, Microsoft provides you with convenient access to Libraries, the Control Panel, and the Network folder window (if applicable) by placing these icons in the Desktop folder window.

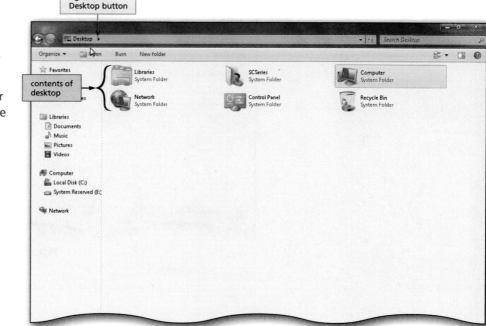

Figure 3–6

3

• Click the arrow to the right of the Desktop button on the Address bar to display a menu containing switching options (Figure 3–7).

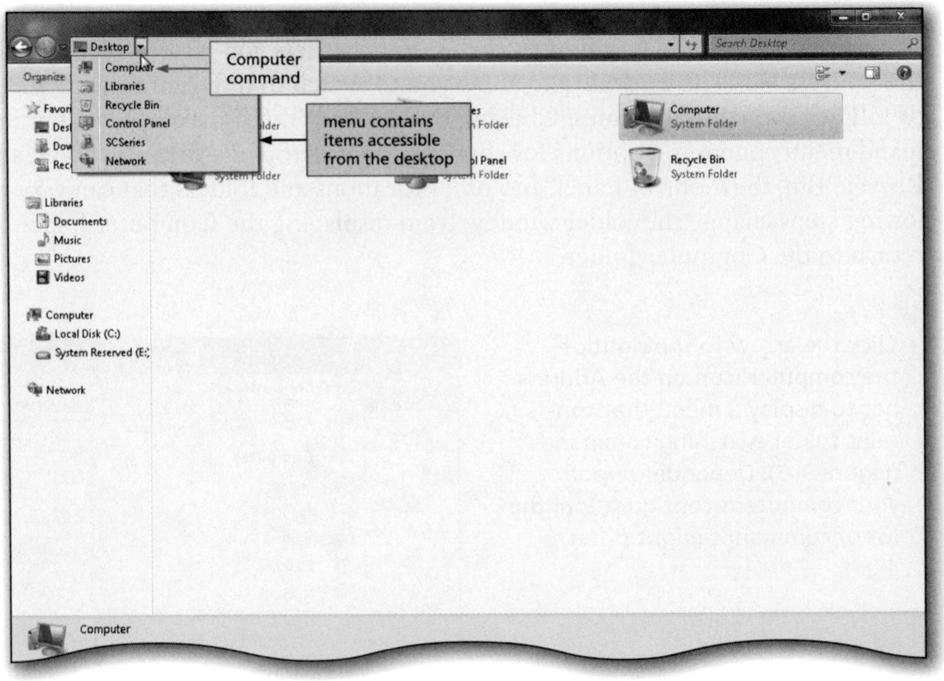

Computer command

menu contains items accessible from the desktop

Figure 3–7

4

• Click the Computer command to switch to the Computer folder (Figure 3–8).

Local Disk (C:) icon

contents of Computer folder

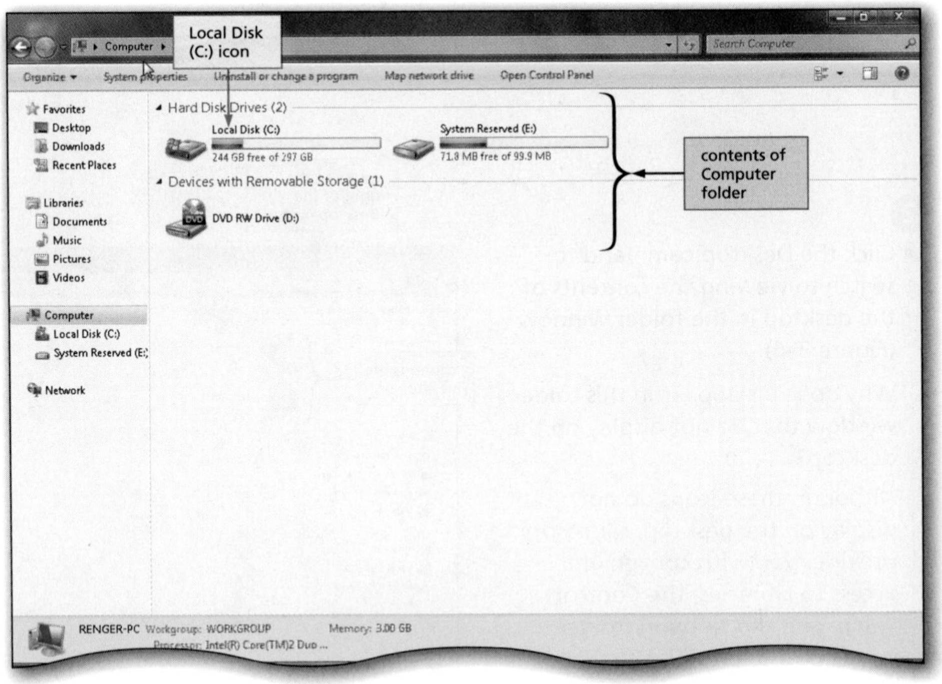

Figure 3–8

To View the Contents of a Drive

In addition to viewing the contents of the Computer folder, you can view the contents of drives and folders. In fact, the contents of any folder or drive on the computer will display in a folder window. By default, Windows 7 uses the active window to display the contents of a newly opened drive or folder. Because only one window displays on the desktop at a time, the clutter of multiple windows on the desktop is eliminated. The following step displays the contents of the C drive in the active window.

1

- Double-click the Local Disk (C:) icon in the Computer folder window to display the contents of the Local Disk (C:) drive (Figure 3–9).

Q&A

Why do I see different folders?

The contents of the Local Disk (C:) window that display on your computer can differ from the contents shown in Figure 3–9 because each computer has its own folders, programs, and documents.

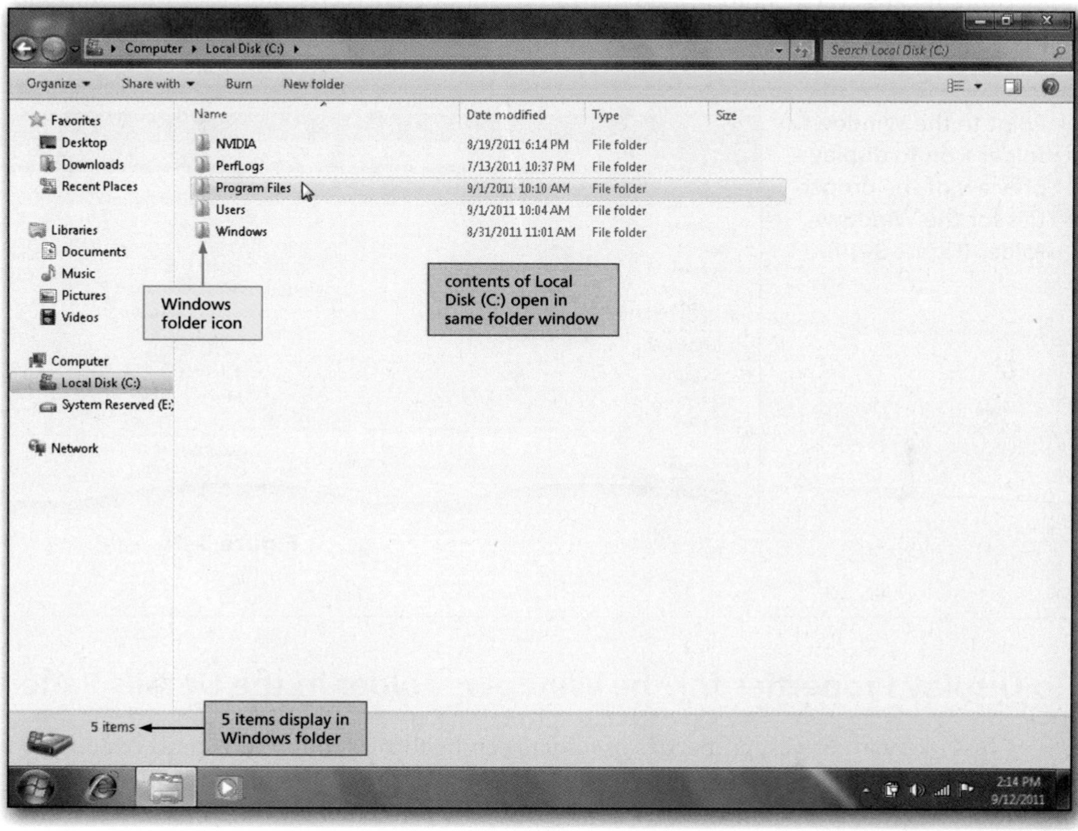

Figure 3–9

Other Ways

1. Right-click Local Disk (C:), click Open
2. Click Local Disk (C:), press ENTER

To Preview the Properties for a Folder

When you move your mouse over a folder icon, a preview of the folder properties will display in a ScreenTip. A **ScreenTip** is a brief description that appears when you hold the mouse over an object on the screen. A ScreenTip does not appear for every object, but when they do, they provide useful information. The properties typically consist of the date and time created, the folder size, and the name of the folder. The Windows folder in the Local Disk (C:) window contains programs and files necessary for the operation of the Windows 7 operating system. As such, you should exercise caution when working with the contents of the Windows folder because changing the contents of the folder might cause the operating system to stop working correctly. The following step shows a preview of the properties for the Windows folder.

- Point to the Windows folder icon to display a preview of the properties for the Windows folder (Figure 3–10).

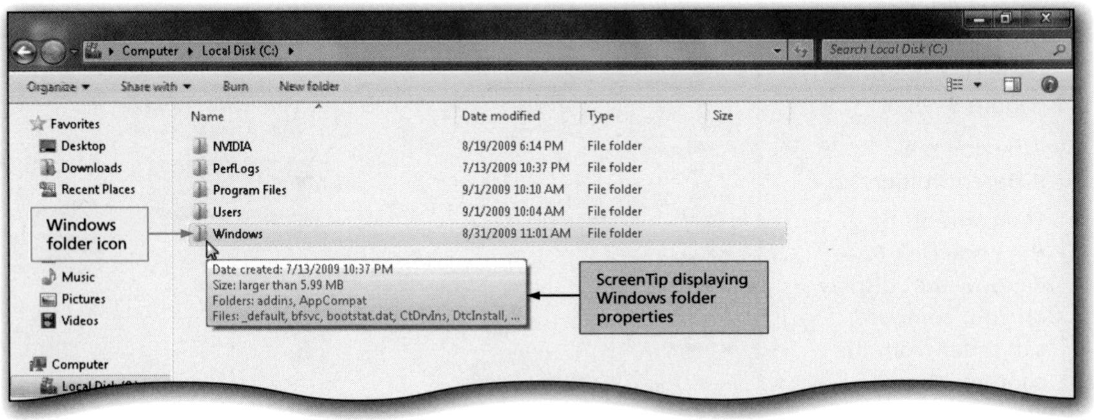

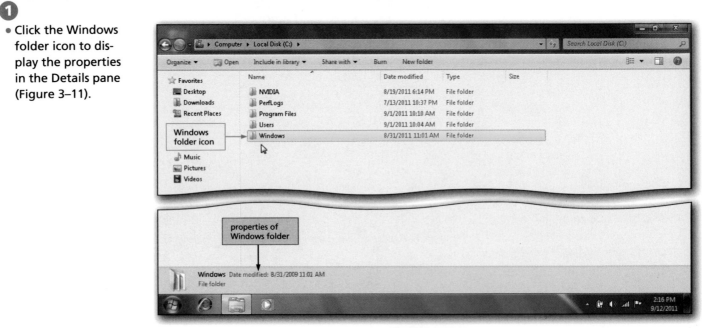

Figure 3–10

To Display Properties for the Windows Folder in the Details Pane

Just like with drives, properties of folders can be displayed in the Details pane. The following step displays the properties for the Windows folder in the Details pane of the Computer folder window.

- Click the Windows folder icon to display the properties in the Details pane (Figure 3–11).

Figure 3–11

To Display All of the Properties for the Windows Folder

If you want to see all of the properties for the Windows folder, you will need to open the Properties dialog box. The following steps display the Properties dialog box for the Windows folder.

1

- Right-click the Windows folder icon to display a shortcut menu (Figure 3–12). (The commands on your shortcut menu might differ.)

Figure 3–12

2

- Click the Properties command to display the Windows Properties dialog box (Figure 3–13).

🔎 **Experiment**

- Click the various tabs in the Properties dialog box to see the different properties available for a folder.

Q&A Why might you want to look at the properties of a folder?

When you are working with folders, you might need to look at folders' properties to make changes, such as configuring a folder for sharing over a network or hiding folders from users who do not need access to them. You even can customize the appearance of a folder to be different than the default Windows folder view.

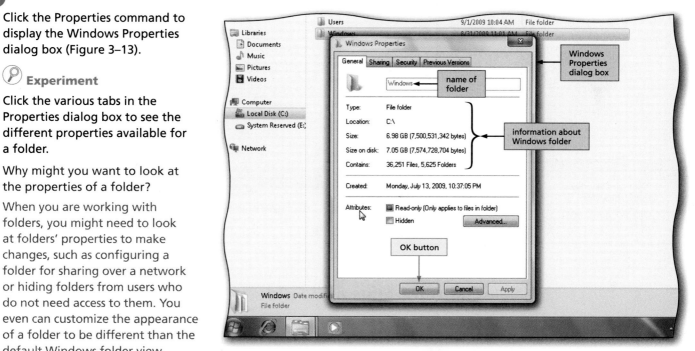

Figure 3–13

Q&A Why are the tabs of the Windows folder properties different from the Local Disk (C:) properties?

Drives, folders, and files have different properties and, therefore, need different tabs. A folder's Properties dialog box typically shows the General, Sharing, Security, and Previous Versions tabs; however, depending upon your Windows 7 version and installed programs, the tabs may differ. The Properties dialog box always will have the General tab, although what it displays also may differ.

To Close the Windows Properties Dialog Box

Now that you have seen the Windows folder properties, you should close the Windows Properties dialog box.

1 Click the OK button to close the Windows Properties dialog box.

To View the Contents of a Folder

The following step opens the Windows folder so that you can view its contents.

1

- Double-click the Windows folder icon to display the contents of the Windows folder (Figure 3–14).

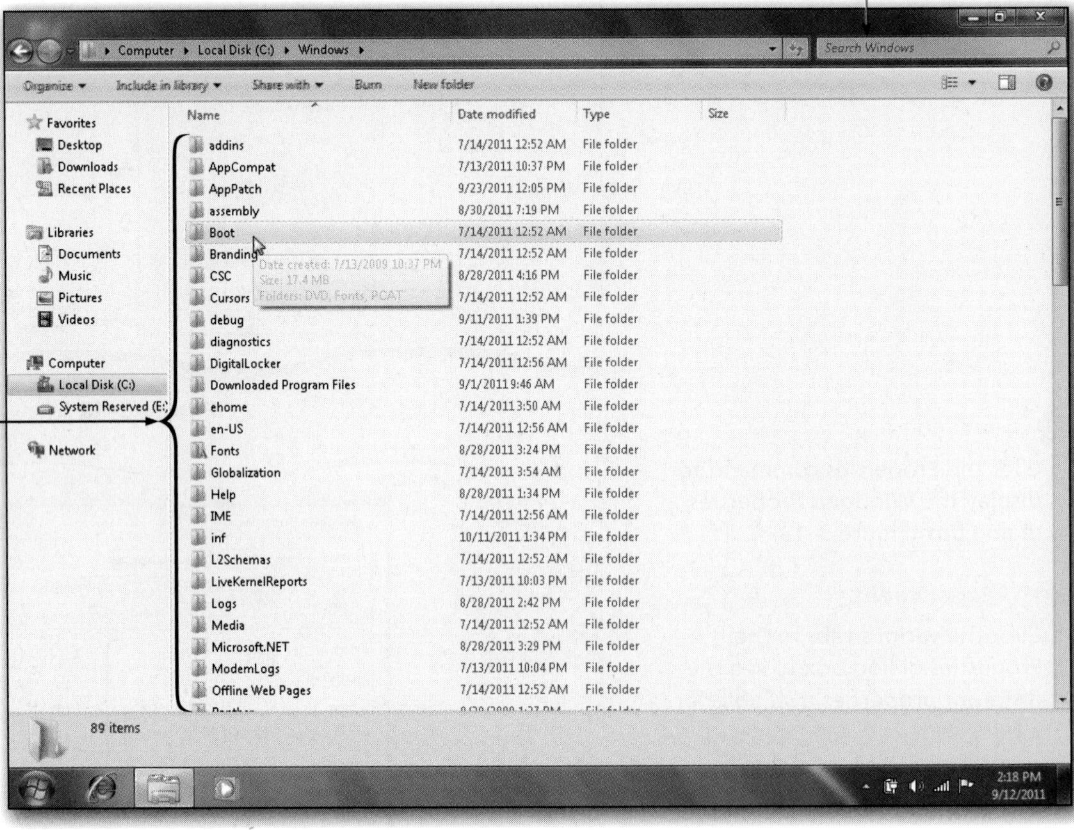

Search box

contents of Windows folder

Figure 3–14

Searching for Files and Folders

The majority of objects displayed in the Windows folder, as shown in Figure 3–14, are folder icons. Folder icons always display in alphabetical order at the top of the list of objects in a folder window, before the icons for programs or files.

Folders such as the Windows folder can contain many files and folders. When you want to find a particular file or folder but do not know where it is located, you can use the Search box to find the file or folder quickly. Similar to the Search box on the Start menu, as soon as you start typing, the window updates to show search results that match what you are typing. As Windows 7 is searching for files or folders that match your search criteria, you will see a searching message displayed in the list area, an animated circle attached to the pointer, and an animated progress bar on the Address bar which provides live feedback as to how much of the search has been completed. When searching is complete, you will see a list of all items that match your search criteria.

If you know only a portion of a file's name and can specify where the known portion of the name should appear, you can use an asterisk in the name to represent the unknown characters. For example, if you know a file starts with the letters MSP, you can type msp* in the Search box. All files that begin with the letters msp, regardless of what letters follow, will display. However, with Windows 7's powerful search capabilities, you would get the same results if you did not include the asterisk. If you want to search for all files with a particular extension, you can use the asterisk to stand in for the name of the files. For example, to find all the text files with the extension .rtf, you would type *.rtf in the Search box. Windows 7 will find all the files with the .rtf extension.

BTW

Hidden Files and Folders
Hidden files and folders usually are placed on your hard disk by software vendors such as Microsoft and often are critical to the operation of their programs. Rarely will you need to designate a file or folder as hidden. You should not delete a hidden file or folder, as doing so might interrupt how or whether a program works. By default, hidden files and folders are not displayed in a file listing.

To Search for a File and Folder in a Folder Window

The following step uses the Search box to search the Windows folder for all the objects that contain "aero" in the file name.

1

• Type aero in the Search box to search for all files and folders that match the search criteria (Figure 3–15).

Q&A How can I stop a search while it is running?

If you decide to stop a search before it is finished running, click the Stop button that appears next to the Address bar in place of the Refresh button. The Stop button only appears while Windows is performing a search. Once a search is complete, the Refresh button is displayed again.

Figure 3–15

Q&A What does the message, "Searches might be slow in non-indexed locations" mean?

Windows 7 maintains an index of certain locations on the computer, such as the libraries, to make searches perform faster. The Windows folder is a very large folder with many items and is not part of the index. This message appears to let you know that the search will take extra time.

To Search for Files Using Search Filters

When searching using the Search box in a folder window, you also can use search filters. A **search filter** is an advanced searching tool that Windows 7 provides from the Search box. Once you select a search filter, you then will be able to select from provided options. For example, if you use the Date modified search filter, you will be shown options such as "Select a date or date range," "A long time ago," or "Earlier this month." The following steps add the Size search filter to the aero search already performed.

1

- Click in the Search box to display search filter options (Figure 3–16).

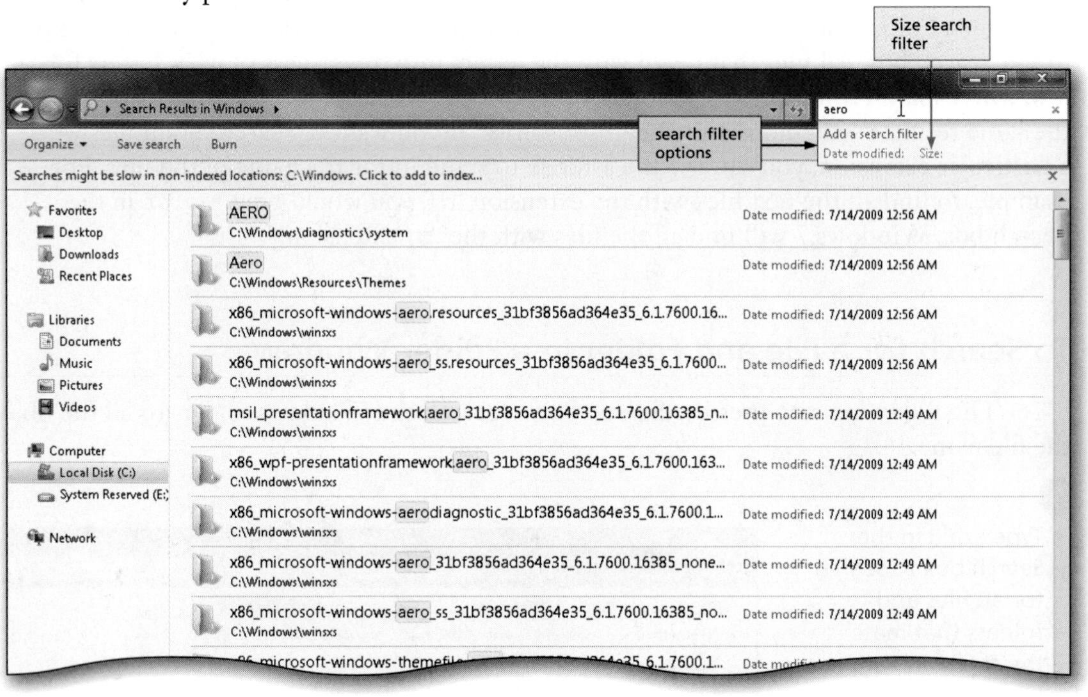

Figure 3–16

2

- Click the Size search filter to add the Size search filter and display filter options (Figure 3–17).

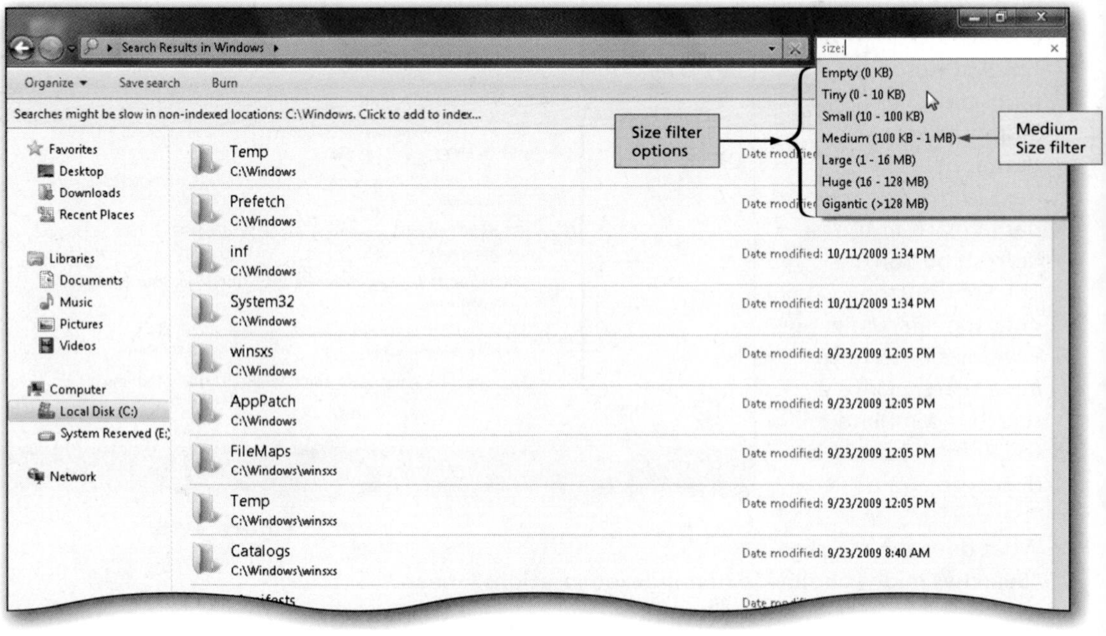

Figure 3–17

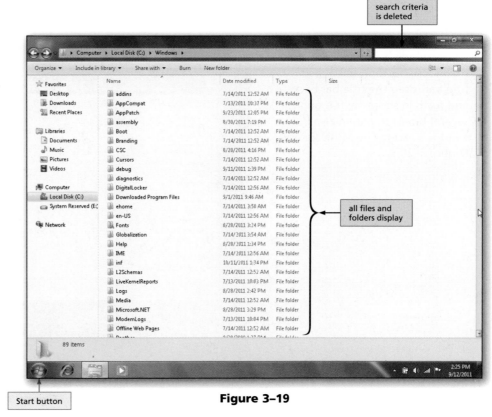

3

- Click the Medium size filter to see files between 100 KB and 1 MB (Figure 3–18).

modified search criteria

x in Search box

files between 100 KB and 1 MB

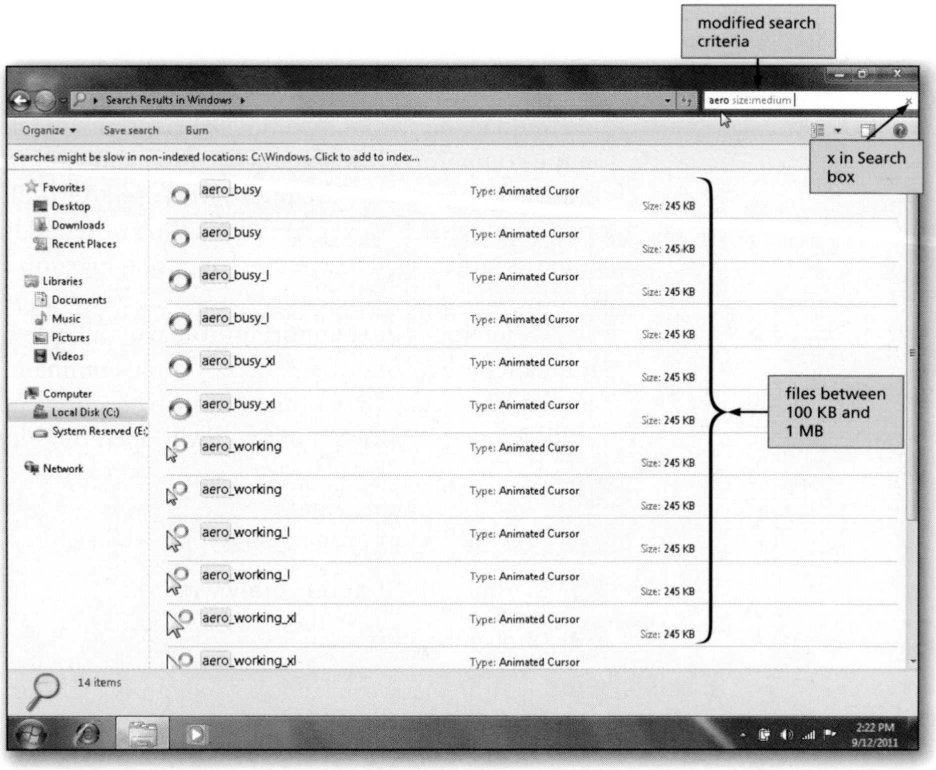

Figure 3–18

To Clear the Search Box

When you finish searching, you can end the search by clearing the Search box. The following step clears the Search box.

1

- Click the x in the Search box to remove the search text from the Search box and redisplay all files and folders in the Windows folder (Figure 3–19).

search criteria is deleted

all files and folders display

Start button

Figure 3–19

To Open Windows

In this chapter, you have been working with one window open. Windows 7 allows you to open many more windows depending upon the amount of RAM you have installed on the computer. However, too many open windows on the desktop can become difficult to use and manage. In Chapter 1, you used Aero Flip 3D to navigate through multiple open windows. However, Windows 7 provides additional tools for managing open windows. You already have used one tool, maximizing a window. When you maximize a window, it occupies the entire screen and cannot be confused with other open windows.

Sometimes, it is important to have multiple windows appear on the desktop simultaneously. Windows 7 offers simple commands that allow you to arrange multiple windows in specific ways. The following sections describe the ways that you can manage multiple open windows. First you will open the Pictures and Music libraries.

1 Display the Start menu.

2 Click the Pictures command to open the Pictures library.

3 Maximize the Pictures library window.

4 Display the Start menu.

5 Click the Music command to open the Music library.

To Use Aero Shake to Minimize and Restore All Windows Except the Active Window

Aero Shake lets you minimize all windows except the active window and then restore all those windows just by shaking the title bar of the active window. The following steps use Aero Shake to minimize all windows except the Music library and then restore those windows.

1

• Click the title bar of the Music library window, and, holding the mouse button, shake the title bar (drag the title bar back and forth in short, swift motions several times) to minimize all windows except the Music library (Figure 3–20).

Figure 3–20

2

- Click the title bar of the Music library window, and, while holding the mouse button, shake the title bar to restore all the windows (Figure 3–21).

- Maximize the Music library window.

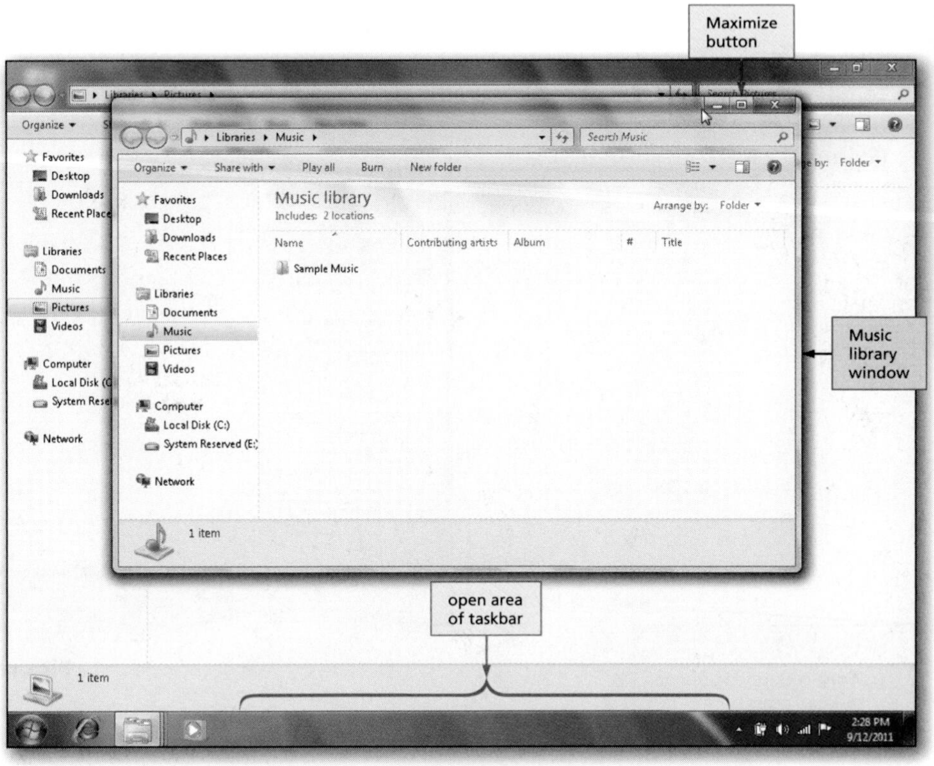

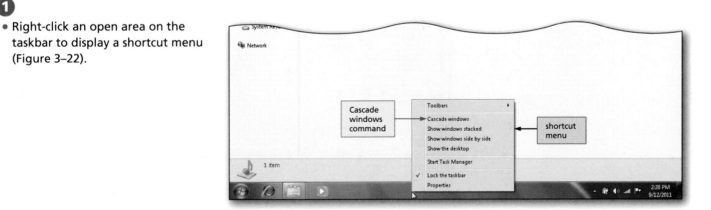

Figure 3–21

To Cascade Open Windows

One way to organize windows on the desktop is to display them in a cascade format, where they overlap one another in an organized manner. In Windows 7, only open windows will be displayed in cascade format: Windows that are minimized or closed will not appear in the cascade. When you cascade open windows, the windows are resized to be the same size to produce the layered cascading effect. The following steps cascade the open windows on the desktop.

1

- Right-click an open area on the taskbar to display a shortcut menu (Figure 3–22).

Figure 3–22

2

- Click the Cascade windows command on the shortcut menu to cascade the open windows (Figure 3–23).

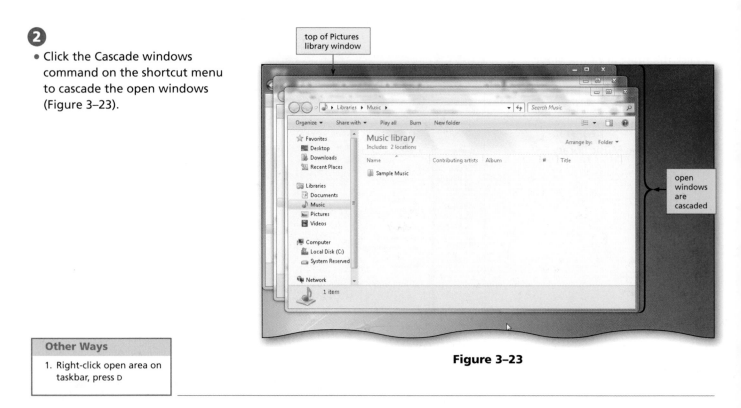

top of Pictures library window

open windows are cascaded

Figure 3–23

Other Ways

1. Right-click open area on taskbar, press D

To Make a Window the Active Window

When windows are cascaded, as shown in Figure 3–23, they are arranged so that you can see them easily. To work with one of the windows, you first must make it the active window. When you make the Pictures library window the active window, it will remain the same size and remain in the same relative position as placed by the Cascade windows command. The following step makes the Pictures library window the active window.

1

- Click the top of the Pictures library window to make it the active window (Figure 3–24).

Q&A

What happens if I click the wrong window?

Click the remaining windows until the Pictures library window displays in the foreground.

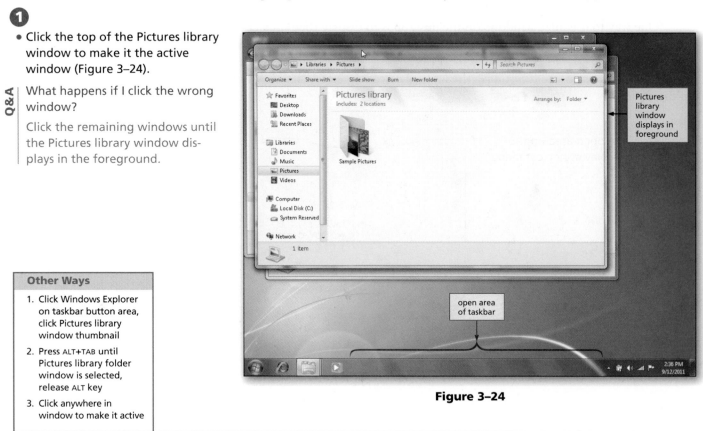

Pictures library window displays in foreground

open area of taskbar

Other Ways

1. Click Windows Explorer on taskbar button area, click Pictures library window thumbnail
2. Press ALT+TAB until Pictures library folder window is selected, release ALT key
3. Click anywhere in window to make it active

Figure 3–24

To Undo Cascading

Now that you have seen the effect of the Cascade windows command, you will undo the cascade operation and return the windows to the size and location they were before cascading. The following steps return the windows to their previous size and location.

1
● Right-click an open area on the taskbar to display the shortcut menu (Figure 3–25).

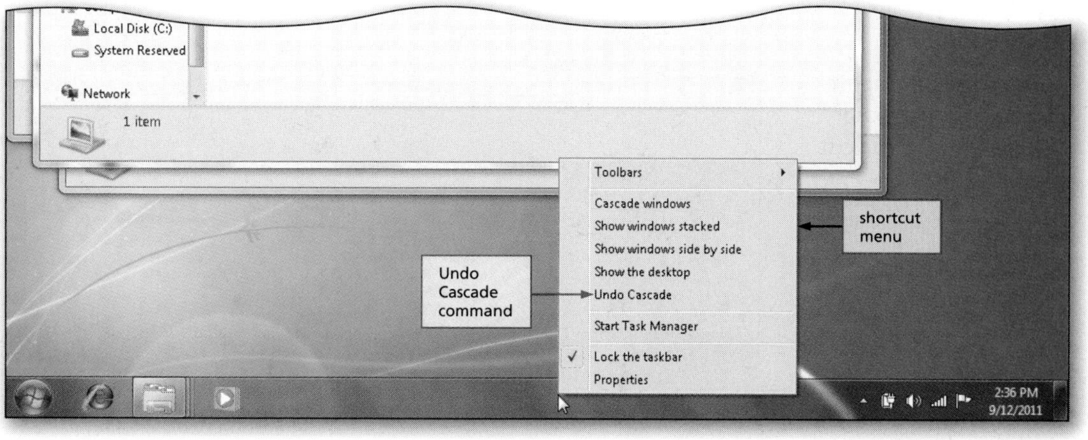

Figure 3–25

2
● Click the Undo Cascade command to return the windows to their original sizes and locations (Figure 3–26).

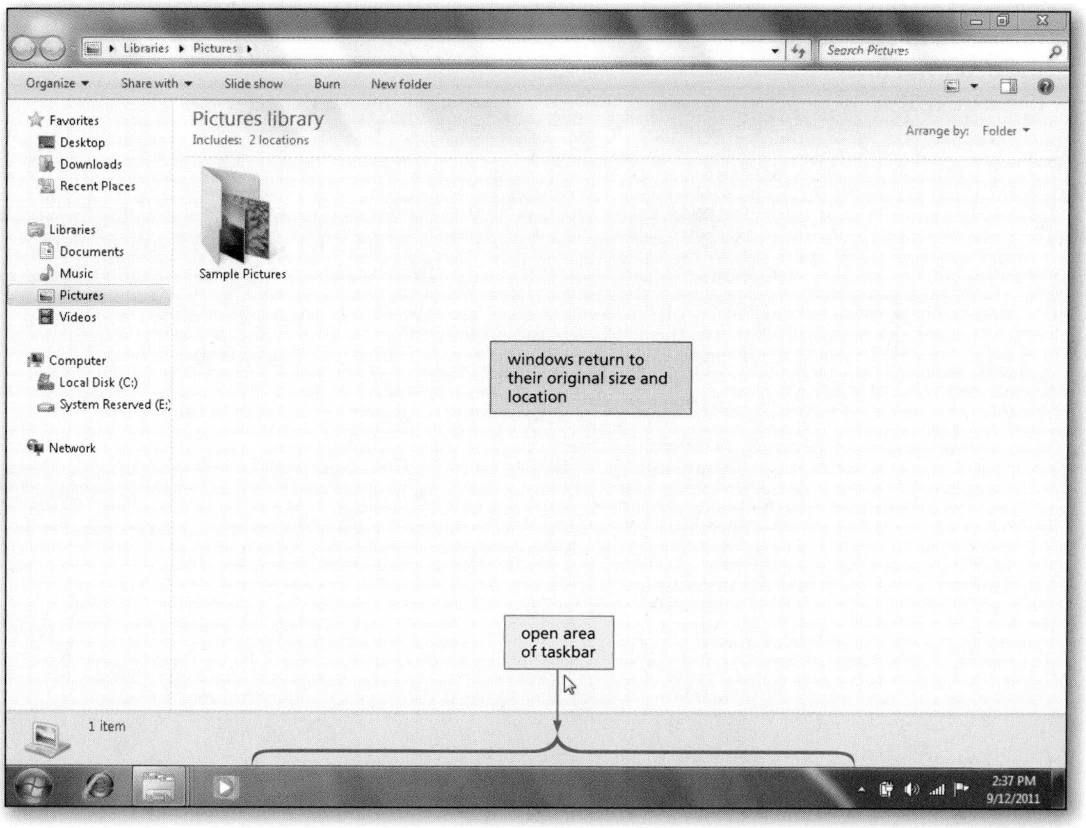

Figure 3–26

Other Ways

1. Right-click open area on taskbar, press U
2. Press CTRL+Z

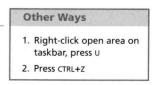

To Stack Open Windows

Although cascading arranges the windows on the desktop so that each of the windows' title bars is visible, it is impossible to see the contents of each window. Windows 7 also can stack the open windows, which allows you to see partial contents of each window. When stacking windows, the windows will be resized to the full width of the screen and arranged on top of each other vertically. Each window will be the same size, and you will be able to see a portion of each window. The following steps stack the open windows.

1

- Right-click an open area of the taskbar to display a shortcut menu (Figure 3–27).

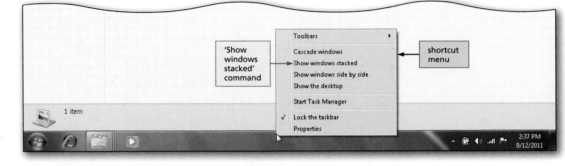

Figure 3–27

2

- Click the 'Show windows stacked' command to stack the open windows (Figure 3–28).

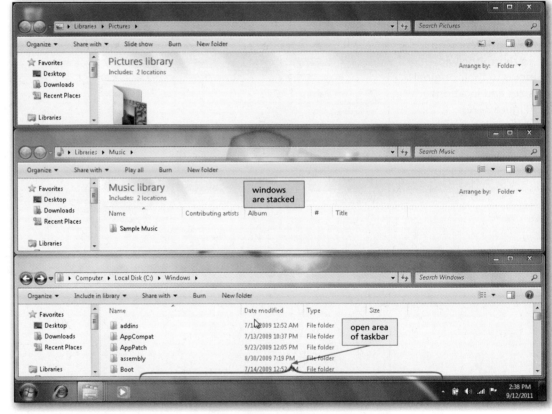

Figure 3–28

Other Ways

1. Right-click open area on taskbar, press T until 'Show windows stacked' is selected, press ENTER

To Undo Show Windows Stacked

Although the stacked windows are arranged so that you can view all of them, you find that the reduced size of an individual window makes working in the window difficult. You will undo the stacking operation to return the windows to the size and position they occupied before stacking. If you want to work in a particular window, you should maximize the window. The following steps return the windows to their original size and position.

1

- Right-click an open area of the taskbar to display the shortcut menu (Figure 3–29).

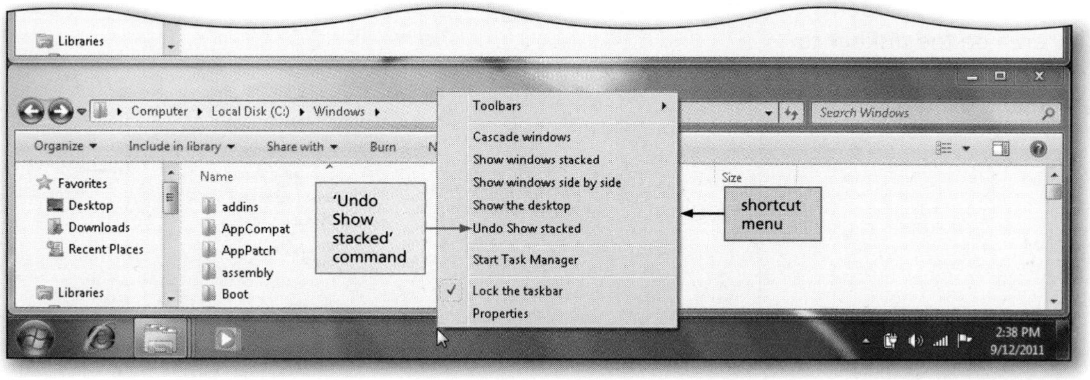

Figure 3–29

2

- Click the 'Undo Show stacked' command to return the windows to their original sizes and locations (Figure 3–30).

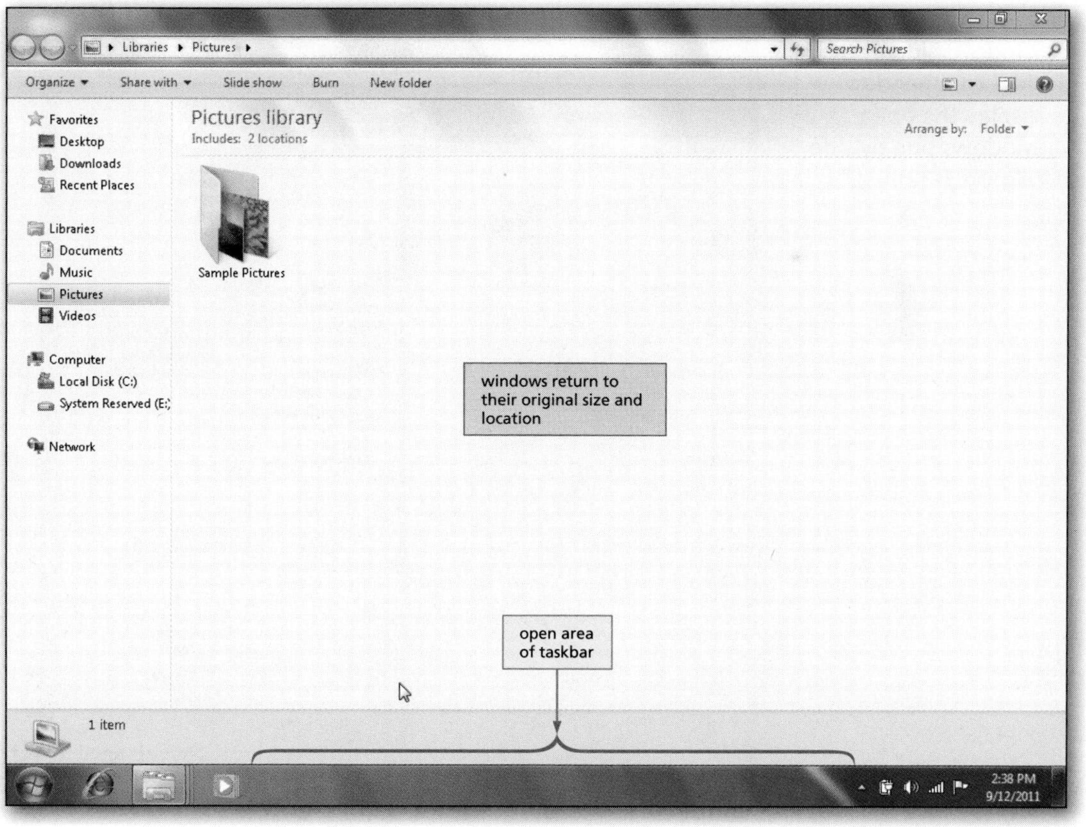

Figure 3–30

Other Ways

1. Right-click open area on taskbar, press U
2. Click CTRL+Z

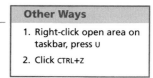

To Show Windows Side by Side

Although stacking arranges the windows vertically above each other on the desktop, it also is possible to arrange them horizontally from left to right, or side by side, like books on a bookshelf. The 'Show windows side by side' command allows you to see partial contents of each window horizontally. The following steps show the open windows side by side.

1
- Right-click an open area on the taskbar to display the shortcut menu (Figure 3–31).

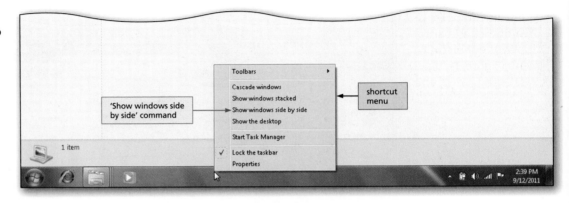

Figure 3–31

2
- Click the 'Show windows side by side' command to display the open windows side by side (Figure 3–32).

Figure 3–32

Other Ways
1. Right-click open area on taskbar, press I

To Undo Show Windows Side by Side

The following steps undo the side by side operation and return the windows to their original arrangement.

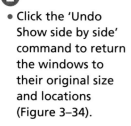

- Right-click an open area on the taskbar to display the shortcut menu (Figure 3–33).

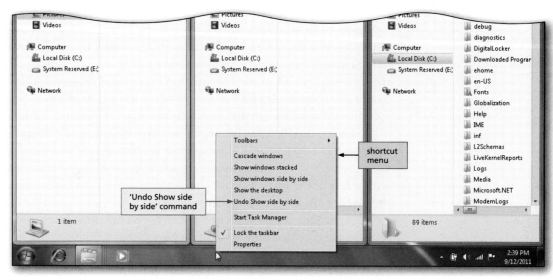

Figure 3–33

2

- Click the 'Undo Show side by side' command to return the windows to their original size and locations (Figure 3–34).

Figure 3–34

Other Ways

1. Right-click open area on taskbar, press U
2. Press CTRL+Z

The Pictures Library

You can organize your pictures and share them with others using the Pictures library. By putting all your pictures in the Pictures library, you will always know where to find them. When you save pictures from a digital camera, scanner, or the Internet, they are saved to the Pictures library by default. More specifically, they are saved to the My Pictures folder. The My Pictures folder is part of the Pictures library and is set as the default save location to be used when working with the library. Recall that when documents were created in the Documents library in Chapter 2, they automatically were saved in the My Documents folder. Each library has a default save location; the default save location for the Documents library is the My Documents folder.

Using the Pictures library allows you to organize pictures, preview pictures, share your pictures with others, display your pictures as a slide show, print your pictures, attach your pictures to e-mail messages, or burn your pictures to an optical disc. You will work with a few of the options now, and the rest will be covered in a later chapter when multimedia files are covered in greater depth.

There are many different formats for picture files. Some pictures have an extension of .bmp to indicate that they are bitmap files. Other pictures might have the .gif extension, which indicates that they are saved in the Graphics Interchange Format. There are too many file types to mention; however, some common types include .bmp, .jpg, .gif, .png, and .tif.

When working with pictures, you should be aware that most pictures that you did not create yourself, including other multimedia files, are copyrighted. A **copyright** means that a picture belongs to the person who created it. The pictures that come with Windows 7 are part of Windows 7 and you are allowed to use them; however, they are not yours. You only can use them according to the rights given to you by Microsoft. Pictures that you take using your digital camera are yours because you created them. Before using pictures and other multimedia files, you should be aware of any copyrights associated with them, and you should know whether you are allowed to use them for your intended purpose.

To View the Save Location for the Pictures Library

To see the default save location for a library, you need to display the properties for the library. You then can change the save location if you so desire. The following steps display the default save location for the Pictures library.

1

- Right-click an open area in the list area of the Pictures library to display the shortcut menu.

- Click the Properties command on the shortcut menu to display the Pictures Properties dialog box (Figure 3–35).

2

- After viewing the save location, click the OK button to close the Pictures Properties dialog box.

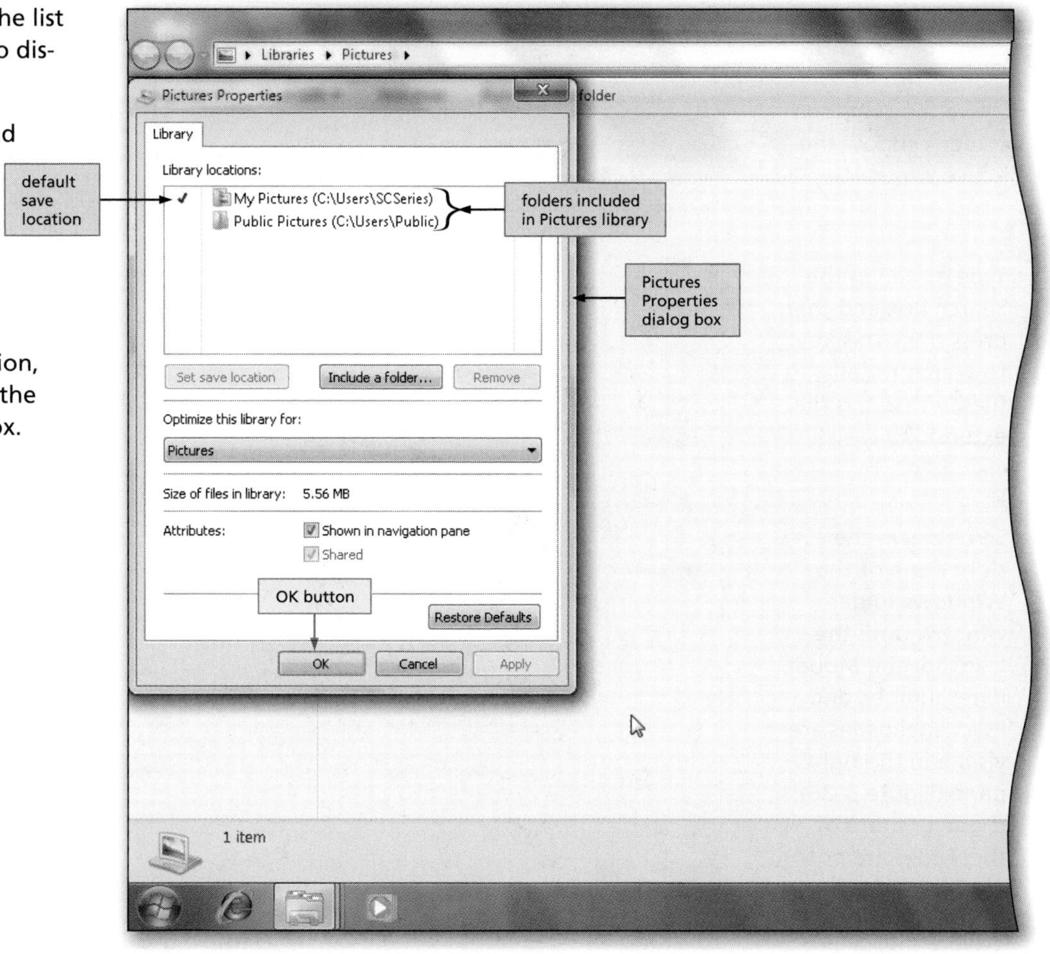

Figure 3–35

To Search for Pictures

You want to copy three files, Monet, Psychedelic, and Pine_Lumber, from the Windows folder to the Pictures library; but first, you have to find these files. Because the three files all have the .jpg extension, you can search for them using an asterisk (*) in place of the file name, as discussed earlier in this chapter. The following steps open the Windows folder window and display the icons for the files you want to copy.

1
- Make the Windows folder window the active window.

2
- Type *.jpg in the Search box and then press the ENTER key to search for all files with a .jpg file extension.

3
- Scroll down the right pane of the Windows folder window until the icons for the Monet, Pine_Lumber, and Psychedelic files are visible in the right pane (Figure 3–36). If one or more of these files are not available, select any of the other picture files.

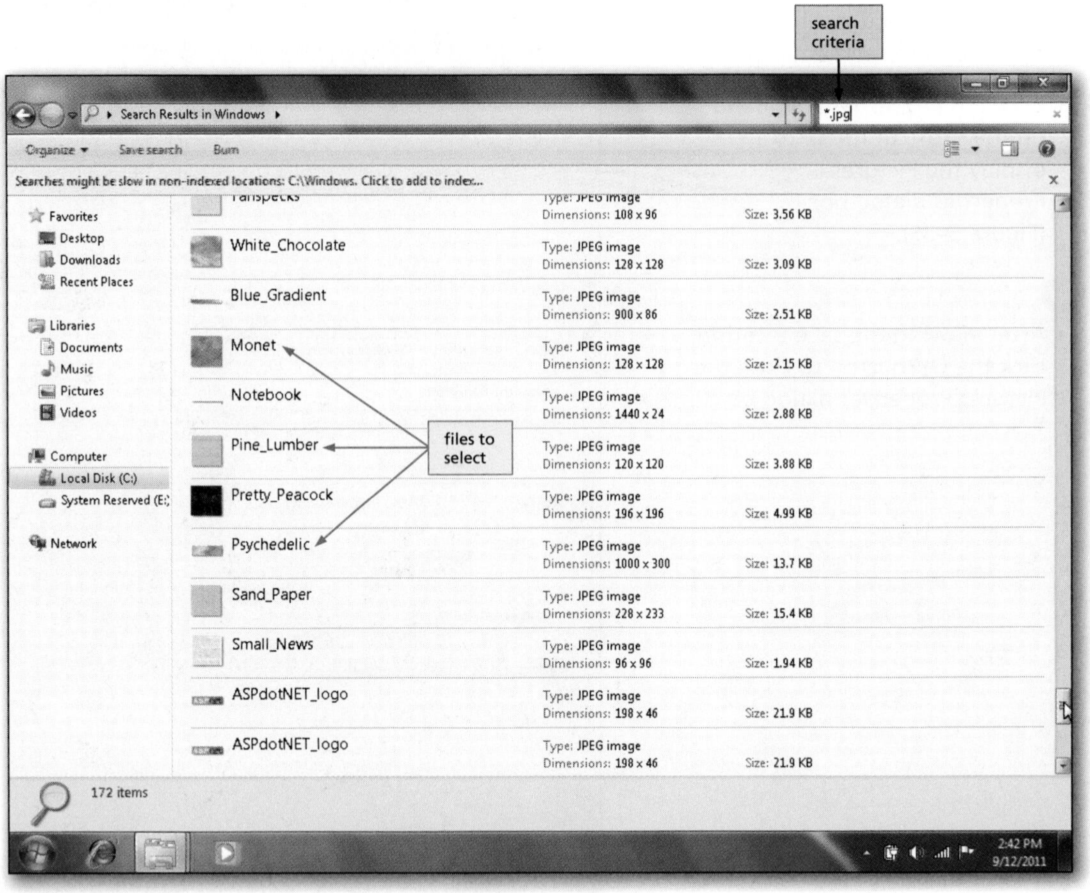

Figure 3–36

To Copy Files to the Pictures Library

In Chapter 2, you learned how to move and copy document files to a folder, how to copy a folder onto a USB flash drive, and how to delete files. Another method you can use to copy a file or folder is the **copy and paste method.** When you **copy** a file, you place a copy of the file in a temporary storage area of the computer called the **Clipboard.** When you **paste** the file, Windows 7 copies it from the Clipboard to the location you specify, giving you two copies of the same file.

Because the search results include the pictures you were looking for, you now can select the files and then copy them to the Pictures library. Once the three files have been copied into the Pictures library, the files will be stored in both the My Pictures folder (the default save location) and Windows folder on drive C. Copying and moving files are common tasks when working with Windows 7. If you want to move a file instead of copying a file, you would use the Cut command on the shortcut menu to move the file to the Clipboard, and the Paste command to copy the file from the Clipboard to the new location. When the move is complete, the files are moved into the new folder and no longer are stored in the original folder.

The following steps copy the Monet, Pine_Lumber, and Psychedelic files from the Windows folder to the Pictures library.

1

- Hold down the CTRL key and then click the Monet, Pine_Lumber, and Psychedelic icons.

- Release the CTRL key.

- Right-click any high-lighted icon to dis-play a shortcut menu (Figure 3–37).

Q&A

Are copying and moving the same?

No. When you copy a file, it is located in both the place to which it was copied and in the place from which it was copied. When you move a file, it is located only in the location to which it was moved.

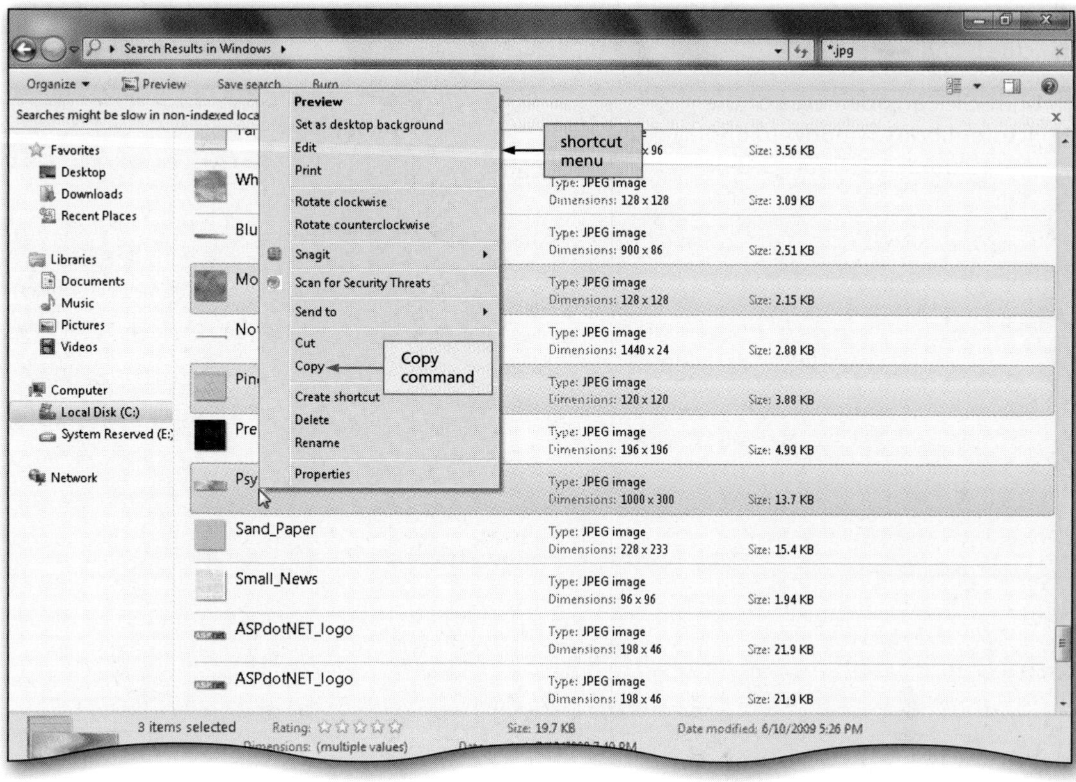

Figure 3–37

2

- Click the Copy command on the shortcut menu to copy the files to the Clipboard (Figure 3–38).

Figure 3–38

3

- Make the Pictures library the active window.

- Right-click an open area of the Pictures library window to display a shortcut menu (Figure 3–39).

Figure 3–39

4

- Click the Paste command on the shortcut menu to paste the files in the Pictures library (Figure 3–40).

Other Ways

1. Select file icons, press ALT, on Edit menu click Copy, display window where you want to store file, press ALT, on Edit menu click Paste

2. Select file icons, press ALT, on Edit menu click Copy to folder, click arrow next to your user name, click My Pictures, click Copy

3. Select file icons, press CTRL+C, display window where you want to store files, press CTRL+V

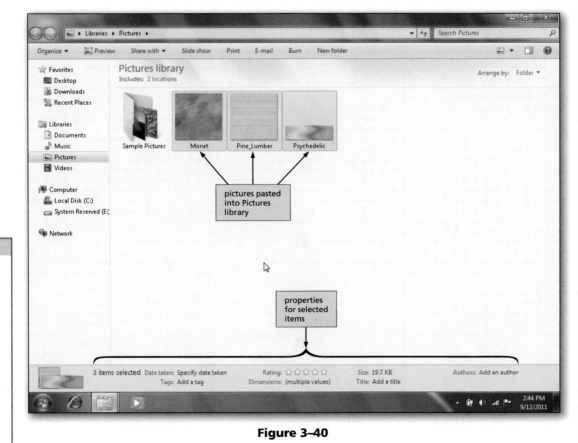

Figure 3–40

To Close the Search Results Window

You no longer need the Search Results window open, so you can close it. Whenever you are not using a window, it is a good idea to close it so as not to clutter your desktop. The following steps close the Search Results window.

1 Display the Search Results window.

2 Close the Search Results window.

To Create a Folder in the Pictures Library

When you have several related files stored in a folder with a number of unrelated files, you might want to create a folder to contain the related files so that you can find and reference them easily. To reduce clutter and improve the organization of files in the Pictures library, you will create a new folder in the Pictures library and then move the Monet, Pine_Lumber, and Psychedelic files into the new folder. The following steps create the Backgrounds folder in the Pictures library.

1

- Make the Pictures library the active window.

- Right-click any open part of the list area of the Pictures library to display a shortcut menu (Figure 3–41). (The commands on the shortcut menu on your computer might differ slightly.)

Figure 3–41

2

- Point to the New command on the shortcut menu to display the New submenu (Figure 3–42). (The commands on the New submenu on your computer might differ slightly.)

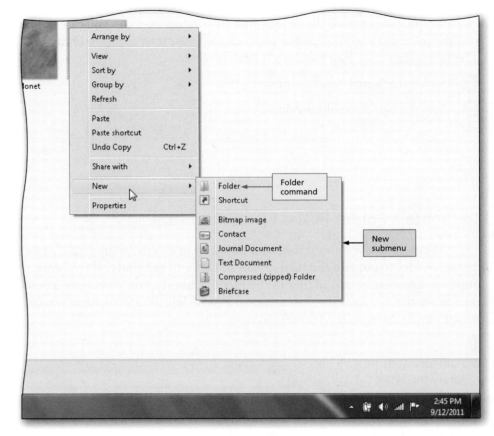

Figure 3–42

3

- Click the Folder command on the New submenu to create a new folder in the Pictures library.

- Type Backgrounds in the icon title text box, and then press the ENTER key to assign the name to the new folder (Figure 3–43).

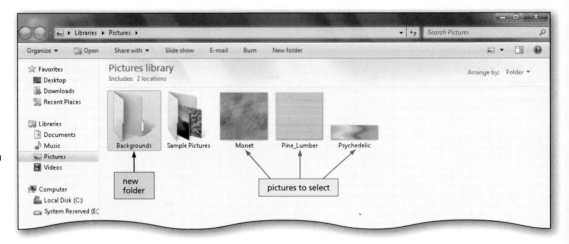

Figure 3–43

Other Ways

1. Click New folder button, type folder name, press ENTER

2. Press ALT, click File menu, point to New, click Folder, type folder name, press ENTER

3. Press ALT+F, press W, press F, type folder name, press ENTER

To Move Multiple Files into a Folder

After you create the Backgrounds folder in the Pictures library, the next step is to move the three picture files into the folder. The following steps move the Monet, Psychedelic, and Pine_Lumber files into the Backgrounds folder.

1

- Click the Monet icon, hold down the CTRL key, and then click the Pine_Lumber and Psychedelic icons to select all three icons (Figure 3–44).

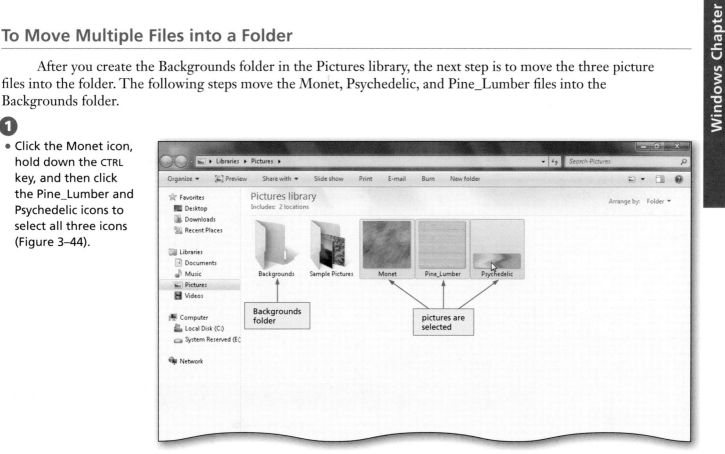

Figure 3–44

2

- Drag the selected icons to the Backgrounds folder, and then release the mouse button to move the files to the Backgrounds folder (Figure 3–45).

Figure 3–45

Other Ways

1. Drag icons individually to folder icon
2. Right-click icon, click Cut, right-click folder icon, click Paste

To Refresh the Image on a Folder

After moving the three files into the Backgrounds folder, it still appears as an empty open folder icon. To replace the empty folder icon with a live preview of the three files stored in the Backgrounds folder (Monet, Pine_Lumber, Psychedelic), the Pictures library must be refreshed. The following steps refresh the Pictures library to display the live preview for the Backgrounds folder.

1

- Right-click any open part of the list area to display a shortcut menu (Figure 3–46).

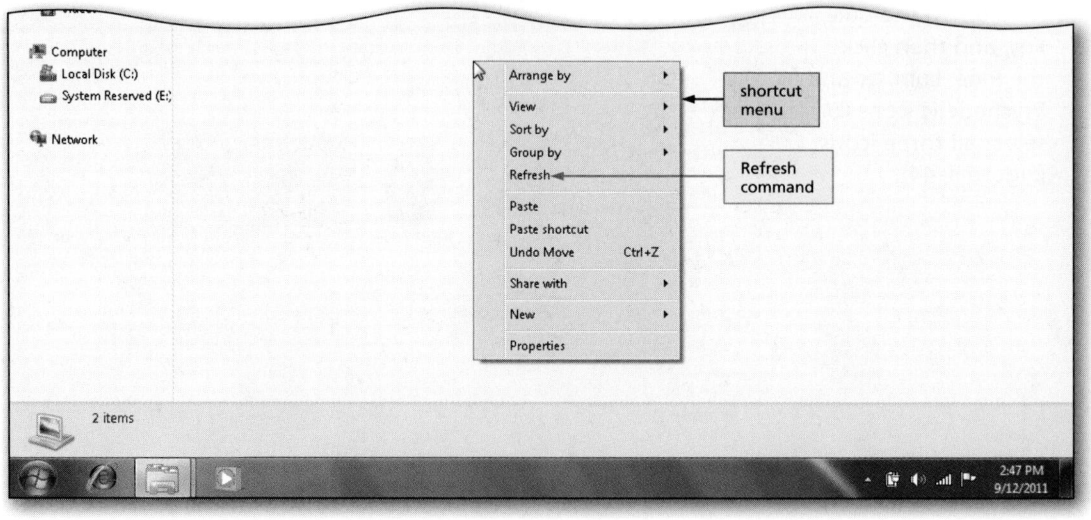

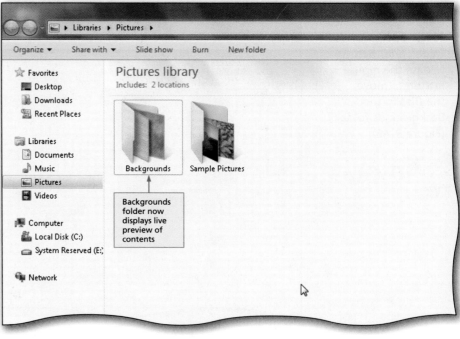

Figure 3–46

2

- Click the Refresh command to refresh the list area (Figure 3–47).

Figure 3–47

Other Ways
1. Press ALT, click View, click Refresh

To View and Change the Properties of a Picture

As mentioned earlier in the chapter, in Windows 7, all objects have properties. You already have explored the properties of a drive, and now you will review the properties of a picture. Picture properties include the Size, Title, Authors, State, Date taken, Tags, Rating, and Dimensions. State refers to whether or not the picture is shared with other users on the computer. Date taken refers to the date the person created the picture.

Tags are keywords you associate with a picture file to aid in its classification. For example, you could tag a family photo with the names of the people in the photo. When you create a tag, it should be meaningful. For example, if you have pictures from a family vacation at the beach and you add a title of vacation; later on, you will be able to find the file using the tag "vacation" in a search. Be aware that you only can search for tags that you already have created. If your family vacation photo was saved as "photo1.jpg" and tagged with the tag "vacation", you will not find it by searching for "beach" as it is not part of the name or tag. Rating refers to the ranking, in stars, that you assign to a picture. You can rate a picture from zero to five stars. Date taken, Tags, and Rating all can be changed using the Details pane. Because you do not know when the Background pictures were created, you only will change the Tags and Rating properties. The following steps display and change the Tags and Rating properties of the Monet image in the Backgrounds folder.

1

- Display the contents of the Backgrounds folder.

- Click the Monet icon to select it (Figure 3–48).

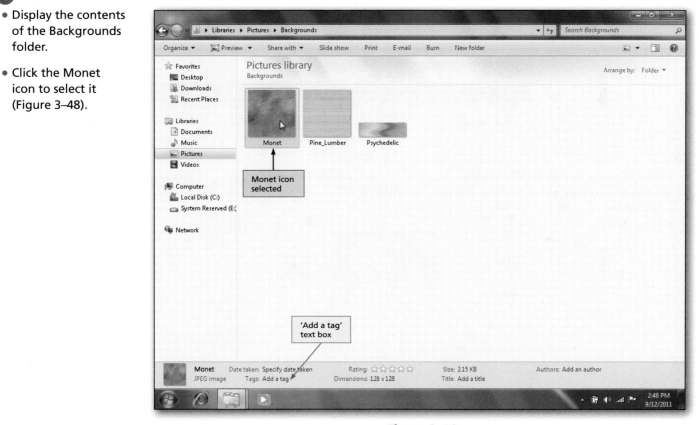

Figure 3–48

2

- Click the 'Add a tag' text box in the Details pane to activate it (Figure 3–49).

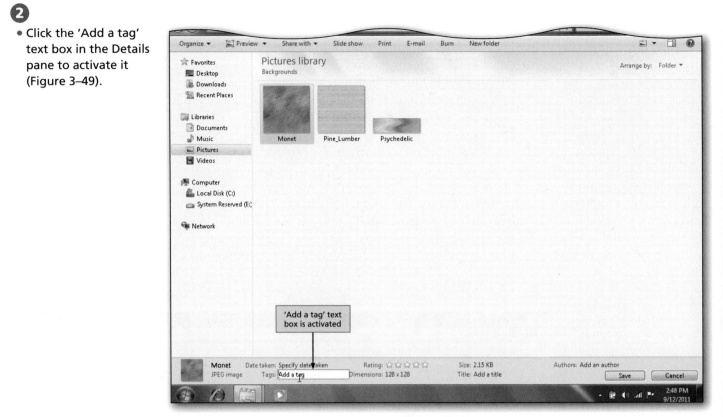

Figure 3–49

3

- Type A Work of Art in the text box to create a tag for the picture (Figure 3–50).

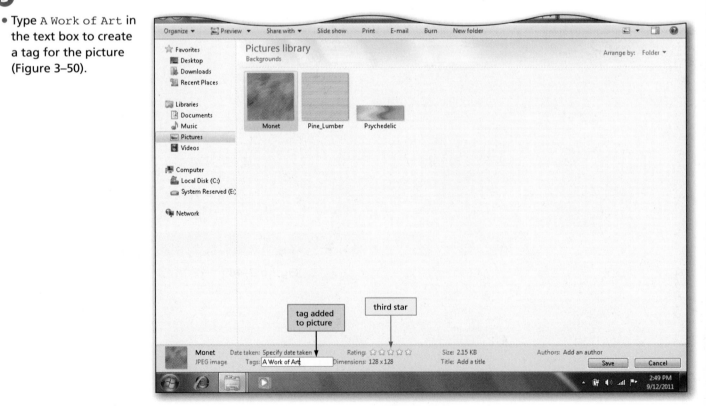

Figure 3–50

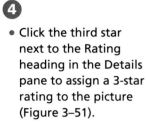

4

• Click the third star next to the Rating heading in the Details pane to assign a 3-star rating to the picture (Figure 3–51).

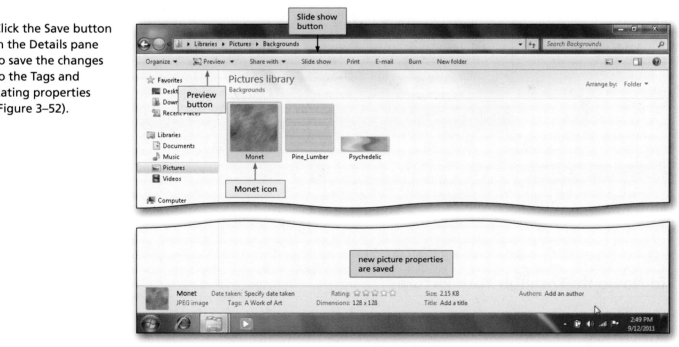

Figure 3–51

5

• Click the Save button in the Details pane to save the changes to the Tags and Rating properties (Figure 3–52).

Figure 3–52

Other Ways

1. Right-click icon, click Properties, click Details tab, click third star next to Rating, enter text next to Tags, click OK

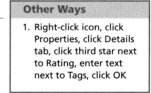

To Open a Picture in Windows Photo Viewer

You can view the images in a folder in Windows Photo Viewer or as a slide show. **Windows Photo Viewer** is a program that allows you to view, print, e-mail, burn, and open the pictures in your Pictures library. You can view pictures individually or as part of a slide show.

The buttons on the toolbar at the bottom of the Windows Photo Viewer window allow you to move through the pictures and rotate a picture clockwise or counterclockwise. The following step displays the Monet picture in the Backgrounds folder in Windows Photo Viewer.

1

- If necessary, select the Monet icon.

- Click the Preview button on the toolbar to open the Monet picture in Windows Photo Viewer (Figure 3–53).

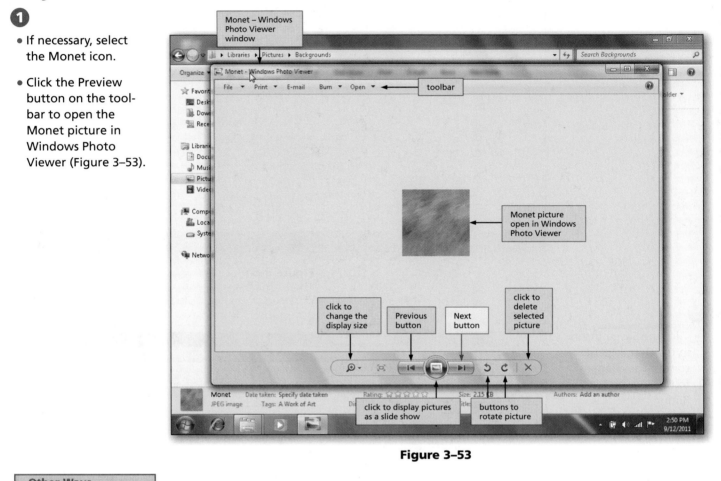

Figure 3–53

Other Ways

1. Right-click icon, click Preview

To Navigate Through Your Pictures

To navigate through your pictures, you use the buttons at the bottom of the Windows Photo Viewer window. The Next (right arrow) button allows you to move to the next picture, and the Previous (left arrow) button allows you to move to the previous picture in the folder. You also can rotate a picture clockwise or counterclockwise using the Rotate buttons, change the display size of a picture, or even delete a picture. The following steps navigate through the pictures in the Backgrounds folder using Windows Photo Viewer.

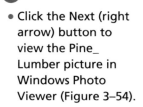

● Click the Next (right arrow) button to view the Pine_Lumber picture in Windows Photo Viewer (Figure 3–54).

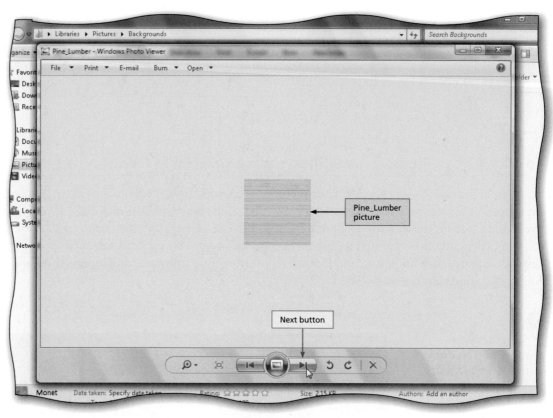

Figure 3–54

● Click the Next (right arrow) button to view the Psychedelic picture in Windows Photo Viewer (Figure 3–55).

Figure 3–55

To Close Windows Photo Viewer

Now that you have seen all of the pictures, the next step is to close Windows Photo Viewer.

1 Click the Close button to close Windows Photo Viewer.

To View Your Pictures as a Slide Show

In Windows 7, you can view your pictures as a **slide show**, which displays each image in the folder in a presentation format on your computer screen. The slide show will automatically display one picture at a time while everything else on the desktop is hidden from sight. The slide show allows you to select whether the pictures will loop in order or will be shuffled to appear in random order. You also can select the speed at which the pictures are displayed, pause the slide show, and exit the slide show. The following step opens the images in the Backgrounds folder as a slide show.

1

• Click the Slide show button on the Pictures library toolbar to view the selected files as a slide show (Figure 3–56).

• Watch the show for a few seconds while the pictures change.

Q&A Can I change the slide show speed?

Yes, you can right-click and then select speeds of Slow, Medium, and Fast.

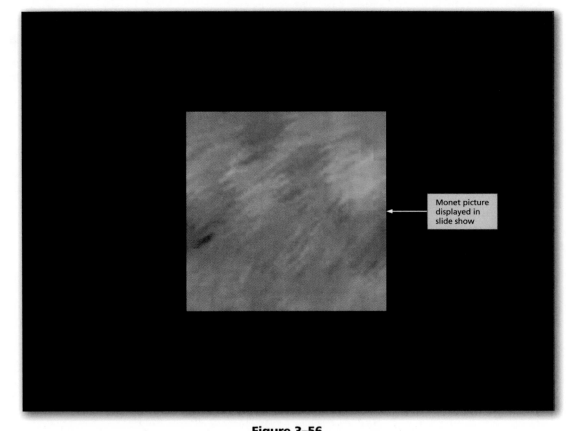

Monet picture displayed in slide show

Figure 3–56

To End a Slide Show

When you are done viewing the slide show, the next step is to end it. The following step exits the slide show.

1
- Press ESC to end the slide show (Figure 3–57).

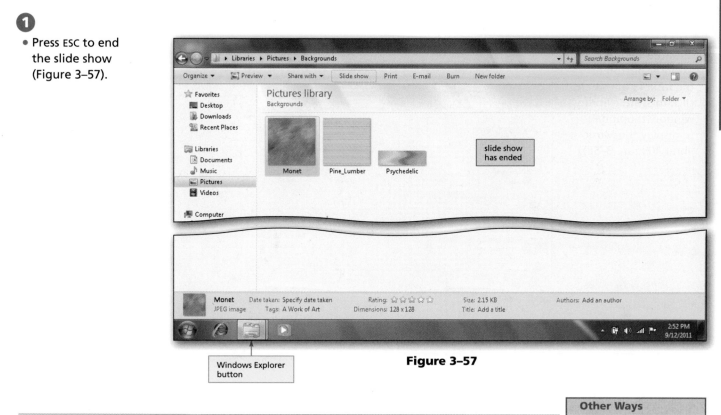

Figure 3–57

Windows Explorer button

Other Ways
1. Right-click, click Exit

The Music Library

The **Music library** can be used to view, organize, and play your music files. If you have a digital music player installed, it will use the default save location of the Music library when you download, play, rip, and burn music. When you **rip** a file, you extract the audio data from a CD and transfer it to your hard disk. After the file has been ripped, it will be in a format that is compatible with your computer as opposed to a CD player. When you **burn** music, you take files that are compatible with your computer and copy them onto a CD in the format that can be played in CD players. When you burn data files to a CD, the contents of the CD cannot be read by a CD player.

You can arrange your music files into organized collections. The Sample Music folder, installed with Windows 7, contains samples of music for you to experiment with so that you can make sure that your sound card and speakers are working properly. If you use a music program such as iTunes or Windows Media Player, you will be able to add additional music files to your collection. Music files come in a variety of formats, similar to how picture files have different formats. Common music file formats include .wav, .wma, .mp3, .mp4, and .mid. For example, audio podcasts often are saved in the .mp3 format.

As with other media files, you should be aware of copyright issues. If you download music from the Internet, make sure that you have permission to do so. To add music files to your Music library, you can obtain permission by paying a small fee to download the song. It is illegal to download and share music that you do not have the rights to download and share.

To Switch to the Music Library

You want to view the contents of the Music library to understand how music is stored and arranged. To see this, you will switch to the Music window. The following step makes the Music library the active window.

1

- Click the Windows Explorer button on the taskbar and then click the Music library window thumbnail to display the Music library (Figure 3–58).

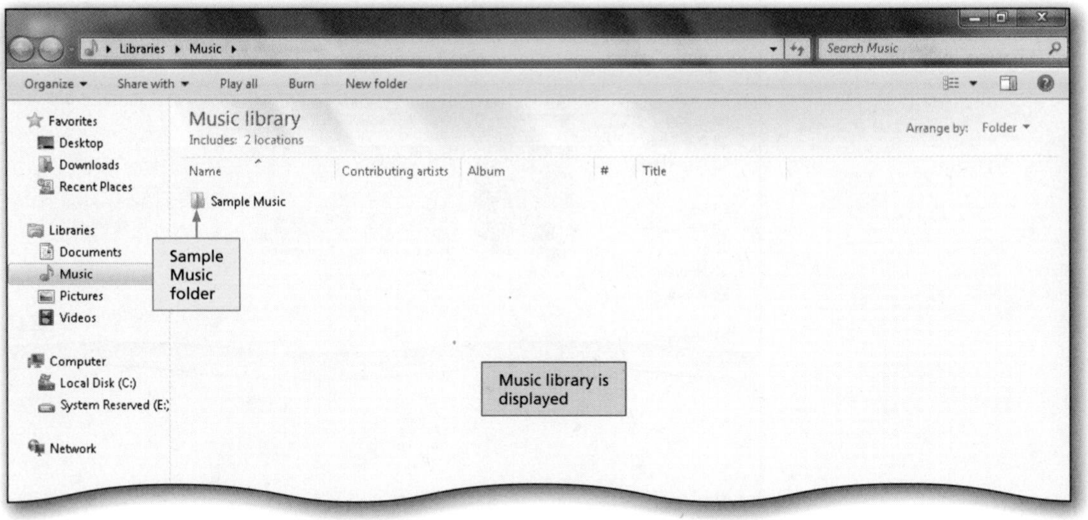

Figure 3–58

To Open the Sample Music Folder

To see the sample music files, you need to open the Sample Music folder. The Sample Music folder is located in the Public Music folder, although a shortcut to the Sample Music folder appears in the Music library. This demonstrates the power of a library; you do not actually need to know where a particular folder is located when working with a library. The library keeps track of that for you. When you view the contents of the Sample Music folder, notice that the Address bar reflects the fact that you are in the library (not the actual storage location). The following step opens the Sample Music folder.

1

- Double-click the Sample Music folder to display the Sample Music folder contents (Figure 3–59).

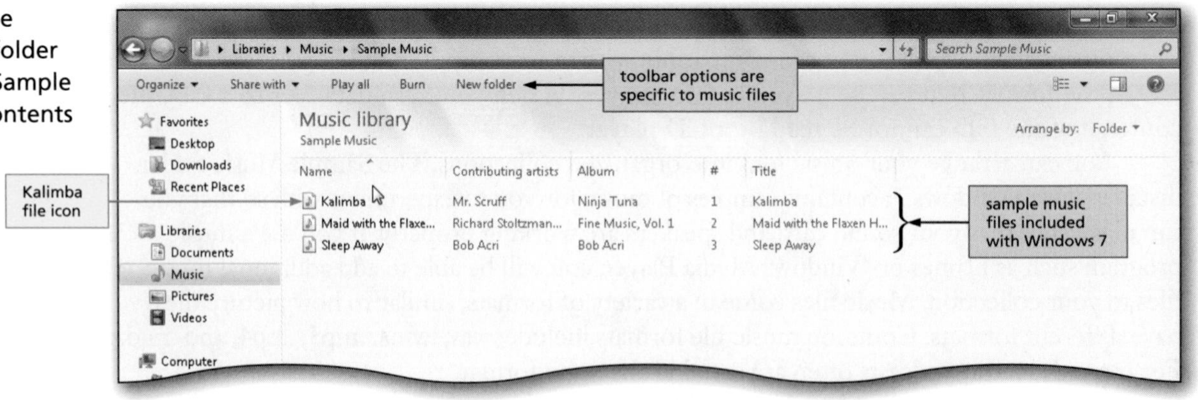

Figure 3–59

To View Information about a Music File

Similar to the Pictures library, when you view a folder that contains music files, the folder structure and options are specific to music files. In the Music library, after the column titled Name, all of the remaining columns, Contributing artists, Album, #, and Title, are properties of the music files. The Contributing artists column contains the name or names of the recording artist(s), whereas the Album column contains the name of the album that includes the song. The number symbol (#) indicates the track number of the song on the album, whereas Title displays the full title of the song.

You might see the album cover image in the Details pane. For an album cover to be displayed, your music files must include the album cover image, which usually occurs when the music files are created. If you download music files, they often will have the album art included, but not every music file will have this.

Once you select a file, its properties display in the Details pane. As with picture files, you can use the Details pane to change the properties. The following steps display the properties of the Kalimba music file in the Details pane and change the genre to New Age.

1
- Click the Kalimba file icon to select the music file (Figure 3–60).

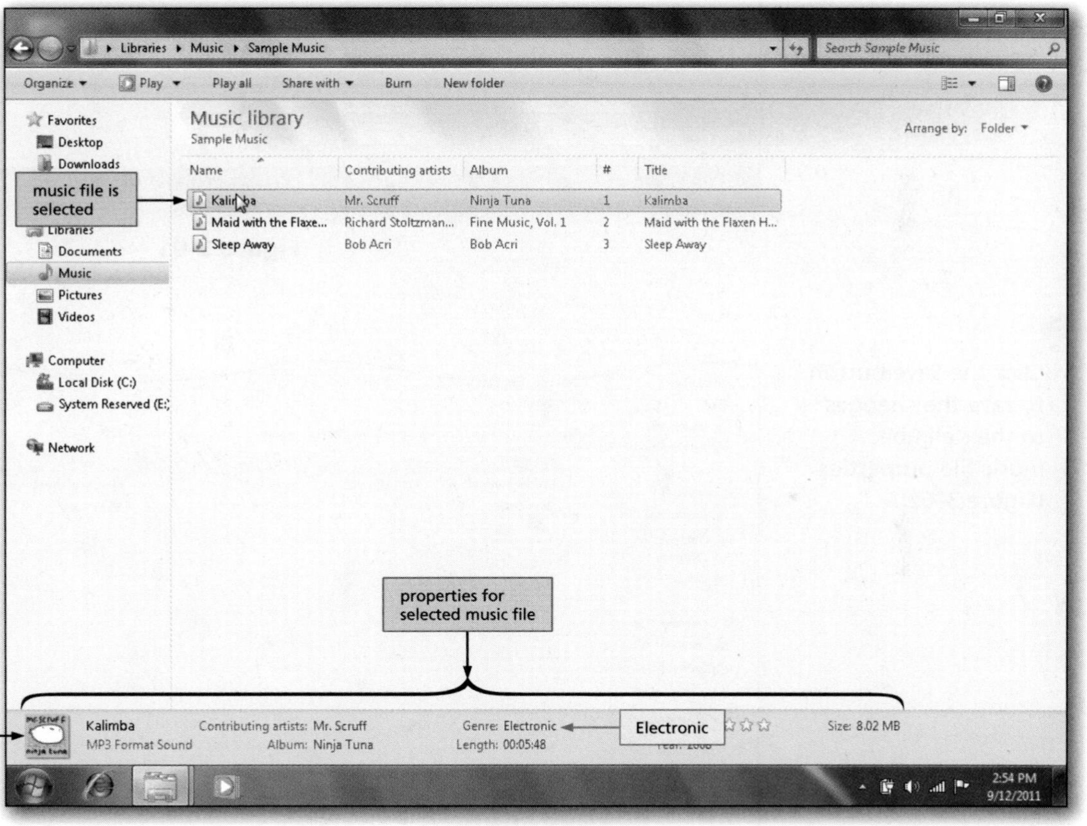

Figure 3–60

2

- Click Electronic in the Genre property to select it.

- Type New Age to change the Genre property (Figure 3–61).

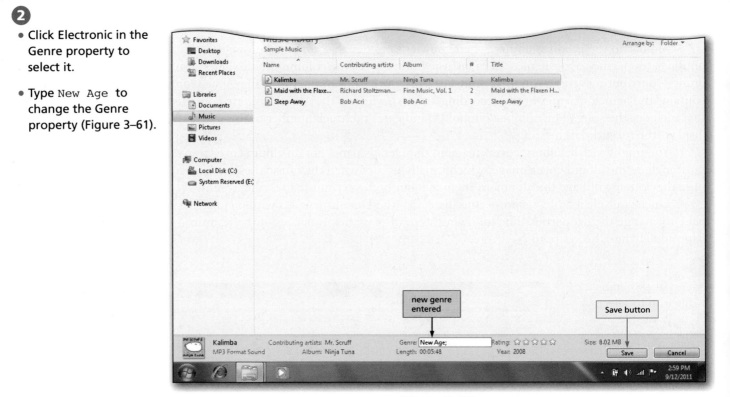

Figure 3–61

3

- Click the Save button to save the changes to the Kalimba music file properties (Figure 3–62).

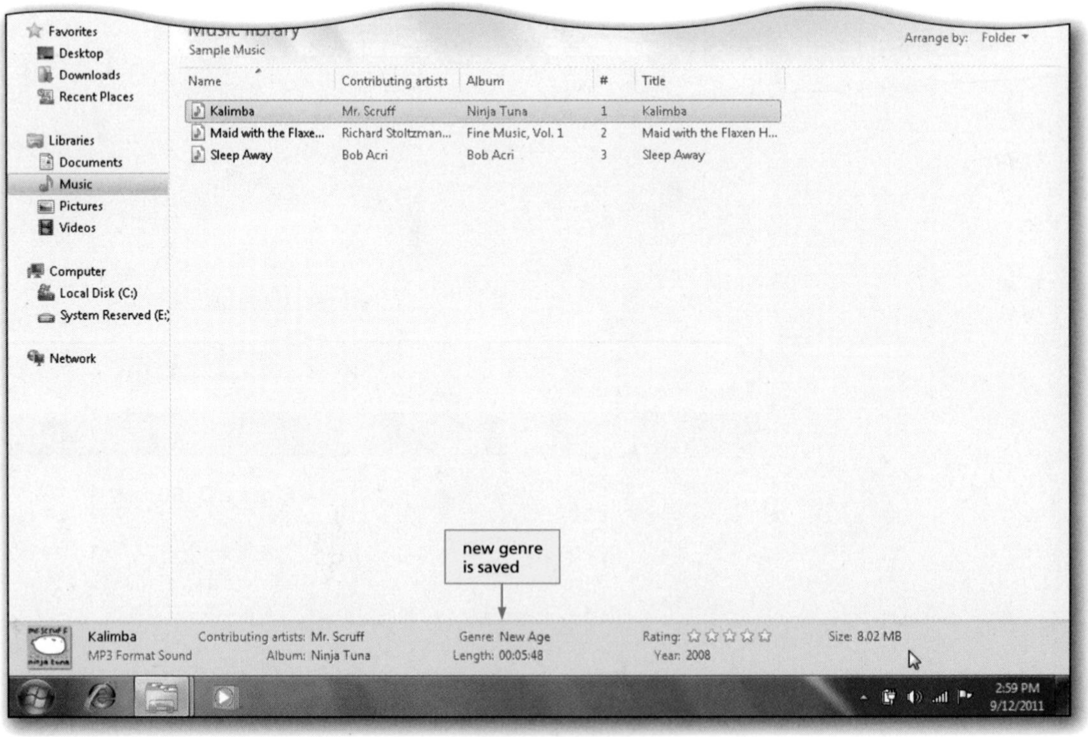

Figure 3–62

To Reset the Genre for a Music File

Because the Kalimba file is in the Sample Music folder that is shared by everyone who uses this computer, you should undo your genre change. However, if you are working on your own computer and you agree with the new genre, you could leave it alone. The following step will reset the genre of the Kalimba file back to its original value.

1

- Click the mouse at the left edge of the genre info.

- Delete New Age from the Genre list.

- Type `Electronic` to enter the original genre value.

- Click the Save button to save the changes to the Kalimba music file properties (Figure 3–63).

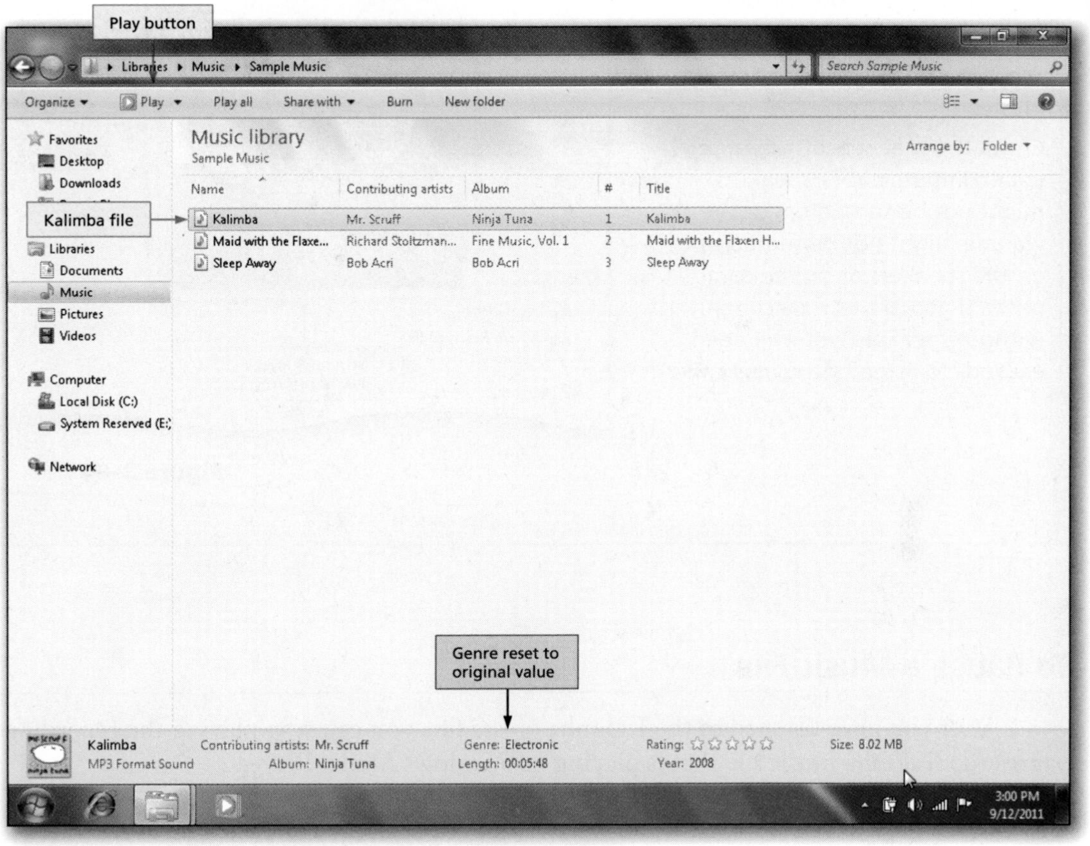

Figure 3–63

To Play a Music File in Windows Media Player

There are several ways to play a music file. The easiest way is to use the Music library toolbar. If you click the Play button, you play the selected song. Clicking the Play all button plays all the music files in the folder. **Windows Media Player** is the default Windows 7 program for playing and working with digital media files such as music or video files.

In addition to playing music files, Windows Media Player can rip and burn music, maintain a music library, sync with portable media players, and even download music. Windows Media Player also works with other multimedia files, including movies. These features of Windows Media Player are discussed in a later chapter.

In Windows Media Player, there are buttons for controlling the playback of the music file. The step on the following page plays the Kalimba music file in Windows Media Player.

1

- If necessary, select the Kalimba file.

- Click the Play button on the toolbar to open and play the Kalimba music file in Windows Media Player (Figure 3–64).

Q&A

Why am I unable to hear any music?

Check the speakers attached to your computer. Your speakers might not be turned on, or the volume might not be turned up on the speakers or on the computer. If you are using a computer without speakers, you will need earbuds to listen to the music file.

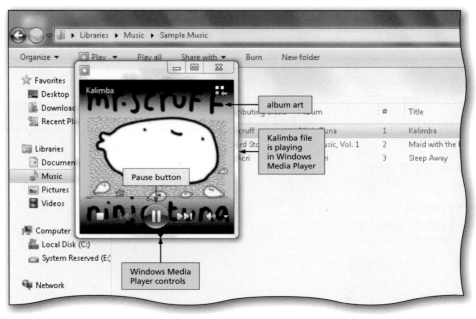

Figure 3–64

To Pause a Music File

After you have listened to the Kalimba music file, you can stop playing the recording. The following step pauses the Kalimba music file that is playing in Windows Media Player.

1

- Click the Pause button on the toolbar at the bottom of the window to pause the song in Windows Media Player (Figure 3–65).

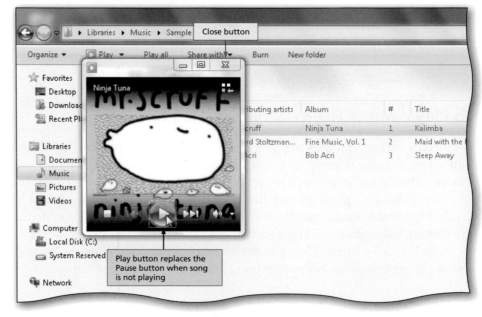
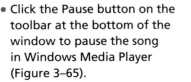

Figure 3–65

To Close Windows Media Player

Now that you are done using the Windows Media Player and the Sample Music folder, you should close them.

1 Close Windows Media Player.

2 Close the Sample Music folder window.

Backing Up Files and Folders

It is very important that you make backups of your important files and folders. A **backup** is a copy of files and folders that are stored at a different location than the originals. Backing up files and folders is a security aid; if something happens to the primary copy of a file or folder, you can restore it from the backup.

Although you can back up files and folders on the same drive where they were created, it is not considered as safe as backing them up to a separate drive. For example, you should not back up your C drive files and folders on the C drive. If something goes wrong with the C drive, it would affect any backups stored there as well. Depending upon the size of the files and folders you are backing up, you might use a USB flash drive, an optical disc, an external hard disk, or any other available storage device to back up your files. You might even consider creating a scheduled backup. A **scheduled backup** is a backup that is made according to predetermined dates and times.

After you have created a backup, you should store your backup away from the computer. Many people store their backups right by their computer, which is not a good practice. If a mishap occurs where the computer area is damaged, someone steals the computer, or any other number of events occurs, the backup still will be safe if it is stored in a different location. Most corporations make regular backups of their data and store the backups off-site.

When you **restore** files or folders from a backup, you copy the files or folders from the backup location to the original location. If your hard disk crashes, a virus infects your computer, or an electrical surge damages your computer, you can restore the files and folders that you have stored on the backup. Before restoring files or folders, make sure that the location to where you are restoring the files is now secure. For example, before restoring files on a hard disk that has been infected by a virus, first make sure the virus is gone.

First, you will back up your files and folders to a USB flash drive. A USB flash drive is handy for backing up files and folders created on a computer in a classroom, computer lab, or cybercafé, where you have to remove your files before you leave.

To Insert a USB Flash Drive and Open It in a Folder Window

First, you need to insert the USB flash drive so that you can back up your data to your USB flash drive. The following steps insert a USB flash drive and open it in a folder window.

1 Insert a USB flash drive into any available USB port on your computer to display the AutoPlay window. If the AutoPlay window does not appear, click the Start button, click the Computer command to open the Computer folder window, and then click the drive letter representing your USB flash drive.

2 Under the General Options heading, click the 'Open folder to view files' command to open a folder window.

To Create a Backup on a USB Flash Drive

With the USB flash drive connected, you are ready to make a backup. You decide to back up your Backgrounds folder. By copying this folder to the USB flash drive, you will be adding a measure of security to your data. The following steps copy the Backgrounds folder from the Pictures library to the USB flash drive.

1

- Make the Backgrounds window the active window (Figure 3–66).

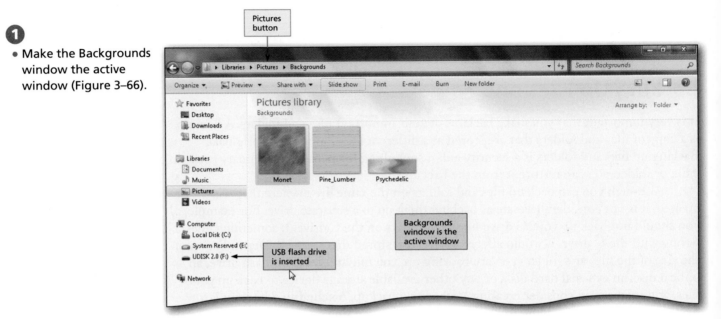

Figure 3–66

2

- Click the Pictures button on the Address bar to change the location to the Pictures library (Figure 3–67).

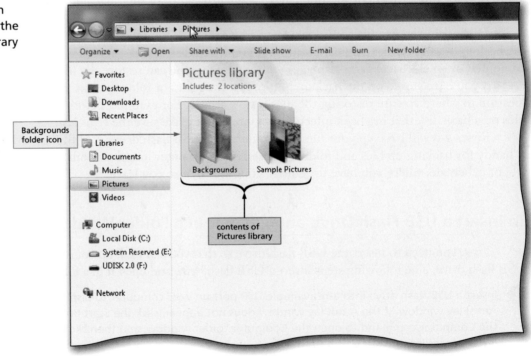

Figure 3–67

3

- If necessary, click the Backgrounds folder icon to select the Backgrounds folder.

- Right-click the Backgrounds folder to display a shortcut menu (Figure 3–68).

- Click the Copy command on the shortcut menu to copy the folder to the Clipboard.

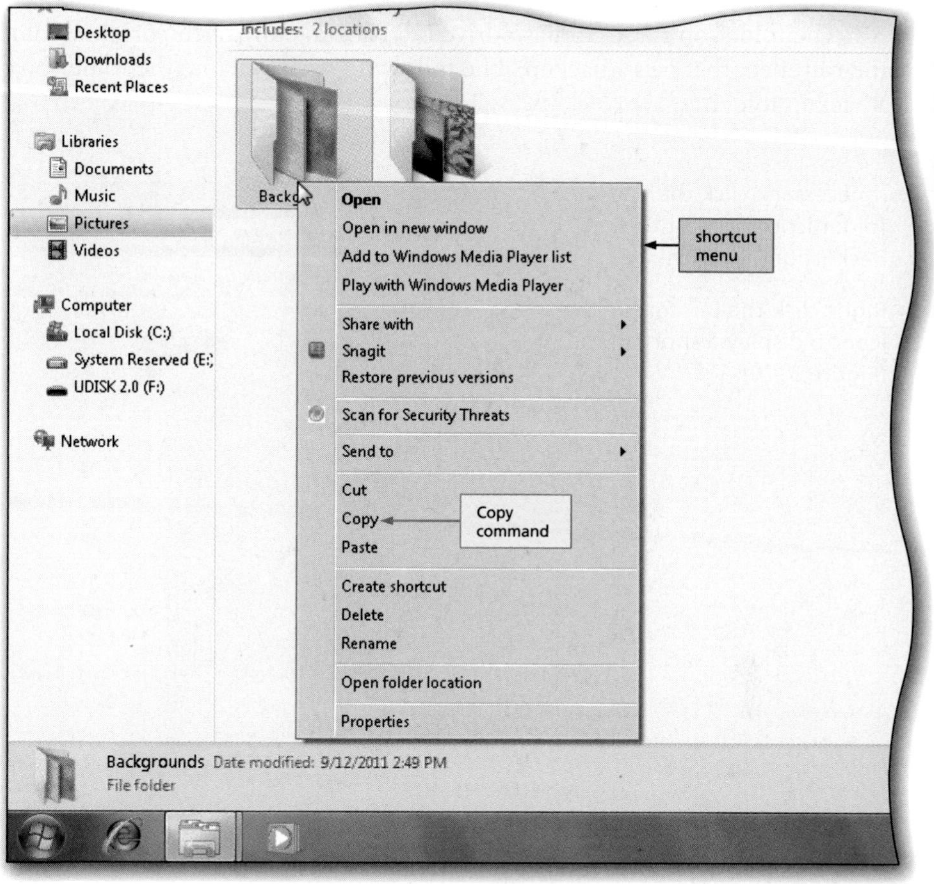

Figure 3–68

4

- Make the UDISK 2.0 (F:) window the active window.

Q&A

Why do I not have a UDISK 2.0 (F:) window?

UDISK 2.0 refers to the name of the USB flash drive, and (F:) refers to the drive letter. If either the name of your USB flash drive or drive letter are different, the window containing your USB flash drive's contents would be named to reflect these differences.

- Right-click an open area in the list area to display a shortcut menu.

- Click the Paste command on the shortcut menu to paste a copy of the Backgrounds folder onto the USB flash drive (Figure 3–69).

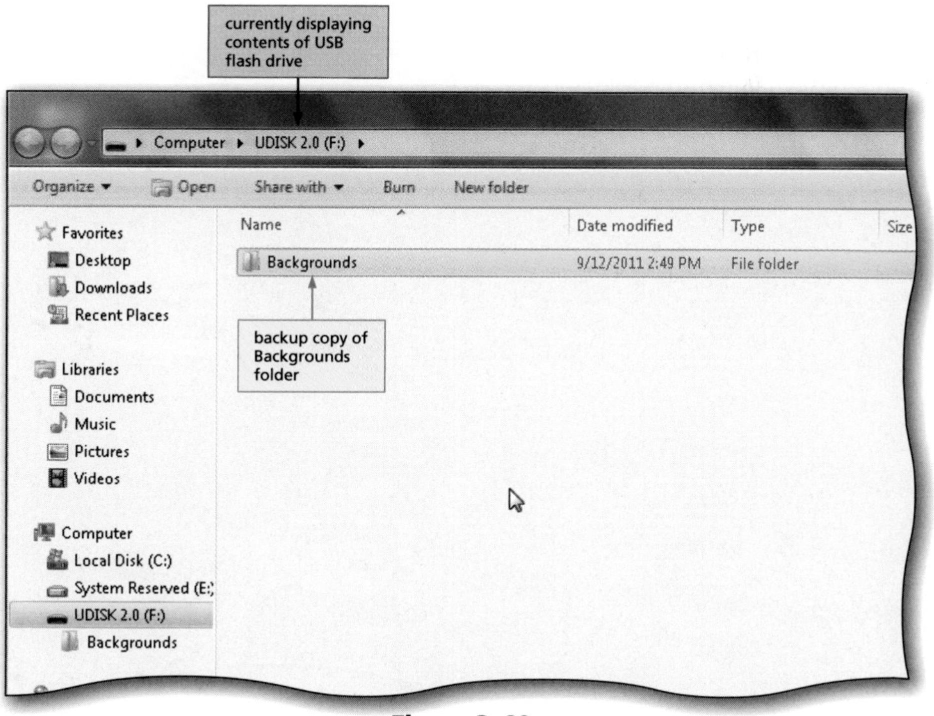

Figure 3–69

To Rename a Folder

The folder on the USB flash drive is a backup copy of the original folder, so it is a good idea to change its name to reflect that it is a backup. The following steps rename the folder on the USB flash drive to indicate that it is a backup folder.

1

- If necessary, click the Backgrounds folder icon to select the Backgrounds folder.

- Right-click the Backgrounds icon to display a shortcut menu (Figure 3–70).

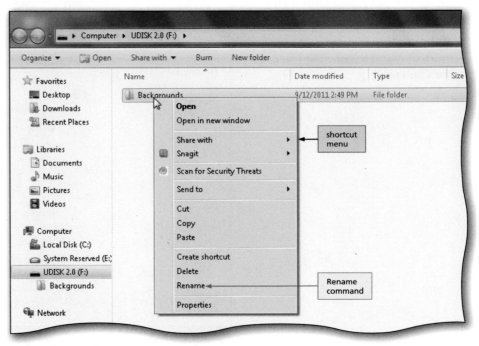

Figure 3–70

2

- Click the Rename command to open the name of the folder in a text box (Figure 3–71).

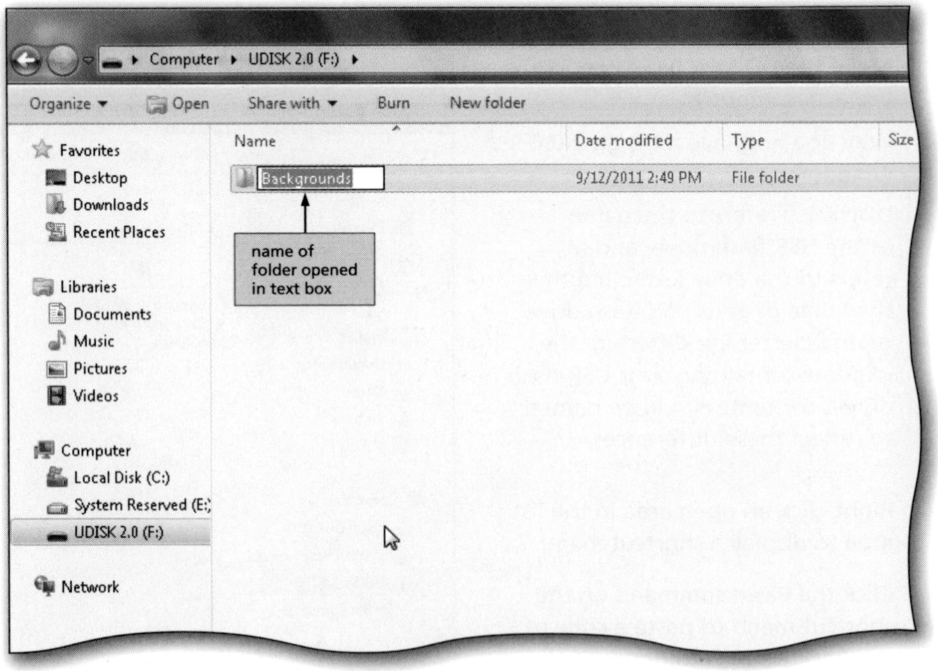

Figure 3–71

● Type Backgrounds – Backup
as the new name for the folder
(Figure 3–72).

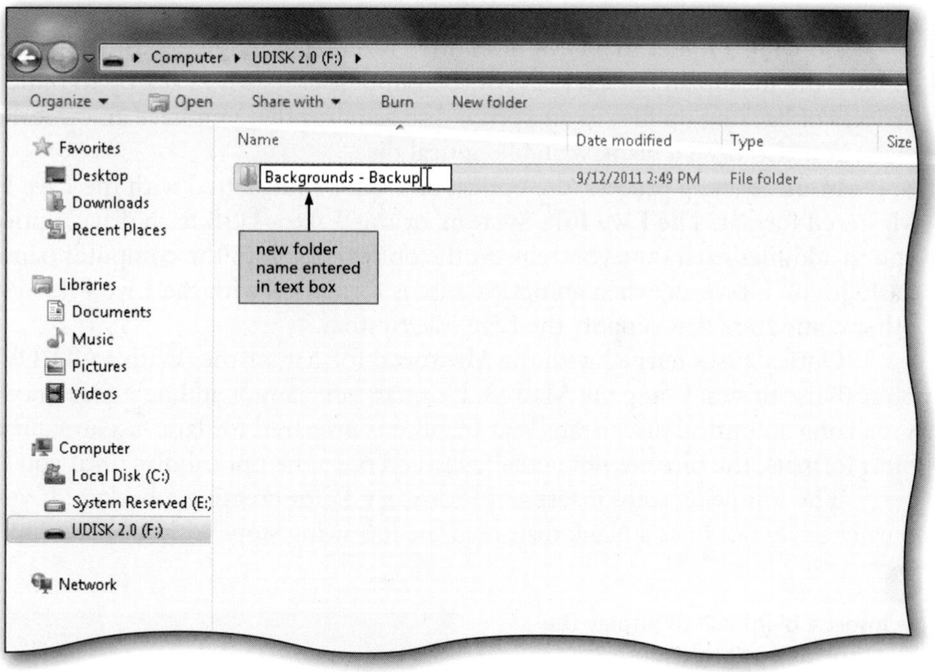

Figure 3–72

4

● Press the ENTER key
to apply the new
name to the folder
(Figure 3–73).

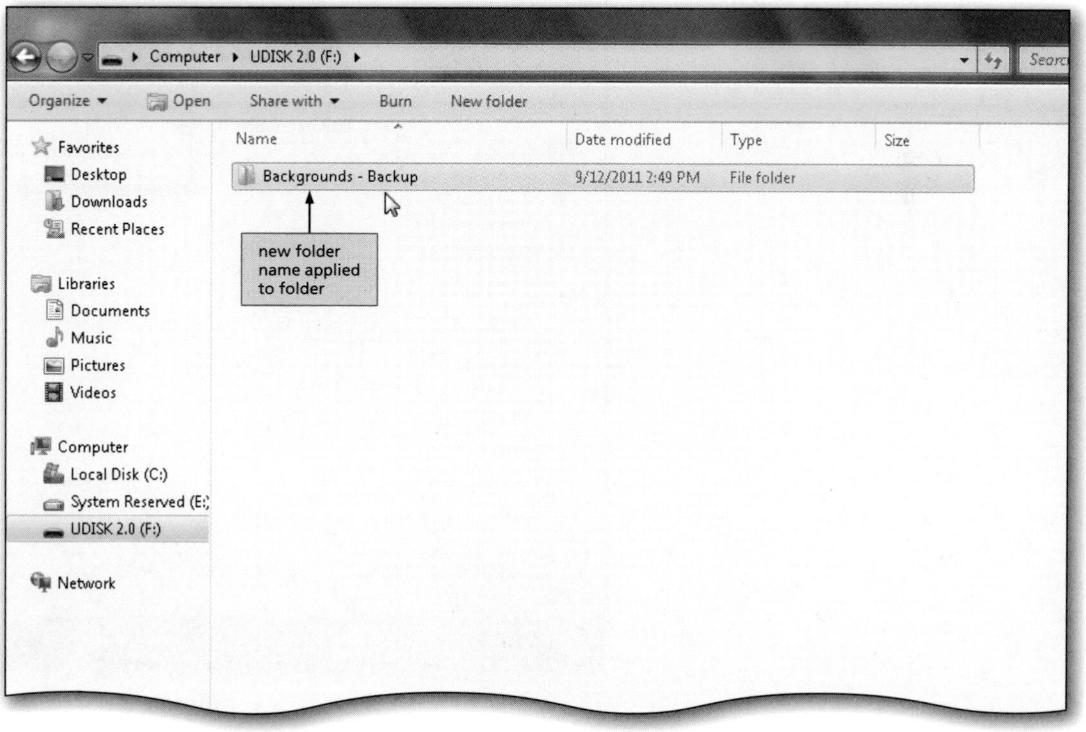

Figure 3–73

To Insert and Format an Optical Disc for Backup

Copying a folder to a USB flash drive is one method of creating a backup. Another way to make a backup is to burn the files to an optical disc. Most computer users who back up to optical discs either use a CD or DVD. The process of backing up files to an optical disc requires that you have an optical disc drive that can write data to optical discs. You also need a blank writable optical disc.

In this backup process, the optical disc can be formatted with the Live File System or formatted with the Mastered format. The **Live File System**, or the 'Like a USB flash drive' option, is a file storage system that allows you to add files each time you reinsert the optical disc into the computer (similar to how you can add files to a USB flash drive). However, when an optical disc is formatted with the Live File System, the files only are readable on other computers that support the Live File System.

Optical discs burned with the **Mastered** format, or the 'With a CD/DVD player' option, are readable on all optical disc drives. Using the Mastered format, you cannot add new files once the optical disc has been finalized. Finalizing an optical disc means that the disc is prepared for later use in your computer or another computer. With both formats, the files are not actually burned onto the optical disc until you eject the optical disc.

The following steps insert and format a CD for creating a backup. If you do not have access to an optical disc burner or do not have a blank disc, read the following steps without performing them.

1

- Insert a blank CD to display the AutoPlay options (Figure 3–74).

- If the AutoPlay window does not appear, open the Computer folder window and then double-click the drive letter representing your optical disc drive to display the Burn a Disc dialog box. Next, skip to Step 3.

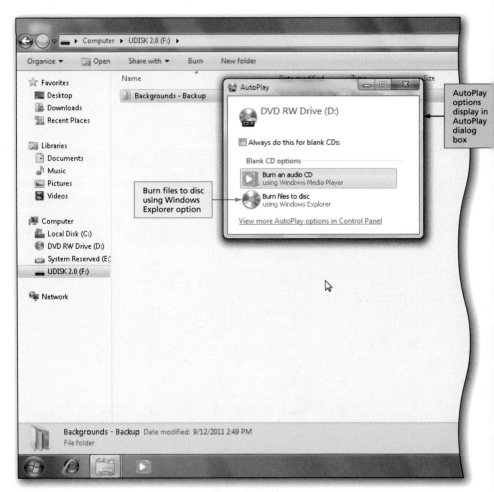

Figure 3–74

2

- Click the 'Burn files to disc using Windows Explorer' option to display the Burn a Disc dialog box.

- If necessary, click the 'Like a USB flash drive' option button to select it (Figure 3–75).

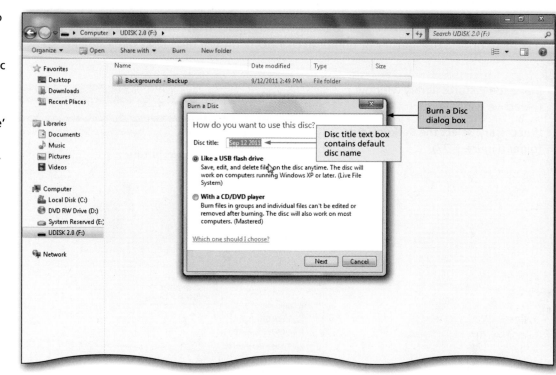

Figure 3–75

3

- Type Backup – Sep in the Disc title text box to provide a name for the disc (Figure 3–76).

- Click the Next button to format the disc. If the AutoPlay dialog box displays after the formatting is complete, click the Close button to close the AutoPlay dialog box.

Backgrounds - Backup   9/12/2011 2:49 PM   File folder

Burn a Disc

How do you want to use this disc?

Disc title: Backup - Sep ← *new name of disc*

○ **Like a USB flash drive**
 Save, edit, and delete files on the disc anytime. The disc will work on computers running Windows XP or later. (Live File System)

○ **With a CD/DVD player**
 Burn files in groups and individual files can't be edited or removed after burning. The disc will also work on most computers. (Mastered)

Which one should I choose?

Next button

[Next] [Cancel]

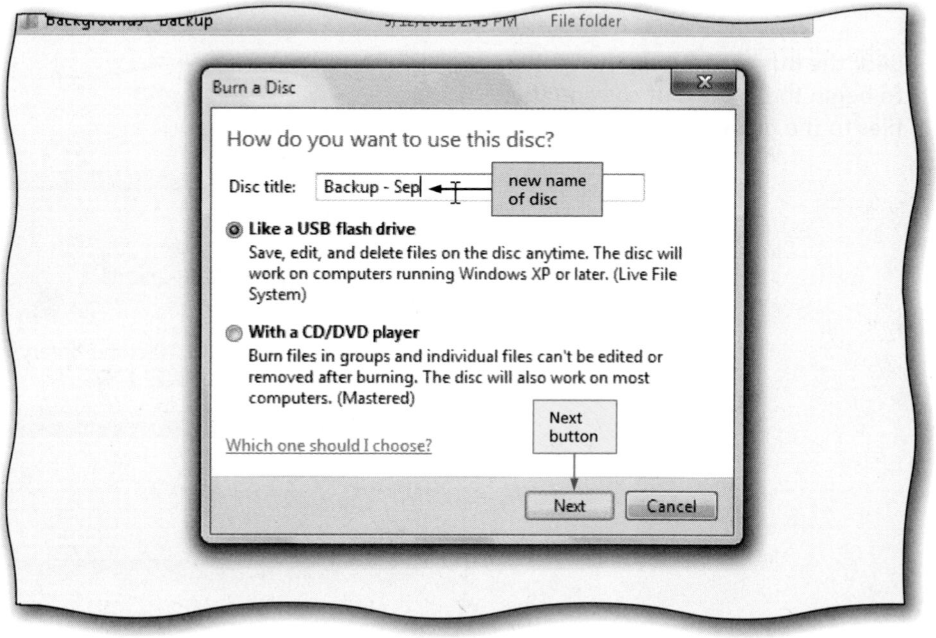

Figure 3–76

To Create a Backup on an Optical Disc

The following steps back up the Backgrounds folder from the Pictures library to the disc. If you do not have access to an optical disc burner or do not have a blank optical disc, read the following steps without performing them.

1
- Make the Pictures library window the active window.
- If necessary, select the Backgrounds folder (Figure 3–77).

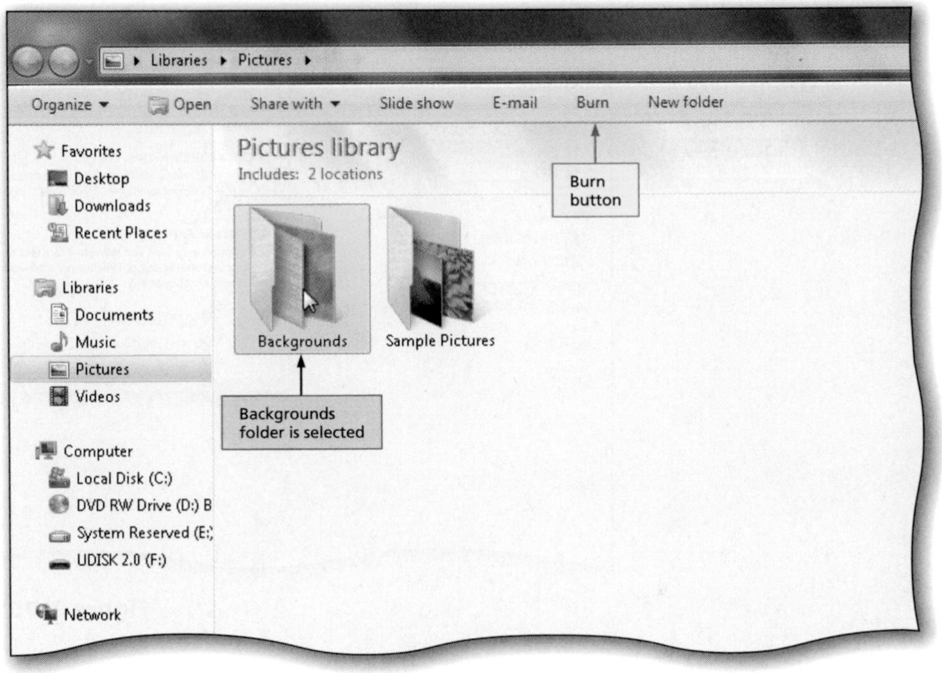

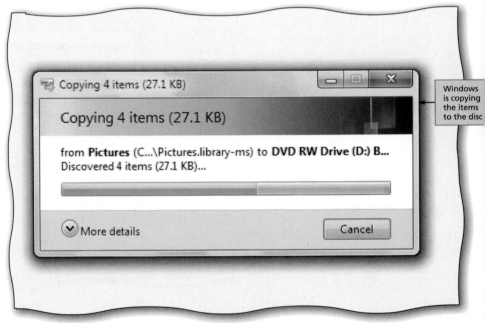

Figure 3–77

2
- Click the Burn button on the toolbar to begin the process of copying the files to the disc (Figure 3–78).

Figure 3–78

3

- Once the copy process has completed, the contents of the Backup – Sep disc appear in a new folder window (Figure 3–79).

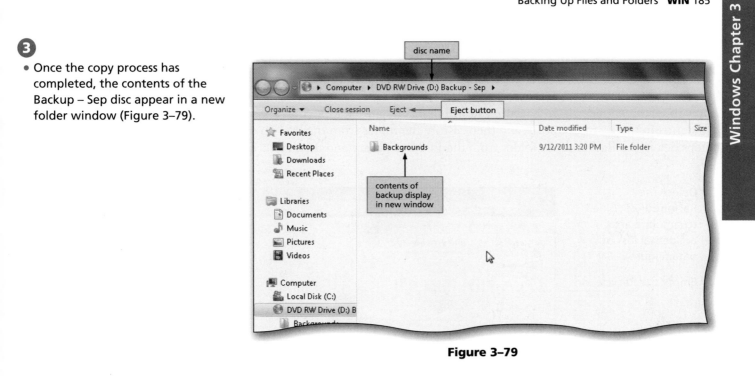

Figure 3–79

To Eject an Optical Disc

Now that the backup process is complete, the Backup - Sep folder is shown in a new folder window (Figure 3–79). You can continue to add files to this disc until you run out of storage space on the disc. Once you are ready to remove the disc, you eject it. Before the computer ejects the disc, it will be finalized. The following step ejects and finalizes the optical disc.

1

- Click the Eject button on the toolbar to have Windows 7 finalize and eject the CD (Figure 3–80).

- Remove the disc from computer's optical disc drive.

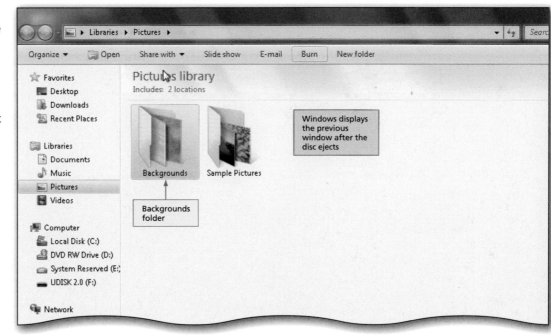

Figure 3–80

To Restore a Folder from a Backup

Whenever you need to restore a file or folder from a backup copy, you need to insert the removable media (where the backup copy was stored), and then you can copy the backup to the destination drive or folder. To learn how to restore a folder from backup, you will first simulate an accidental loss of data by deleting the Backgrounds folder from the Pictures library, and then restore the folder from the backup on your USB flash drive. The following steps delete the Backgrounds folder from the Pictures library and then restore it from your backup copy.

1

- Delete the Backgrounds folder to simulate an accidental loss of data (Figure 3–81).

- Empty the Recycle Bin.

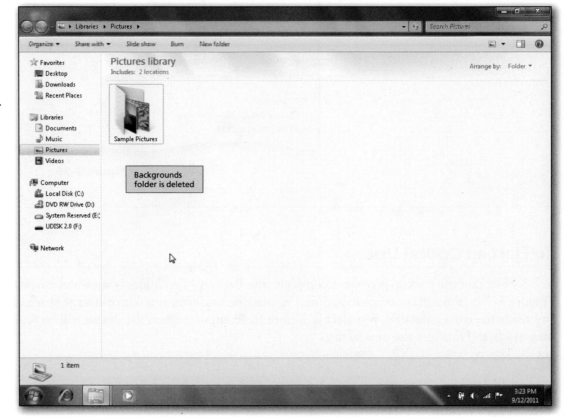

Figure 3–81

2

- Make the UDISK 2.0 (F:) window, or the window representing your USB flash drive, the active window.

- Copy the Backgrounds - Backup folder to place a copy on the Clipboard.

- Make the Pictures library window the active window.

- Paste the Backgrounds - Backup folder to place a copy in the Pictures library (Figure 3–82).

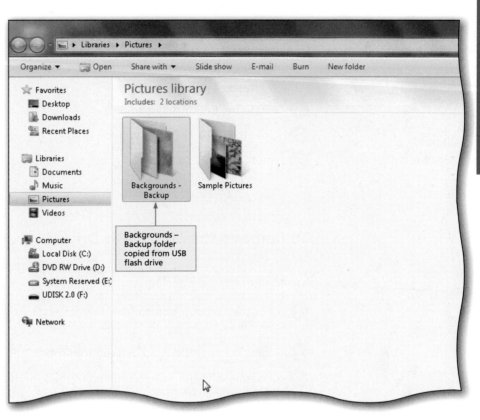

Figure 3–82

3

- Rename the folder Backgrounds to finish the restoration process (Figure 3–83).

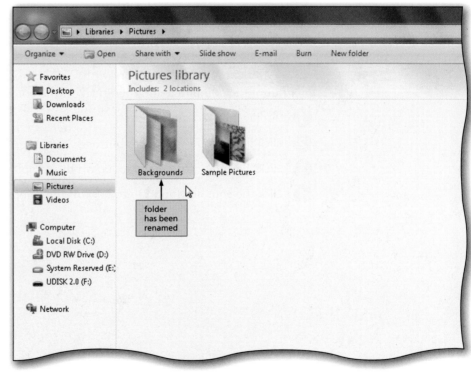

Figure 3–83

To Delete a Folder from the Pictures Library

You now have restored the Backgrounds folder after a mishap. This process would be the same if you were working from an optical disc backup. To return the Pictures library to its original state, you will delete the Backgrounds folder. The following steps delete the Backgrounds folder.

1 Delete the Backgrounds folder.

2 Close the Pictures library window.

3 Empty the Recycle Bin.

To Remove the USB Flash Drive

Now that you are done working with the USB flash drive, you should safely remove it. The following steps safely remove the USB flash drive.

1 Click the Computer button on the Address bar of the UDISK 2.0 (F:) window to display the Computer folder window.

2 Right click the UDISK 2.0 (F:) icon to display a shortcut menu.

3 Click the Safely Remove command to prepare the drive to be removed. If the Safely Remove command does not display on the shortcut menu, click the Eject command.

4 Remove the USB flash drive from your computer.

5 Close the Computer folder window.

To Log Off from and Turn Off the Computer

After completing your work with Windows 7, you should end your session by logging off of the computer, and then turn off the computer.

1 Display the Start menu.

2 Click the Shut down options button.

3 Click the Log off command to log off the computer.

4 Click the Shut down button to turn off the computer.

Chapter Summary

In this chapter, you learned about the Computer folder window. You learned how to view the properties of drives and folders, as well as how to view their content. You worked with files and folders in the Pictures library, reviewed and changed their properties, and viewed images in Windows Photo Viewer and as a slide show. As part of this process, you also learned how to copy and move files as well as how to create folders. Next, you saw how to work with files and folders in the Music library. You changed the genre of a music file and learned how to listen to a music file using the Windows Media Player. Finally, you gained knowledge of how to make a backup of files and restore the files, including how to copy, rename, and delete files and folders. The items listed below include all of the new Windows 7 skills you have learned in this chapter.

1. Display Properties for the Local Disk (C:) Drive in the Details Pane (WIN 136)
2. Display the Local Disk (C:) Properties Dialog Box (WIN 137)
3. Close the Local Disk (C:) Properties Dialog Box (WIN 138)
4. Switch Folders Using the Address Bar (WIN 139)
5. View the Contents of a Drive (WIN 141)
6. Preview the Properties for a Folder (WIN 142)
7. Display Properties for the Windows Folder in the Details Pane (WIN 142)
8. Display All of the Properties for the Windows Folder (WIN 143)
9. View the Contents of a Folder (WIN 144)
10. Search for a File and Folder in a Folder Window (WIN 145)
11. Search for Files Using Search Filters (WIN 146)
12. Clear the Search Box (WIN 147)
13. Use Aero Shake to Minimize and Restore All Windows Except the Active Window (WIN 148)
14. Cascade Open Windows (WIN 149)
15. Make a Window the Active Window (WIN 150)
16. Undo Cascading (WIN 151)
17. Stack Open Windows (WIN 152)
18. Undo Show Windows Stacked (WIN 153)
19. Show Windows Side by Side (WIN 154)
20. Undo Show Windows Side by Side (WIN 155)
21. View the Save Location for the Pictures Library (WIN 157)
22. Search for Pictures (WIN 158)
23. Copy Files to the Pictures Library (WIN 158)
24. Create a Folder in the Pictures Library (WIN 161)
25. Move Multiple Files into a Folder (WIN 163)
26. Refresh the Image on a Folder (WIN 164)
27. View and Change the Properties of a Picture (WIN 165)
28. Open a Picture in Windows Photo Viewer (WIN 168)
29. Navigate Through Your Pictures (WIN 168)
30. View Your Pictures as a Slide Show (WIN 170)
31. End a Slide Show (WIN 171)
32. Switch to the Music Library (WIN 172)
33. Open the Sample Music Folder (WIN 172)
34. View Information about a Music File (WIN 173)
35. Reset the Genre for a Music File (WIN 175)
36. Play a Music File in Windows Media Player (WIN 175)
37. Pause a Music File (WIN 176)
38. Create a Backup on a USB Flash Drive (WIN 178)
39. Rename a Folder (WIN 180)
40. Insert and Format an Optical Disc for Backup (WIN 182)
41. Create a Backup on an Optical Disc (WIN 184)
42. Eject an Optical Disc (WIN 185)
43. Restore a Folder from a Backup (WIN 186)

Learn It Online

Test your knowledge of chapter content and key terms.

Instructions: To complete the Learn It Online exercises, start your browser, click the Address bar, and then enter the Web address scsite.com/win7/learn. When the Windows 7 Learn It Online page is displayed, click the link for the exercise you want to complete and then read the instructions.

Chapter Reinforcement TF, MC, and SA
A series of true/false, multiple-choice, and short-answer questions that test your knowledge of the chapter content.

Flash Cards
An interactive learning environment where you identify chapter key terms associated with displayed definitions.

Practice Test
A series of multiple-choice questions that test your knowledge of chapter content and key terms.

Who Wants To Be a Computer Genius?
An interactive game that challenges your knowledge of chapter content in the style of a television quiz show.

Wheel of Terms
An interactive game that challenges your knowledge of chapter key terms in the style of the television show *Wheel of Fortune*.

Crossword Puzzle Challenge
A crossword puzzle that challenges your knowledge of key terms presented in the chapter.

Apply Your Knowledge

Reinforce the skills and apply the concepts you learned in this chapter.

File and Program Properties

Instructions: You want to demonstrate to a friend how to display the properties of an image, display the image using the Paint program instead of the Windows Photo Viewer program, and print the image. You also want to demonstrate how to display the properties of an application program.

Part 1: Displaying File Properties
1. Click the Start button and then click the Computer command.
2. Double-click the Local Disk (C:) icon. If necessary, click 'Show the contents of this folder' link.
3. Double-click the Windows icon. If necessary, click the 'Show the contents of this folder' link.
4. Search for the Penguins picture file. If the Penguins icon is not available on your computer, find the icon of another image file.
5. Right-click the Penguins icon. Click Properties on the shortcut menu. Answer the following questions about the Penguins file.
   a. What type of file is Penguins?

   _____

   b. What program is used to open the Penguins image?

   _____

   c. What is the path for the location of the Penguins file?

   _____

d. What is the size (in bytes) of the Penguins file?

_____

e. When was the file created?

_____

f. When was the file last modified?

_____

g. When was the file last accessed?

_____

Part 2: Using the Paint Program to Display an Image

1. Click the Change button in the Penguins Properties dialog box. Answer the following questions.

   a. What is the name of the dialog box that displays?

   _____

   b. Which program is used to open the Penguins file?

   _____

   c. List the other program(s) you can use to open the file.

   _____

2. Click the Paint icon in the Open with dialog box.
3. Click the OK button in the Open with dialog box.
4. Click the OK button in the Penguins Properties dialog box.
5. Double-click the Penguins icon to launch the Paint program and display the Penguins image in the Penguins – Paint window (Figure 3–84).

Figure 3–84

Continued >

Apply Your Knowledge *continued*

6. Print the Penguins image by clicking the Paint button on the menu bar, clicking the Print command, and then clicking the Print button in the Print dialog box.

7. Click the Close button in the Penguins – Paint window. Do not save the changes.

Part 3: Resetting the Program Selection in the Open with Dialog Box

1. Right-click the Penguins icon. Click Properties on the shortcut menu. Answer the following question.

   a. What program is used to open the Penguins image?

   _____

2. Click the Change button in the Penguins Properties dialog box.

3. If necessary, click the Windows Photo Viewer icon in the Open with dialog box to select the icon.

4. Click the OK button in the Open with dialog box.

5. Click the OK button in the Penguins Properties dialog box.

Part 4: Displaying Program Properties

1. Return to the Search Results in the Windows folder and clear the Search box.

2. Scroll the right pane of the Windows folder window until the HelpPane icon displays. If the HelpPane icon does not appear, scroll to display another file.

3. Right-click the icon. Click Properties on the shortcut menu. Answer the following questions.

   a. What type of file is selected?

   _____

   b. What is the file's description?

   _____

   c. What is the path of the file?

   _____

   d. What size is the file when stored on disk?

   _____

4. Click the Cancel button in the Properties dialog box.

5. Close the Windows window.

Extend Your Knowledge

Extend the skills you learned in this chapter and experiment with new skills. You might need to use Help to complete the assignment.

Creating a Picture

Instructions: You want to use Paint to design a Congratulations image for a friend and then print the message. The file name of the Paint program is paint, but you do not know the location of the program on the hard disk. You first will use Search to find the paint file on the hard disk.

Part 1: Searching for the Paint Program

1. Click the Start button.

2. Type paint in the Search box.

3. Click the Paint icon.

Part 2: Creating a Bitmap Image
1. Launch Paint and display the Untitled – Paint window (Figure 3–85).

2. Use the Pencil tool shown in Figure 3–85 to write the message Congratulations Graduate! in the Untitled – Paint window. *Hint:* Hold the left mouse button down to write and release the left mouse button to stop writing. If you make a mistake and want to start over, click the Undo button.

3. Click the Paint button on the menu bar and then click Save as. When the Save As dialog box displays, type Congratulations Graduate in the File name text box, click the Pictures library in the Navigation pane, and then click the Save button in the Save As dialog box to save the file in the Pictures library.

4. Close the Congratulations Graduate - Paint window.

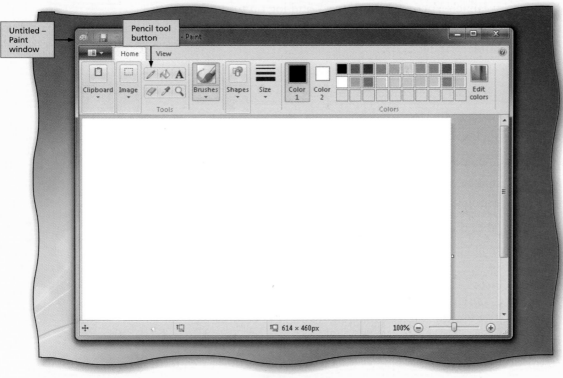

Figure 3–85

Part 3: Previewing and Printing the Congratulations Graduate Image
1. Open the Pictures library folder.

2. Click the Congratulations Graduate icon in the Pictures window to select the icon.

3. Click Preview on the toolbar.

4. After viewing the image in Windows Photo Viewer, click the Print button on the toolbar to view printing options.

5. Click Print to open the Print Pictures dialog box.

6. Click Print to print the image.

7. Close Windows Photo Viewer.

Part 4: Deleting the Congratulations Graduate Image
1. Click the Congratulations Graduate icon to select the file.

2. Click Organize on the toolbar, and then click Delete.

3. Click the Yes button in the Delete File dialog box.

4. Close the Pictures library window.

In the Lab

Use the guidelines, concepts, and skills presented in this chapter to increase your knowledge of Windows 7. Labs are listed in order of increasing difficulty.

Lab 1: Using Search to Find Picture Files

Instructions: You know that searching is an important feature of Windows 7. You decide to use the Search text box to find the images on the hard disk. You will store the files in a folder in the Pictures library, print the images, and copy them to a USB flash drive.

Part 1: Searching for Files in the Search Results Window

1. If necessary, launch Microsoft Windows 7 and log on to the computer.
2. Click the Start button on the taskbar and then click the Computer command. Maximize the Computer folder window.
3. Double-click Local Disk (C:), and then double-click the Windows folder to open it.
4. In the Search box, type Lighthouse as the entry.
5. Copy the image to the Pictures library using the Navigation pane.
6. If necessary, close all open windows.

Part 2: Searching for Files from Another Window

1. Click the Start button and then click the Pictures command.
2. Click the Search box.
3. Type Koala as the entry.
4. Copy the image to the Pictures library.
5. Close the Pictures library window.

Part 3: Searching for Groups of Files

1. Click the Start button and then click the Computer command.
2. Double-click Local Disk (C:), and then double-click the Windows folder to open it.
3. In the Search box of the Windows folder, type tu* as the search term (Figure 3–86).
4. Answer the following question.
    a. How many files were found?

    _____

5. Scroll to find the Tulips icon. Click the Tulips icon to select the icon. If the Tulips icon does not display, select another icon.
6. Copy the image to the Pictures library.

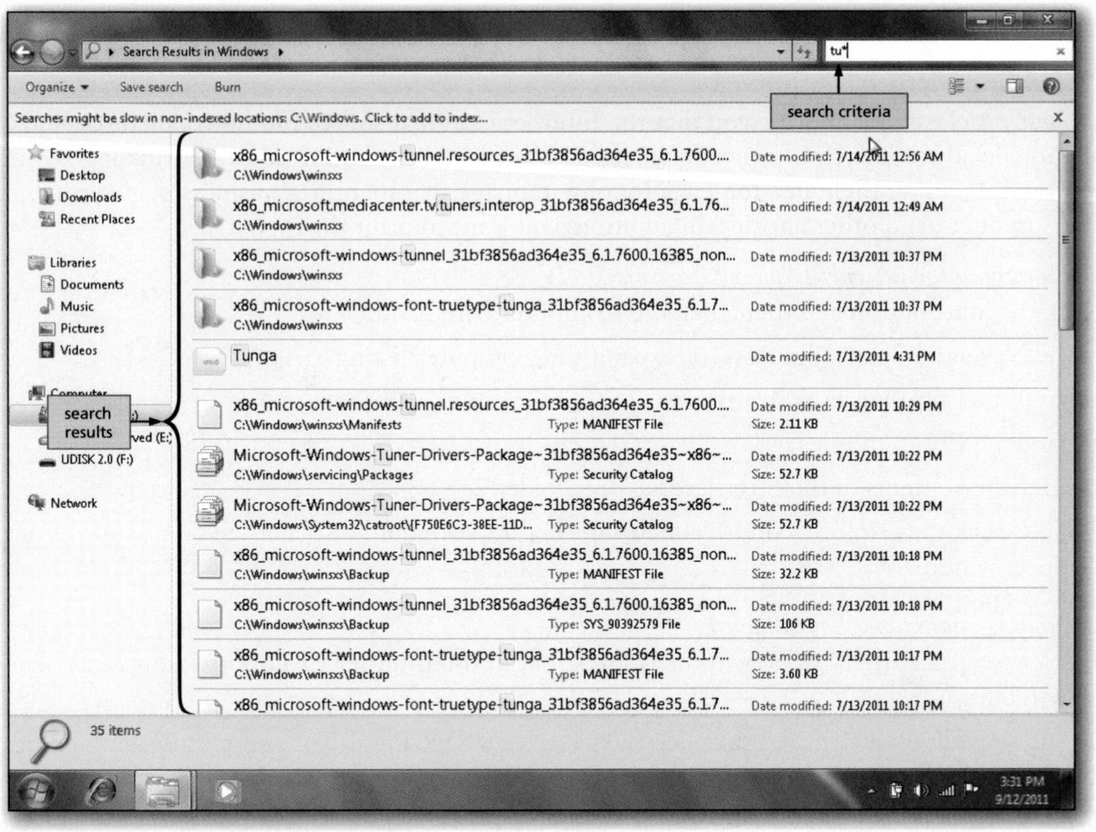

Figure 3–86

Part 4: Creating the More Backgrounds Folder in the Pictures Library

1. Click the New folder button, type More Backgrounds in the icon title text box and then press the ENTER key.

2. Select the icons of the images you copied to the Pictures library and then move the images to the More Backgrounds folder.

3. Right-click an open area of the window and refresh the thumbnail image on the More Backgrounds folder.

Part 5: Printing the Images

1. Open the More Backgrounds folder.

2. Select the pictures.

3. Click Print on the toolbar to display the Print Pictures dialog box.

4. Use the scroll bar to select the Wallet option.

5. Type 3 in the Copies of each picture text box.

6. Click the Print button to print the pictures.

Part 6: Moving the More Backgrounds Folder to a USB Flash Drive

1. Insert a USB flash drive into an available USB port and then click the 'Open folder to view files' command.

2. Switch to the Pictures window.

3. Select the More Backgrounds icon in the Pictures window.

4. Right-click the More Backgrounds icon.

5. Click Send to and then click USB flash drive.

6. Close the Pictures library.

7. Safely remove the USB flash drive from the computer.

Continued >

STUDENT ASSIGNMENTS

In the Lab *continued*

Lab 2: Finding Pictures Online

Instructions: A classmate informs you that the Internet is a great source of photos, pictures, and images. You decide to launch Internet Explorer, search for well-known candy and drink logos on the Internet, and then save them in a folder. A **logo** is an image that identifies businesses, government agencies, products, and other entities. In addition, you want to print the logos.

Part 1: Launching the Internet Explorer Program
1. Click the Start button and then click the Computer command.
2. In the Navigation pane, if necessary, expand the Computer listing.
3. Expand the Local Disk (C:) list.
4. Expand the Program Files list.
5. Display the contents of the Internet Explorer folder.
6. Double-click the iexplore icon to launch Internet Explorer and display the Windows Internet Explorer window.

Part 2: Finding and Saving Logo Images
1. Type www.jellybelly.com in the Address bar in the Internet Explorer window, and then click the Go button.
2. Locate the Jelly Belly icon. Right-click the icon, click Save Picture As on the shortcut menu, and then click the Save button to save the logo in the Pictures library.
3. Type www.smarties.com in the Address bar and then click the Go button. Locate the Smarties picture that matches the one in Figure 3–87 and use the file name, Smarties logo, to save the Smarties logo in the Pictures library.

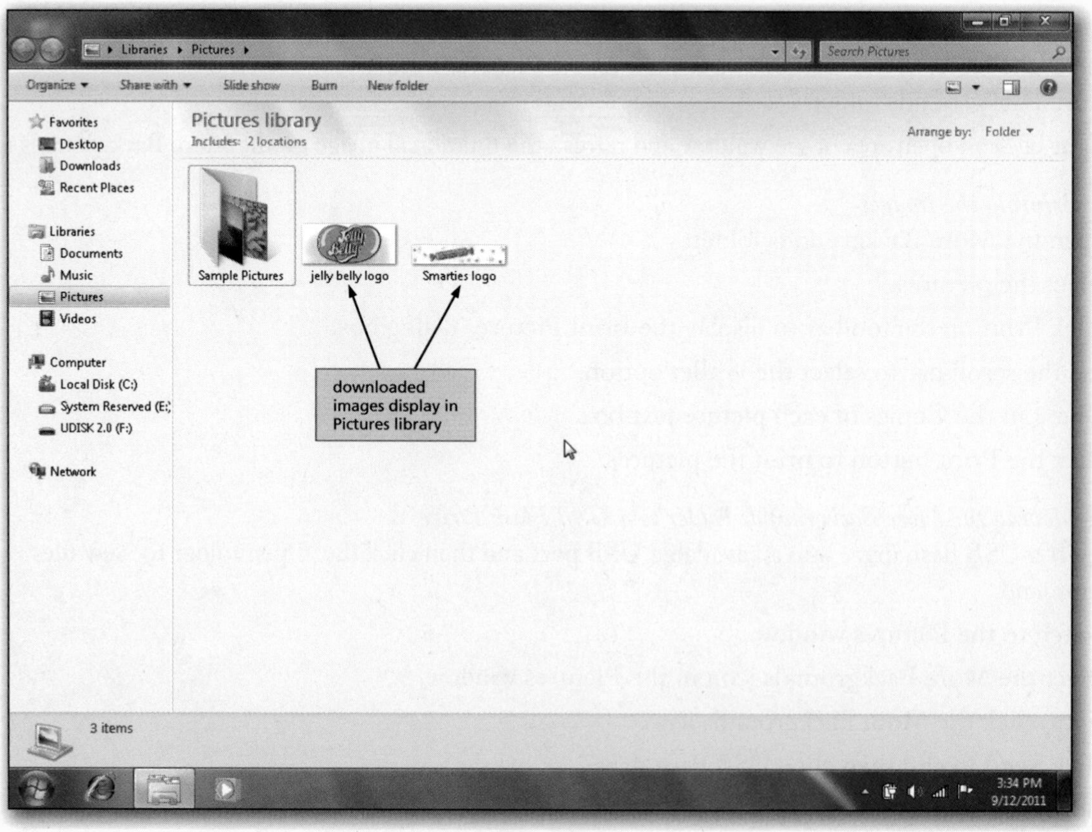

Figure 3–87

4. Close Internet Explorer and close the Internet Explorer folder window.

5. Click the Start button and then click Pictures. The Jelly Belly logo and Smarties image display in the Pictures window (Figure 3–87). The logos in the Pictures library window on your computer might be different from the logos shown in Figure 3–87 if the businesses have changed their logos.

Part 3: Displaying File Properties
1. Right-click each logo file in the Pictures library, click Properties, answer the following question about the logo, and then close the Properties dialog box.

   a. What type of file is the Jelly Belly logo file?

   _____

   b. What type of file is the Smarties logo file?

   _____

2. Click an open area of the Pictures library to deselect the Smarties logo file.

Part 4: Creating the Candy Logos Folder in the Pictures Library
1. Make a new folder in the Pictures library, type Candy Logos in the icon title text box, and then press the ENTER key.

2. Click the Jelly Belly logo, hold down the CTRL key, and then click the Smarties logo.

3. Right-drag the icons to the Candy Logos icon and then click Move here on the shortcut menu.

4. Refresh the image on the Candy Logos folder.

Part 5: Printing the Logo Images
1. Open the Candy Logos folder.

2. Select both of the logos.

3. Click Print on the toolbar to display the Print Pictures dialog box. Choose the option for printing both logos on a single page.

4. Click the Print button to print the pictures.

Part 6: Moving the Candy Logos Folder to a USB Flash Drive
1. Insert a USB flash drive into an available USB port.

2. Copy the Candy Logos folder to the USB flash drive.

3. Safely remove the USB flash drive from the computer.

4. Delete the Candy Logos folder from the Pictures library.

5. Close the Pictures library.

Lab 3: Managing Your Music

Instructions: You want to investigate the different ways you can organize the music stored on your computer. Once you determine which method of organizing your music you prefer, you decide that you want to add to your music collection. First you will learn about the copyright laws that pertain to digital music and then you will research a few Web sites that allow you to download music files.

Part 1: Organizing Your Music
1. Open the Start menu and then open the Music library. Open the Sample Music folder and answer the following questions.

   a. How many files are there?

   _____

   b. To which album does Sleep Away belong?

   _____

Continued >

c. Which song is the longest running? (*Hint:* Play in Windows Media Player.)

_____

Part 2: Researching Copyright Laws Regarding Digital Music Files
1. Click the Internet Explorer icon on the taskbar. Type `www.copyright.gov` in the Address bar and then press the ENTER key.

   a. What copyright laws exist concerning music files?

   _____

   b. What should you know before downloading music files?

   _____

   c. What are the legal ramifications of downloading and sharing illegal music files?

   _____

Part 3: Finding Music Online
1. Type `www.netmusic.com` in the Address bar and press the ENTER key.

   a. What types of music can be downloaded from this Web site?

   _____

   b. What are the fees?

   _____

   c. Are there any free, legal downloads available?

   _____

   d. Would you use this service?

   _____

2. Type `rhapsody.com` in the Address bar of Internet Explorer and press the ENTER key. (Figure 3–88).

   a. What program do you need to download music from this Web site?

   _____

   b. What are the fees for using the program? for shopping?

   _____

   c. How are music files downloaded from within the program?

   _____

   d. Would you use this service?

   _____

Figure 3–88

3. Type www.apple.com/itunes in the Address bar of Internet Explorer and press the ENTER key. Click the learn how to get started link.

a. What program do you need to download music from this Web site?

_____

b. What are the fees for using the program? for shopping?

_____

c. How are music files downloaded from within the program?

_____

d. Would you use this service?

_____

Cases and Places

Apply your creative thinking and problem-solving skills to design and implement a solution.

• EASIER   •• MORE DIFFICULT

• 1 Finding Programs

You are interested in identifying which programs are installed on your computer. To find all the programs, you decide to search the Program Files folder on your computer. Using techniques you learned in this chapter, open the Program Files folder on the C drive. Search for *.exe files. Summarize your findings in a brief report. Be sure to indicate the number of programs you found.

• 2 Filter Searching

Your employer suspects that someone has used your computer during off-hours for non–company business. She has asked you to search your computer for files that have been created or modified during the last week. Search for files in the Windows 7 libraries using the Date modified filter. When you find the files, determine if any are WordPad files or Paint files that you did not create or modify. Summarize the number and date they were created or modified in a brief report.

•• 3 Researching Backups

Backing up files is an important way to protect data and ensure that it is not lost or destroyed accidentally. You can use a variety of devices and techniques to back up files from a personal computer. Using Windows Help and Support, research the Backup and Restore. Determine what backup tools Windows 7 provides. Write a brief report of your findings.

•• 4 Researching Photo Printing Sites

Make It Personal

Now that you know how to work with the Pictures library, you want to find Web sites where you can upload and print your photos. Using the Internet, search for three photo printing Web sites. Find the prices per 4 x 6 photo, which file formats are required, and explore any other photo products that you would be interested in purchasing. Write a brief report that compares the three Web sites and indicate which one you would use.

•• 5 Researching Data Security

Working Together

Data stored on disk is one of a company's most valuable assets. If that data were to be stolen, lost, or compromised so that it could not be accessed, the company could go out of business. Therefore, companies go to great lengths to protect their data. Working with classmates, research how the companies where you each work handle their backups. Find out how each one protects its data against viruses, unauthorized access, and even against natural disasters such as fire and floods. Prepare a brief report that describes the companies' procedures. In your report, point out any areas where you find a company has not protected its data adequately.

Appendix A
Comparison of the New Features of Windows 7 Editions

The Microsoft Windows 7 operating system is available in a variety of editions. The six editions that you most likely will encounter are Windows 7 Starter, Windows 7 Home Basic, Windows 7 Home Premium, Windows 7 Professional, Windows 7 Enterprise, and Windows 7 Ultimate. Because not all computers have the same hardware or are used for the same functions, Microsoft provides these various editions so that each user can have the edition that meets his or her needs. Table A–1 compares features in the various editions. Windows 7 Ultimate, the most complete version of Windows 7, is used as a baseline for clarifying the features of the other editions. Windows 7 Starter and Windows 7 Home Basic are not included in this table as they are more limited in their offerings.

Table A–1 Comparison of Windows 7 Editions

Ultimate Features	Home Premium	Professional	Enterprise
64-bit Support	✓	✓	✓
Action Center	✓	✓	✓
Aero Peek	✓	✓	✓
Aero Shake	✓	✓	✓
Backup and Restore	✓	✓	✓
BitLocker			✓
DirectX 11	✓	✓	✓
Domain Join		✓	✓
HomeGroup	✓	✓	✓
Internet Explorer 8	✓	✓	✓
Jump Lists	✓	✓	✓
Libraries	✓	✓	✓
Location Aware Printing		✓	✓
Maximum RAM (32-bit)	4 GB	4 GB	4 GB
Maximum RAM (64-bit)	16 GB	192 GB	192 GB
Minimum RAM (32-bit)	1 GB	1 GB	1 GB
Minimum RAM (64-bit)	2 GB	2 GB	2 GB
Multiplayer Games	✓	✓	✓

Table A–1 Comparison of Windows 7 Editions *(continued)*

Ultimate Features	Home Premium	Professional	Enterprise
Parental Controls	✓	✓	✓
Pin	✓	✓	✓
Play To	✓	✓	✓
Power Management	✓	✓	✓
ReadyBoost	✓	✓	✓
Remote Media Streaming	✓	✓	✓
Sleep and Resume	✓	✓	✓
Snap	✓	✓	✓
Sticky Notes	✓	✓	✓
Supports 35 Languages			✓
System Restore	✓	✓	✓
Tablet PC	✓	✓	✓
User Account Control	✓	✓	✓
View Available Networks	✓	✓	✓
Windows Connect Now	✓	✓	✓
Windows Defender	✓	✓	✓
Windows Easy Transfer	✓	✓	✓
Windows Experience Index	✓	✓	✓
Windows Fax and Scan	✓	✓	✓
Windows Firewall	✓	✓	✓
Windows Media Center	✓	✓	✓
Windows Media Player 12	✓	✓	✓
Windows Search	✓	✓	✓
Windows Taskbar	✓	✓	✓
Windows Touch	✓	✓	✓
Windows Troubleshooting	✓	✓	✓
Windows Update	✓	✓	✓
Windows XP Mode		✓	✓
WordPad	✓	✓	✓
XPS	✓	✓	✓

Appendix B
Windows 7 Security

Windows 7 Security Features

According to Microsoft, Windows 7 has been engineered to be the most secure version of Windows ever. It includes a number of updated security features that help you accomplish three important goals: to enjoy a computer free from malware, including viruses, worms, spyware, and other potentially unwanted software; to have a safer online experience; and to understand when a computer is vulnerable and how to protect it from external threats.

Malware, short for malicious software, are computer programs designed to harm your computer, whether displaying inappropriate Web sites to facilitating identity theft. Examples of malware include viruses, worms, and spyware. A **virus** is a program that attaches itself to another program or file so that it can spread from computer to computer, infecting programs and files as it spreads. Viruses can damage computer software, computer hardware, and files. A computer **worm** copies itself from one computer to another by taking advantage of the features that transport data and information between computers. A worm is dangerous because it has the ability to travel without being detected and to replicate itself in great volume. For example, if a worm copies itself to every person in your e-mail address book and then the worm copies itself to the names of all the e-mail addresses of each of your friends' computers, the effect could result in increased Internet traffic that slows down business networks and the Internet. **Spyware** is a program that is installed on your computer that monitors the activity that takes place to gather personal information and send it secretly to its creator. Spyware also can be designed to take control of the infected computer.

A **hacker** is an individual who uses his or her expertise to gain unauthorized access to a computer with the intention of learning more about the computer or examining the contents of the computer without the owner's permission.

To Display the Windows Action Center

The **Action Center** can help you to manage your computer's security by monitoring the status of several essential security features on your computer, including firewall settings, automatic updating, virus protection, spyware and unwanted software protection, Internet security settings, User Account Control settings, and Network Access Protection. The following steps display the Action Center.

1
- Click the Start button on the taskbar to display the Start menu (Figure B–1).

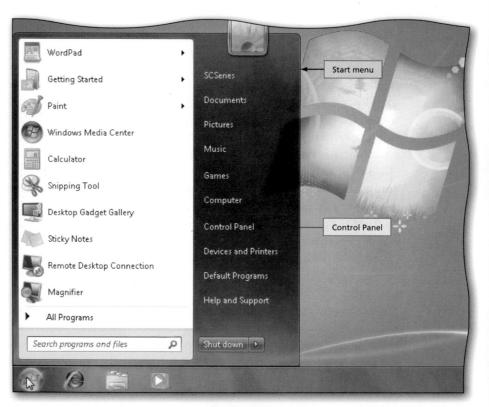

Figure B–1

2
- Click the Control Panel command to open the Control Panel (Figure B–2).

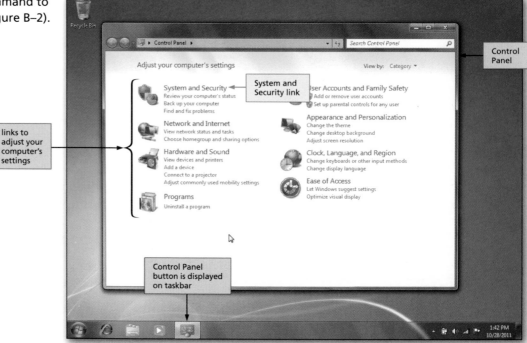

Figure B–2

• Click the System and Security link to display the System and Security window (Figure B–3).

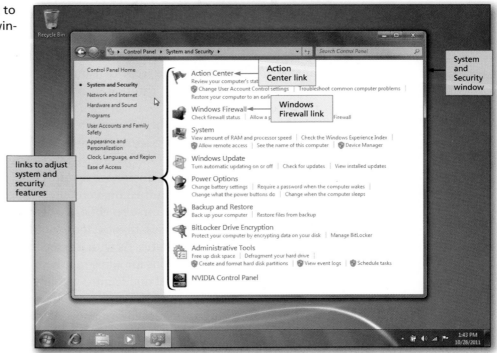

Figure B–3

• Click the Action Center link in the right pane of the System and Security window to display the Action Center (Figure B–4).

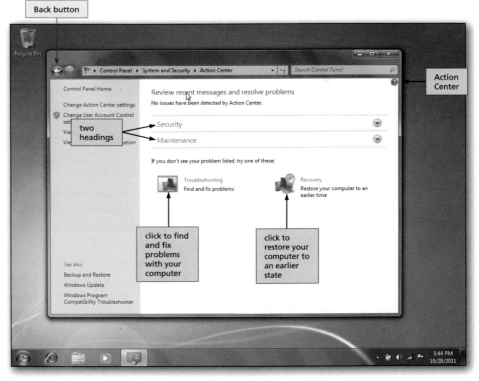

Figure B–4

Understanding the Action Center

The right pane displays options to let you review messages and resolve problems. There are two expandable sections. The first is the Security section. Clicking the arrow to the right of the Security heading expands the section and displays security features. "On" and "OK" mean that the security feature is turned on and working properly. "Off" means that the security feature is turned off and you should turn it on, if appropriate. For features that have settings you can change, you will see options for adjusting them.

The second section is the Maintenance section, which allows you to view maintenance features. Similar to the Security section, "On" means that the maintenance feature is turned on and working, and "Off" means that the feature is turned off and you should turn it on, if appropriate. Not all maintenance features have the same options. For example, if troubleshooting features are turned on, you only will see the message "No action needed." For some of the features, you can also choose whether you want to monitor the messages that pop up when an issue arises. If you choose not to monitor a feature, you will see a "Currently not monitored" status. As with the security features, if there are settings you can change, you will see options for adjusting them.

In the left pane of the Action Center window are links to Control Panel Home, Change Action Center settings, Change User Account Control settings, View archived messages, and View performance information. At the bottom of the left pane are links to related areas of the Control Panel that you might want to visit.

Managing Windows Firewall

Windows Firewall is a program that protects your computer from unauthorized users by monitoring and restricting data that travels between your computer and a network or the Internet. Windows Firewall also helps to block, but does not always prevent, computer viruses and worms from infecting your computer. Windows Firewall automatically is turned on when Windows 7 is launched. It is recommended that Windows Firewall remain on, unless you have another firewall program actively protecting your computer.

To Open Windows Firewall

From the Windows Firewall window's right pane, you can monitor and manage the firewall settings for any network to which you are connected. Connected networks normally are classified as home, work, and public networks. Home and work networks are considered private networks and have settings that are different from public networks that are not considered to be as secure.

From the left pane, you can allow programs or features through Windows Firewall, change notification settings, turn Windows Firewall off, restore default settings, adjust advanced settings, and troubleshoot your network. Windows Firewall is set up with the most secure settings by default, according to Microsoft. The following step opens Windows Firewall.

1

- Click the Back button in the Action Center window to return to the System and Security window.

- Click the Windows Firewall link to display the Windows Firewall window (Figure B–5).

Q&A

Why does my window show a different network?

You can connect to different types of networks. The type of network connection you have will determine whether your home or a public network is displayed.

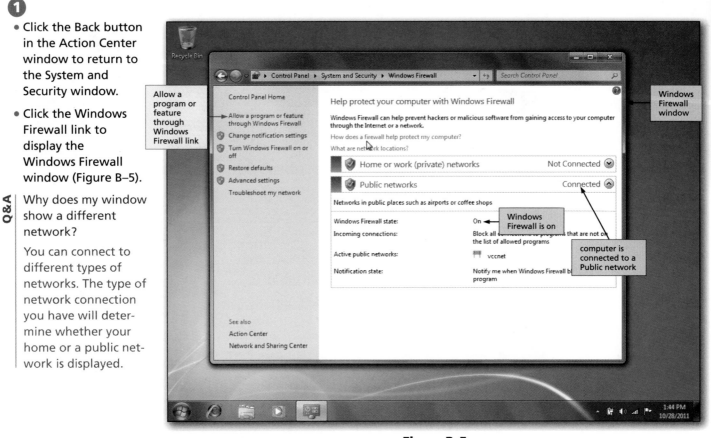

Figure B–5

To Allow a Feature Through the Firewall

You can adjust Windows Firewall settings as needed. For example, if you have a program or feature that you want to allow to communicate through the firewall, you can allow it using the 'Allow a program or feature through Windows Firewall' link. Caution should be used as each program or feature allowed through the firewall carries the risk of making your computer less secure; that is, the computer becomes easier to access and more vulnerable to attacks by hackers. The more programs and features you allow, the more vulnerable is the computer. To decrease the risk of security problems, only allow programs or features that are necessary and recognizable, and promptly remove any program or feature that no longer is required.

One feature that is sometimes allowed for home and work networks is File and Printer Sharing. This feature allows other computers access to files and printers that you choose to share with the network. The steps on the following pages allow File and Printer Sharing through the firewall for home and work networks only.

1

- Click the Allow a program or feature through Windows Firewall link to display the Allowed Programs window (Figure B–6).

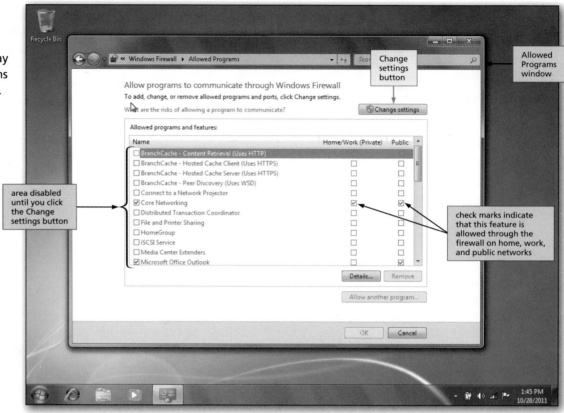

Figure B–6

2

- Click the Change settings button to enable the 'Allowed programs and features' area (Figure B–7).

Figure B–7

3

• Click the Home/Work (Private) check box for File and Printer Sharing to allow the feature through the firewall (Figure B–8).

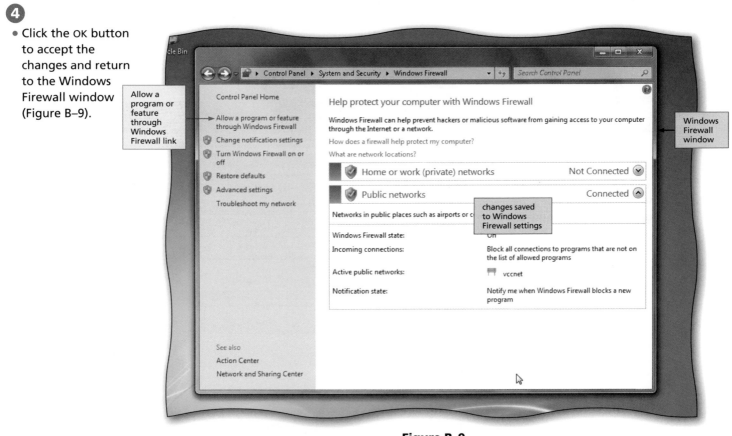

Figure B–8

4

• Click the OK button to accept the changes and return to the Windows Firewall window (Figure B–9).

Figure B–9

To Disallow a Feature Through the Firewall

If you later decide that you do not want to allow a program or feature through the Windows Firewall, you should disallow it. The following steps disallow File and Printer Sharing through the firewall for Home/Work networks only.

1

- Click the Allow a program or feature through Windows Firewall link to display the Allowed Programs window (Figure B–10).

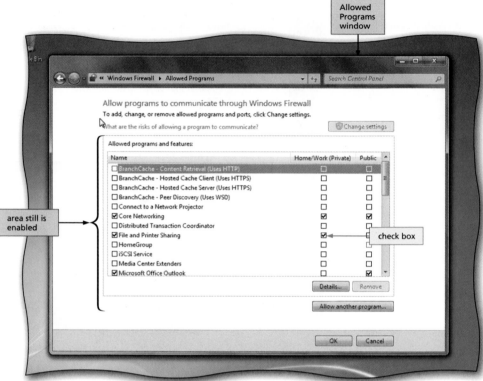

Figure B–10

2

- If necessary, click the Change settings button to enable the 'Allowed programs and features' area.

- Click the Home/Work (Private) check box for File and Printer Sharing to disallow the feature through the firewall (Figure B–11).

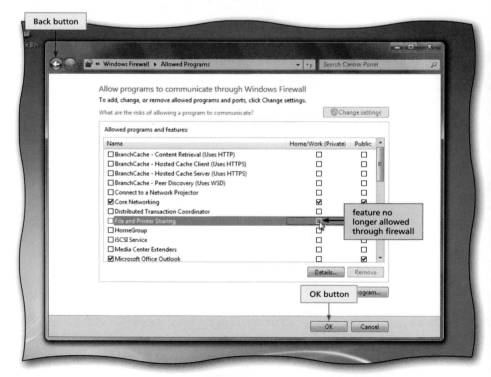

Figure B–11

3

- Click the OK button to accept the changes and return to the Windows Firewall window (Figure B–12).

Figure B–12

Windows Update

Windows Update helps to protect your computer from viruses, worms, and other security risks. When Windows Update is turned on and the computer is connected to the Internet, Windows 7 periodically checks with Microsoft to find updates for your computer, and then automatically downloads them. If the Internet connection is lost while downloading an update, Windows 7 resumes downloading when the Internet connection becomes available.

To Set an Automatic Update

You want to make sure that Windows Update runs once each week, so you decide to set it to run on a specific day and at a specific time. Once you set the day and time, Windows 7 will check with Microsoft to find updates, automatically download any available updates, and install them at the specified day and time. The followings steps configure an automatic update for a day (Friday) and time (6:00 AM).

1

- Click the Back button to return to the System and Security window.

- Click the Windows Update link in the System and Security window to display the Windows Update window (Figure B–13).

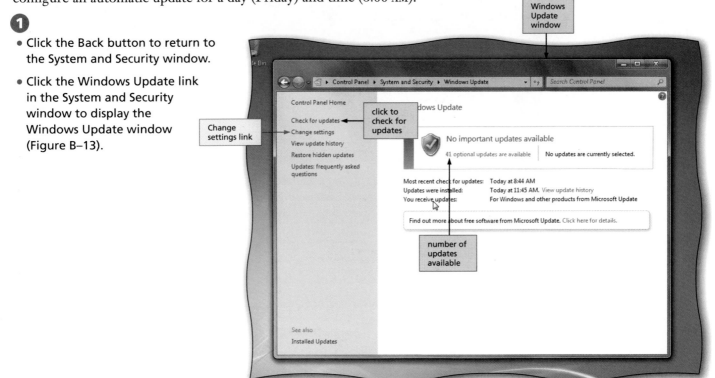

Figure B–13

2

- Click the Change settings link to display the Change settings window (Figure B–14).

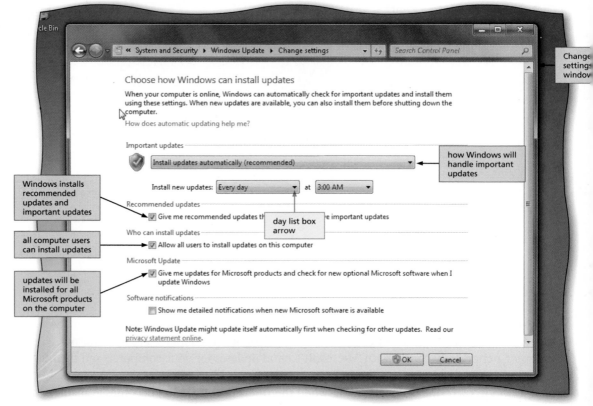

Figure B–14

3

- Click the day list box arrow to display a list of day options (Figure B–15).

Figure B–15

4

- Click the Every Friday list item to set the day to Every Friday.
- Click the time list box arrow to show the list of time options (Figure B–16).

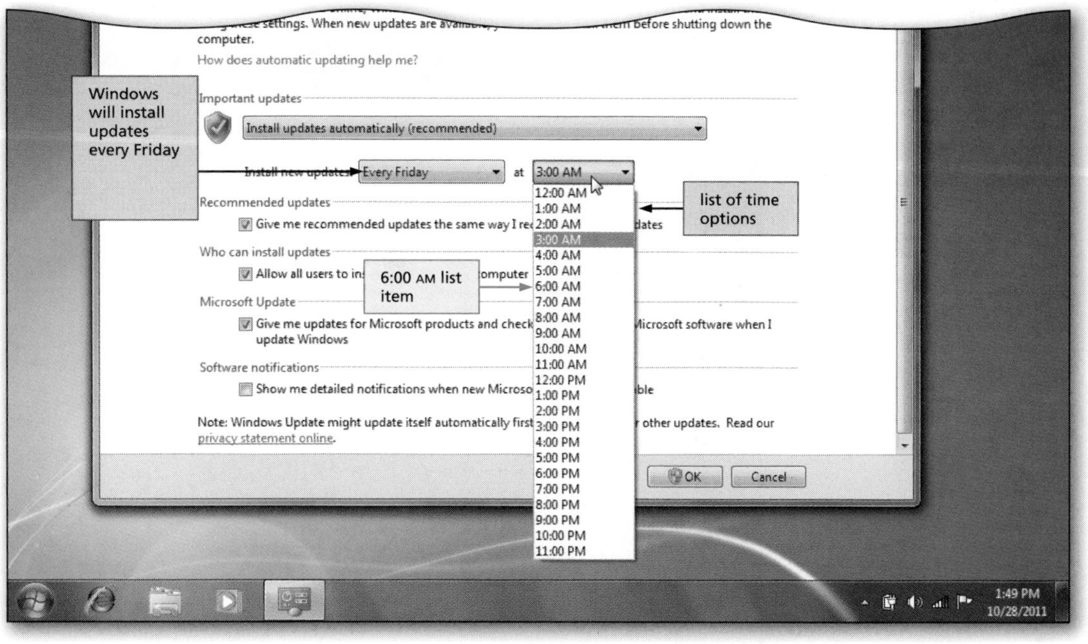

Windows will install updates every Friday

list of time options

6:00 AM list item

Figure B–16

5

- Click the 6:00 AM list item in the time list box to set the time to 6:00 AM (Figure B–17).

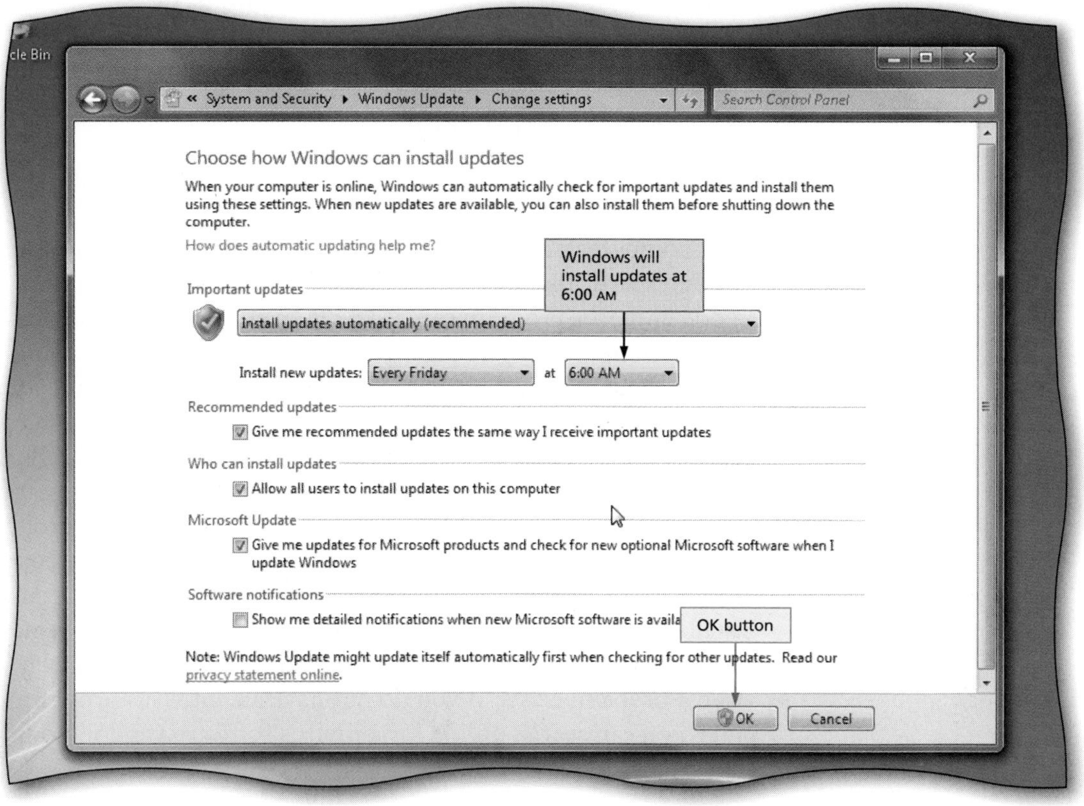

Windows will install updates at 6:00 AM

OK button

Figure B–17

6

- Click the OK button in the Windows Update window to save the changes and return to the Windows Update window (Figure B–18).

7

- Close the Windows Update window.

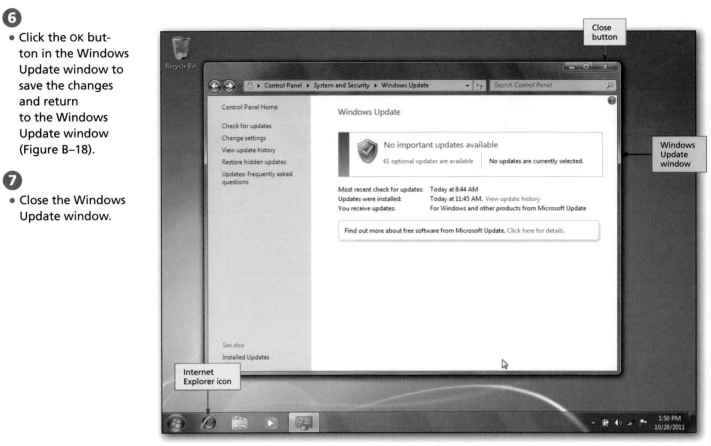

Figure B–18

Protecting Against Computer Viruses

Most computer magazines, daily newspapers, and even the nightly news channels warn of computer virus threats. Although these threats sound alarming, a little common sense and a good antivirus program can ward off even the most malicious viruses.

A computer can be protected against viruses by following these suggestions. First, educate yourself about viruses and how they spread. Downloading a program from the Internet, accessing a Web site, or receiving an e-mail message can cause a virus to infect your computer. Second, learn the common signs of a virus. Observe any unusual messages that appear on the computer screen, monitor system performance, and watch for missing files and inaccessible hard disks. Third, recognize that programs on removable media might contain viruses, and scan all removable media before copying or opening files.

Finally, Windows 7 does not include an antivirus program. You should purchase and install the latest version of an antivirus program and use it regularly to check for computer viruses. Many antivirus programs run automatically and display a dialog box on the screen when a problem exists. If you do not have an antivirus program installed on your computer, you can search online for antivirus software vendors to find a program that meets your needs.

To Search for Antivirus Software Vendors

The following steps go online to display a list of Microsoft-approved consumer security providers.

1
- Click the Internet Explorer icon on the taskbar to open Internet Explorer (Figure B–19).

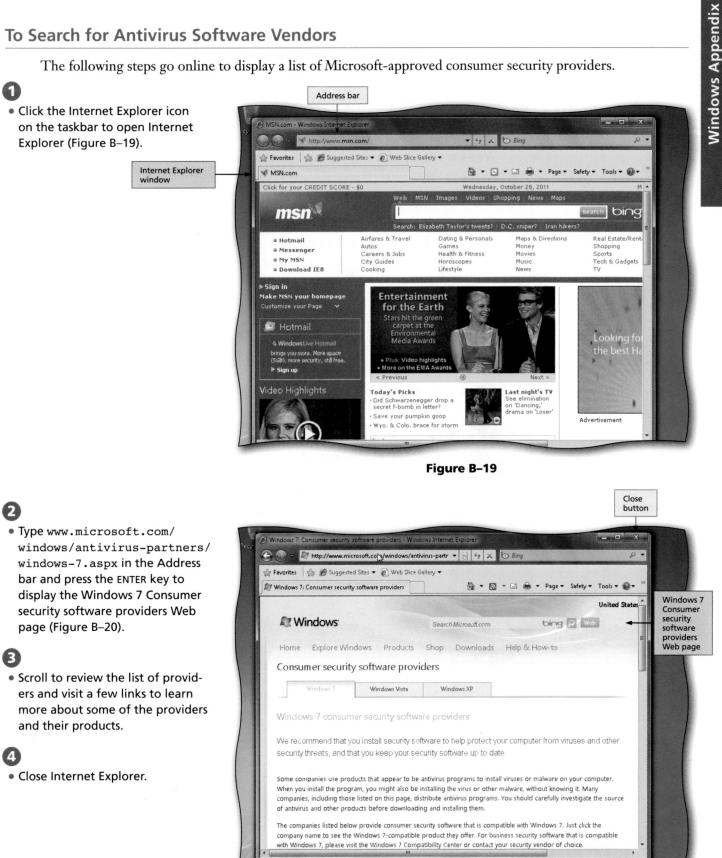

Figure B–19

2
- Type www.microsoft.com/ windows/antivirus-partners/ windows-7.aspx in the Address bar and press the ENTER key to display the Windows 7 Consumer security software providers Web page (Figure B–20).

3
- Scroll to review the list of providers and visit a few links to learn more about some of the providers and their products.

4
- Close Internet Explorer.

Figure B–20

Protecting Against Malware

It is important to run anti-malware software whenever you are using your computer. Malware and other unwanted software can attempt to install itself on your computer any time you connect to the Internet. It also can infect your computer when you install some programs using an optical disc or other removable media. Potentially unwanted or malicious software also can be programmed to run at unexpected times, not just when it is installed.

Windows Defender is installed with Windows 7. Windows Defender uses definitions similar to those used by antivirus programs. A **definition** is a rule for Windows Defender that identifies what programs are malware and how to deal with them. Windows Defender scans your computer regularly to find and remove malware.

To keep up with new malware developments, Windows Defender uses Windows Update to regularly check for definition updates. This helps you to ensure that your computer can handle new threats. It is recommended to allow Windows Defender to run using the default actions. Windows Defender is not a replacement for antivirus software; it is important that in addition to using Windows Defender, you also have current antivirus software installed.

To View the Windows Defender Settings for Automatic Scanning

The following steps display the automatic scanning settings in Windows Defender.

1

- Display the Start menu.

- Type windows defender in the Search box.

- Click the Windows Defender link to open Windows Defender (Figure B–21).

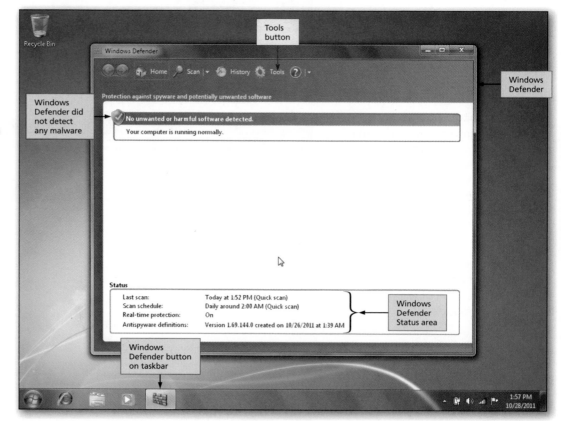

Figure B–21

2

- Click the Tools button on the toolbar to display the Windows Defender Tools and Settings (Figure B–22).

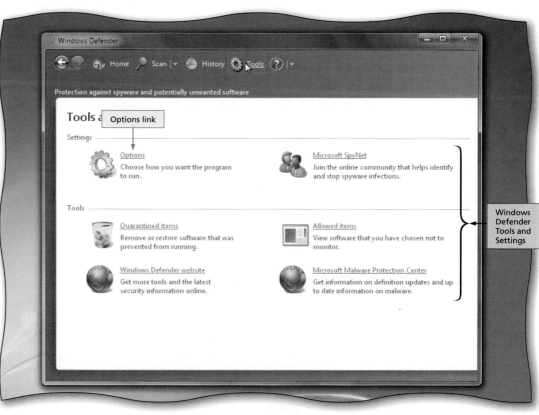

Figure B–22

3

- Click the Options link to view the Windows Defender settings for Automatic scanning (Figure B–23).

- Close the Windows Defender window.

Figure B–23

Security Settings in Internet Explorer

In addition to the security features shown earlier in this appendix, you can configure the security features of Internet Explorer. These security features protect the computer while you browse the Internet or send and receive e-mail messages. The Internet Explorer security settings protect the computer, the computer's contents, and the computer's privacy by blocking viruses and other security threats on the Internet.

To View Pop-Up Settings

One security feature in Internet Explorer is the Pop-up Blocker. **Pop-up Blocker** prevents annoying **pop-up windows**, also referred to as **pop-ups**, from appearing while you view a Web page. Pop-up windows typically advertise products or services. They can be difficult to close, often interrupt what you are doing, and can download spyware, which secretly gathers information about you and your computer, and sends the information to advertisers and other individuals.

By default, Pop-up Blocker is turned on by Internet Explorer and set to a Medium setting, which blocks most pop-up windows. Pop-up Blocker also plays a sound and displays an Information Bar in Internet Explorer when a pop-up window is blocked.

In the Pop-up Blocker Settings dialog box, if you want to allow certain Web sites to display pop-up windows when you visit the site, you can add the site's Web address to the list of allowed sites. Internet Explorer adds the Web site to the Allowed sites list. The following steps display the Pop-up Blocker settings in Internet Explorer.

①

- Open Internet Explorer.
- Click the Tools button on the Command bar to display the Tools menu (Figure B–24).

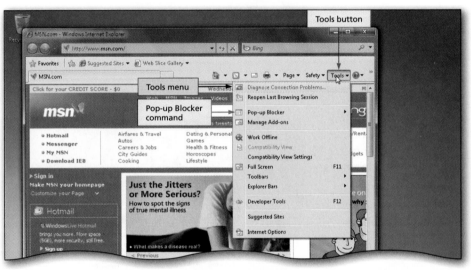

Figure B–24

②

- Point to the Pop-up Blocker command to display the Pop-up Blocker submenu (Figure B–25).

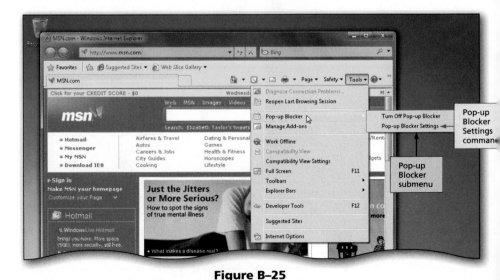

Figure B–25

3

- Click Pop-up Blocker Settings to display the Pop-up Blocker Settings dialog box (Figure B–26).

Q&A How do I block all pop-ups?

If you want to block all pop-ups, click the Blocking level list box arrow, and then click High: Block all pop-ups in the Blocking level list box. If you want to allow more pop-ups, click the Blocking level box arrow, and then click Low: Allow pop-ups from secure sites in the Blocking level list box.

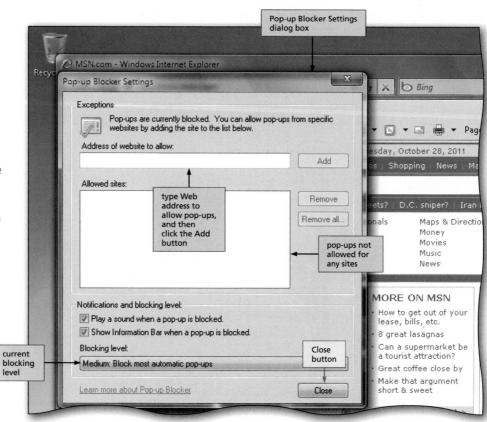

Figure B–26

4

- After viewing the Pop-up Blocker Settings dialog box, close the Pop-up Blocker Settings dialog box (Figure B–27).

Figure B–27

To View Internet Explorer Add-On Settings

Internet Explorer **add-ons** add functionality to Internet Explorer by allowing different toolbars, animated mouse pointers, and stock tickers. Although some add-ons are included with Windows 7, thousands are available from Web sites on the Internet. Most Web site add-ons require permission before downloading the add-on, whereas others are downloaded without your knowledge, and some add-ons do not need permission at all.

Add-ons usually are safe to use, but some might slow down your computer or shut down Internet Explorer unexpectedly. This usually happens when an add-on is poorly built or created for an earlier version of Internet Explorer. In some cases, spyware is included with an add-on and might track your Web browsing habits. The Manage Add-ons window allows you to display add-ons that have been used by Internet Explorer or that run without permission, enable or disable add-ons, and remove downloaded ActiveX controls.

The following steps illustrate how to view the Add-on settings.

1
- Click the Tools button to display the Tools menu.
- Click the Manage Add-ons command to display the Manage Add-ons dialog box (Figure B–28).

2
- When finished viewing the add-ons, close the dialog box.
- Close Internet Explorer.

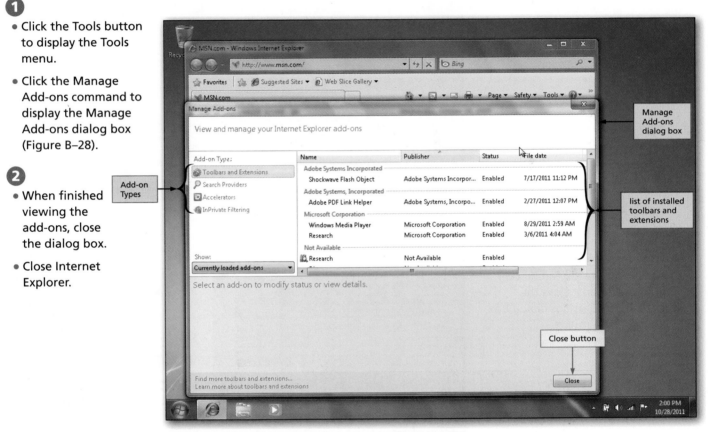

Figure B–28

Summary

Security is an important issue for computer users. You need to be aware of the possible threats to your computer as well as the security features that can be used to protect your computer. The Action Center, along with other security features in Windows 7, allows you to configure the security settings that will help you keep your computer safe.

Exercises

1. Researching Antivirus Software

1. Visit `www.microsoft.com/windows/antivirus-partners/windows-7.aspx` (Figure B–29) in Internet Explorer.

2. Follow the link to Avast. Answer the following questions regarding their antivirus software.

   a. How much does the home antivirus software cost?

   _____

   b. Does Avast offer other malware protection? Spyware protection?

   _____

3. Return to the Windows 7 Consumer security software providers Web page. Follow the link to Trend Micro. Answer the following questions regarding their home antivirus software.

   a. How much does the antivirus software cost?

   _____

   b. Does Trend Micro offer other malware protection? Spyware protection?

   _____

   c. Compare the home version with the other versions offered. How much difference is there between the versions in price? In features?

   _____

   _____

Figure B–29

Continued >

Exercises *continued*

2. Viewing Windows Update

1. Open Windows Update (Figure B–30).

2. It is important to know what has been updated on your computer. You should view your installed updates on a regular basis. Click the 'View update history' link.

3. For Windows Defender, answer the following questions.

   a. What is the definition number of the latest Windows Defender update installed?

   _____

   b. When was the latest update installed?

   _____

   c. Was the latest update successful?

   _____

   d. What was the level of importance of the update?

   _____

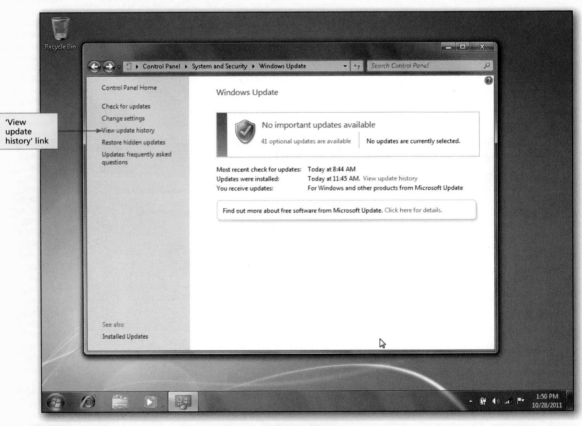

Figure B–30

4. For Windows 7, answer the following questions.

   a. What is the ID number of the latest Windows 7 update installed?

   _____

   b. When was the latest update installed?

   _____

c. Was the latest update successful?

_____

d. What was the level of importance of the update?

_____

5. For Security Updates, answer the following questions.
   a. What is the ID number of the latest Security update installed?

   _____

   b. When was the latest update installed?

   _____

   c. Was the latest update successful?

   _____

   d. What was the level of importance of the update?

   _____

6. Sometimes updates fail to install. Can you find an instance of an update that failed to install? What was it?

_____

_____

_____

Index

Note: **Boldfaced** page numbers refer to pages where key terms are defined.